An Inductive Approach
to English Grammar and Composition
for ESL Students

Second Edition

Regina A. Rochford
Queensborough Community College
City University of New York

KENDALL/HUNT PUBLISHING COMPANY
4050 Westmark Drive   Dubuque, Iowa 52002

Dedicated

to my husband
who is my best friend and advocate,
my daughter
whom I love with all my heart and
in memory of my parents
who taught me the value of education.

Contents

Part I: Grammar

Part II: Composition

Appendix

Part One

Grammar

Main Clauses

1

The objective of this chapter is to teach students:

- *what a main clause is,*

- *how to connect two main clauses in order to avoid run on sentences and comma splices,*

- *how to deal with reduced main clauses,*

- *how to use coordinating conjunctions and conjunctive adverbs.*

Connecting Sentences

Review of Main Clauses

A **simple sentence** contains **one main clause**. It is a complete sentence which makes sense by itself. A **main clause** is also referred to as an **independent clause**.

The following are examples of sentences which contain one main clause each.
- Emma bought a gift for the baby.
- Richard M. Nixon resigned as president of the United States.
- President Kennedy was elected in 1960.

A **compound sentence** contains two **main or independent clauses**.

The following are examples of compound sentences which contain two main clauses.

-       *main clause*   *main clause*
  <u>Emma bought a gift for the baby</u>, but <u>she forgot to bring it with her</u>.

-   *main clause*
  In August 1974, <u>Richard M. Nixon resigned as president of the United States</u>, and
      main clause
  <u>he died in 1994</u>.

-       *main clause*   *main clause*
  <u>President Kennedy was elected in 1960</u>, and <u>he was assassinated in 1963</u>.

Punctuation of Main Clauses

Read the following sentences carefully and answer the questions below. Note that * indicates that there is an error in the sentence.

    1. *a. It was dark and rainy there was a loud blast of thunder.
       *b. Claude watched the game Marie read a book.

*c. We studied French**X**hey studied English.

2. a. It was dark and rainy, and there was a loud blast of thunder.
   b. Claude watched the game, but Marie read a book.
   c. We studied French, so they studied English.

3. a. It was dark and rainy. There was a loud blast of thunder.
   b. Claude watched the game. Marie read a book.
   c. We studied French. They studied English.

How many main clauses does 1.a, 2.a and 3.a contain? _____

Explain why 1.a, b, and c are punctuated incorrectly.
Two main clauses can not be separated by a _____

What is it called when two sentences are separated by a comma?
When two main clauses are separated by a comma, it is called a _____

Explain why 2.a, 2.b and 2.c are punctuated correctly.
Two main clauses can be separated by inserting a _____ after the first main clause and a _____ before the second main clause.

Explain why 3.a, 3.b and 3.c are also punctuated correctly.
Two main clauses can be separated by a_____. The second sentence must start with a _____ letter.

4. a . Oscar was tired. So, he went to bed.
   b. We got in the car. But, it wouldn't start.
   c. I was sick. But, I went to work.

Explain why a comma is used after the conjunction in 4.a, b, and c.
When a conjunction is used to begin a sentence, a _____ is placed immediately after the conjunction.

5. *a. He did not study, but**X**e got an A.
   *b. I ran to the telephone, and**X**he caller hung up.
   *c. They saw the car accident, and **X**hey called for an ambulance.

Explain what punctuation mark _is not needed_ in 5.a, 5.b and 5.c.
When two main clauses are joined by a conjunction, a comma is placed _____ the conjunction. A _comma_ is not placed after the _____.

1

Two simple sentences or main clauses *can not* be separated by a comma .This is called **a comma splice.**

comma splice

example: * She ate dinner X cleaned the house.

Two main clauses *can be separated* by a *period*. The next word after the period must begin with a capital letter.

example: She ate dinner. He cleaned the house.

Two main clauses *can be joined* by using a *comma* after the first main clause and a *conjunction* before the second main clause.

example: She ate dinner, and I cleaned the house.

If the conjunction is the first word of a new sentence, a comma is placed immediately after the conjunction, and the conjunction begins with a capital letter.

example: She ate dinner. But, I cleaned the house.

Reduced Main Clauses

✔ The following sentences are punctuated correctly. Underline the main clause(s) in each sentence.

1. a. I went to bed, but I couldn't sleep.
   b. I went to bed but couldn't sleep.
2. a. He was waving his arms, and he was calling us.
   b. He was waving his arms and calling to us.
3. a. Susan jumped out of the chair, and she yelled at the child.
   b. Susan jumped out of the chair and yelled at the child.

How many main clauses are in 1a, 2a, and 3b?
These sentences contain _____ main clause each.

How many main clauses are in 1b, 2b, and 3b?
These sentences contain _____ main clauses.

What is the second clause called?
This is called a _____ because it omits the _____ or part of the verb.

Explain why these sentences don't need a comma before the conjunction.
Because there is only one _____ in the sentence, a comma is not needed before the _____ .

2

When a sentence contains **only one main clause** and the second main clause is **reduced** (the subject or part of the verb is omitted), do not use a comma to separate the two clauses because the second half of the sentence is no longer a main clause.

(two main clauses)
example: She stood up, and she began to sing.

(one main clause and one reduced clause)
She stood up and began to sing.

Read the following sentences carefully.
Underline the main clause(s) in each example.

1. a. I ate ice cream. He drank coffee.
   b. I ate ice cream, and he drank coffee.
   *c. I ate ice cream he drank coffee.
2. a. I sang a song. Pete played the violin.
   b. I sang a song, and Pete played the violin.
   *c. I sang a song Pete played the violin.

State the rule that explains why 1.a and 2.a are punctuated correctly.
Two main clauses *can be* separated by a _____

State the rule that explains why 1.b and 2.b are punctuated correctly.
Two main clauses can be separated by a _____ and a _____ .

How many main clauses do 1.c and 2.c have? _____

Explain why 1.c and 2.c are incorrect.
Two_____ clauses can not be_____ together without using a comma along with a conjunction or a period.

What is it called when two main clauses are *fused* together?
When two main clauses are fused together, it is called a_____ sentence.

3

Two simple sentences (main clauses) **can not be** fused together. This is called a **run on** sentence or a **fused** sentence.

run on sentence
example: * The children played softball the parents worked in the garden.

Two main clauses **can be joined** by using a **comma** after the first main clause and a **conjunction** before the second main clause.

example: The children played softball, and the parents worked in the garden.

Or, two main clauses can be separated by a *period*.

example: The children played softball. The parents worked in the garden.

6 Main Clauses

Coordinating Conjunctions

Coordinating conjunctions are used to connect two main clauses.

List the words used in this chapter to connect two main clauses.

List some other coordinating conjunctions that could be used to connect two main clauses.

 With a partner or in a small group read the following composition and make any changes necessary to avoid comma splices, run on sentences and unnecessary commas.

I remember the day I was bitten by a dog, I had just arrived in this country I barely spoke any English, and didn't know anyone here. I think this is why this incident was so traumatic.

It was a cold day and my mother took me to a restaurant where she worked. We ate dinner, and left through the back door. We walked outside the restaurant, and walked down the street. Suddenly, I stepped on a dog's tail by accident, he got very mad, and ran after me. He was barking and growling I tried to run back to the restaurant but he was faster than I was. When he finally caught me, he bit me on the leg several times he was so vicious that I thought he was a mad dog.

My mother and I ran back into the restaurant my uncle cleaned the wounds and took me to a local hospital to see an emergency room doctor. The doctor said that I had to receive a series of rabies shots, and stay in the hospital. When I heard I had to stay in the hospital, I hugged my mother, and begged her not to leave. Then the doctor said he wanted to test the dog for rabies. If the dog's test results were negative, I wouldn't have to get the shots. So, he sent my uncle to look for the dog. After a few hours, my uncle returned with the animal. Since the dog didn't have rabies, I didn't have to receive the shots, or stay in the hospital.

This was one of my first experiences in this country it was very frightening for me since I almost had to stay in the hospital where no one spoke my language to get a lot of painful shots.

Write a composition about a time you or someone you know was injured or hurt. Be sure to connect some simple sentences using the techniques just discussed. Before submitting your composition, proof read it carefully to verify there are no comma splices or run on sentences.

Connecting Main Clauses with the Semi-Colon · · · · · · · · · · · ·

A **conjunctive adverb** can also be used to connect two main clauses. The following is a list of conjunctive adverbs:

moreover	furthermore	however	nevertheless	instead
therefore	finally	besides	nonetheless	indeed

 Read the following sentences and underline the main clauses.

1. a. She is taking sixteen credits; moreover, she is working 20 hours a week.
    b. She is taking sixteen credits. Moreover, she is working 20 hours a week.
2. a. Chu is studying in New York; therefore, she'll have to speak English.
    b. Chu is studying in New York. Therefore, she'll have to speak English.
3. a. You are failing this course; however, you're passing the other course.
    b. You are failing this course. However, you're passing the other course.

How many main clauses are in each of the above examples?
There are _____ main clauses in each example.

What type of word is used to connect the two sentences?
A _____ adverb is used to connect the two sentences.

Explain how a semicolon is used to separate two main clauses.
Two main clauses can be joined by using a_____ and a _____ adverb to separate them, and the conjunctive adverb must be followed by a_____ .

Explain what must be used when a conjunctive adverb begins a sentence.
When a conjunctive adverb starts a sentence, it must be followed by a_____ .

Rule

4

Two main clauses can be connected using a **semicolon** and a **conjunctive adverb**, however the conjunctive adverb must be followed by a **comma.**

example: Mary failed three <u>courses; therefore, she</u> was asked to leave the school.

When a sentence begins with a conjunctive adverb, the conjunctive adverb must be followed by a **comma.**

example: Mary failed three <u>courses. Therefore, she</u> was asked to leave the school.

With a partner, correct and or punctuate the following sentences.

1. Alice is always late, however, her husband is always early.
2. John is a janitor; however his father is a doctor.
3. We went to Disney World but we didn't enjoy the amusement park.
4. We went to Disney World. And we really liked the Epcot Center.
5. She is failing her Spanish course. Therefore she is getting a tutor to help her.
6. She is failing her Spanish course; therefore she is getting a tutor to help her.
7. She is failing her Spanish course, therefore, she is getting a tutor to help her.
8. The boy had eaten every piece of candy, and drunk every can of soda.
9. The house is very old and in bad shape. Nevertheless they are going to buy it.
10. She is buying a diamond watch and wearing a fur coat.
11. Sharon ran out of money during her trip therefore she came home early.
12. She finished college however she can't get a job.

 With a partner or in a small group read the following letter which was written to the chairman of the ESL department about a teacher. Wherever possible, connect two sentences using a conjunction or conjunctive adverb and the appropriate punctuation which was just reviewed in this chapter.

Dear Dr. Newton:

At your request, each student in my pre-composition class has been asked to write an evaluation of the professor who taught them last spring.

In the spring, I took a pre-composition course. I took it with Professor Ringle. She was a very unusual teacher. We learned a lot of important points about English grammar. We practiced each point in an essay too. Professor Ringle came to each class with a well planned lesson. She had us figure out the grammatical rules in small groups. Then we were given assignments to do in our groups. We had to use the grammar in a composition she assigned to us at home.

She always came to class on time. She made us stay very late. This upset me because I have to go to my job right after her class. I get docked if I arrive late. Two times I lost an hour of pay because I didn't get out of my class on time. I don't think this is fair. I wish you would ask her to be more considerate of the students' schedules.

I also wish that she would give the class a break. Sometimes the students want to go to the bathroom or get something to eat. We can't do this because she won't let us leave the room during class unless it is an emergency. This is not fair to the students. It is hard to sit in a classroom for an hour and a half. We get bored. Could you please tell Professor Ringle to give us a break? Could you please tell Professor Ringle to let us come in and out whenever we want to?

Thank you.

Alexander Slovanski

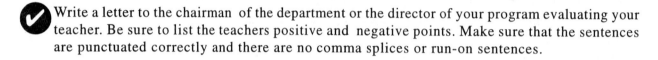

Write a letter to the chairman of the department or the director of your program evaluating your teacher. Be sure to list the teachers positive and negative points. Make sure that the sentences are punctuated correctly and there are no comma splices or run-on sentences.

With a partner or in a small group, revise the following composition to eliminate run-on sentences and comma splices. Be sure to use semi-colons, commas and connecting words correctly.

I was told New York City was once called Fun City, but, today the name has changed to Crime City. The reason is more and more serious crimes are happening around us; moreover no one can stop them. Light prison sentences are the cause of this increase in crime, therefore, we should have capital punishment, I believe this would prevent many serious crimes. Even though the death penalty looks immoral, it justifies the death of innocent people who have been killed by vicious criminals.

Every person has one life no one can get a second chance to live after being murdered. This is why life is so important to us, therefore we will do anything to protect our lives. But the murder rate is increasing rapidly. Our society can not let malicious criminals live among us it will make our lives very unsafe. Sometimes a criminal kills someone, goes to jail and is released in a few years I read a story about a man who was convicted of murdering a young woman, he served a few years in prison, and was released because of his good behavior in jail. Two weeks after his release, he murdered another person. If this criminal had been executed for the first murder he committed, his second victim would not have been killed.

Some folks say the death penalty is immoral and wrong because we have no right to destroy another human life. However did the murderer have the right to kill someone? The answer is no and the only way our society can guarantee that a murderer doesn't kill again is by giving him the death penalty. By letting criminals live, society is being unfair to the people who obey the laws.

No one forces anyone to commit murder, if a person kills someone, he/she should pay for it and be given the death penalty. If we have capital punishment, our lives will become safer. I agree with the death penalty.

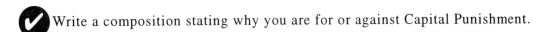 Write a composition stating why you are for or against Capital Punishment.

With a partner or in a small group, revise the following composition to eliminate run-on sentences and comma splices. Be sure to use semi-colons, commas and connecting words correctly.

Most young people grow up with working parents and they feel money is the most important thing in their lives. But, these youngsters must realize life doesn't revolve around material objects but love and concern I believe this focus on money has a negative impact on children.

The first and most important problem is many youngsters are given a lot of money because their parents work and feel guilty for not being more available. These children don't know how to make their lives valuable without a lot of money in their pockets in this century, many young people never spend time with their parents so the children grow up with lots of cash which is supposed to compensate for a close parental relationship. For example, one of my friends got enough money from his parents for his books at school but he didn't buy them, he wasted all his money on junk. His parents didn't know what he did with the money because they didn't spend any time interacting with him. If these parents had been more concerned, they could have taught him appropriate behavior and would have known what he had done.

The second issue is many young people don't realize they are idolizing material things, many of us live in the comfort of material objects but we must recognize that these luxuries can effect us negatively. For example, my friend enjoys buying expensive clothes and jewelry but she can't afford them because she is not a rich woman. I asked her why she isn't more responsible and reasonable. She said, "I learned as a child if I have nice things, I can make good friends." But, in reality friendship doesn't result from what a person owns, friendship comes from the heart

I believe parents must be more involved and concerned about their children they must give them love and care all the time they should teach them money can't buy love or happiness.

 With a partner or in a small group, revise the following composition to eliminate run-on sentences and comma splices. Be sure to use semi-colons, commas and connecting words correctly.

Many young people are very crazy and adventurous they aren't aware of the dangers of drinking and driving, they take chances and sometimes they break the law.

In my country my friend's parents went on a trip and they left him alone in the house. One night my friend got bored he decided to take out the family car for a ride, he picked me up and we went to a party, he did a lot of heavy drinking. When it came time to go, my friend was too drunk to drive, and he didn't believe that I knew how to drive a car, he insisted on driving even though he was very drunk.

As we were returning home, a police officer stopped us he asked my friend for the registration and his driver's license my friend didn't have the required documents, the police officer realized he was drunk and he made us get out of the car. He immediately arrested my friend for driving under the influence of alcohol.

When we got to the police station, I called my parents, they spoke to the policeman, they had us released, fortunately my father was able to resolve the problem. When my friend's parents found out about the incident, they had a long discussion with him and made him promise not to drink and drive.

This incident ended without any tragedy but young people have to be fully aware of the dangers of drinking and driving before they get behind the wheel of a car.

Adverbial Clauses

2

The objective of this chapter is to teach students:

- *how to identify and form adverbial clauses which must be connected to a main clause,*

- *to develop the concept of subordinating conjunctions and fragments.*

Introduction to Dependent Adverbial Clauses

 Read the following sentences. Try to circle the dependent adverbial clauses.

When Nina arrived in the United States, she lived in a small apartment in the city. Although she lived in a very safe neighborhood, she was afraid to leave her apartment since she had heard there was a lot of crime in the city. Everyday she would sit and gaze out the window. One day while she was looking out her kitchen window, a woman named Alla called up to Nina. The two women began to talk every morning. One day Alla invited Nina to her house for lunch. Even though Nina wasn't really interested in eating, she went to Alla's for lunch because she had become bored and depressed when she sat alone by the window all day.

Alla began to escort Nina around the neighborhood and introduced Nina to many people from different countries. Despite Nina's inability to communicate well in English, she started to meet new people and socialize instead of being alone all day. Little by little Nina's English began to improve, and she became more acclimated to her new country.

Alla was Nina's first friend in America, and they eventually became best friends. Moreover, after Nina met Alla, Nina began to study at a local college, and she eventually graduated with a degree. The transition from Nina's country to the United States was not easy. However, because of Alla's friendship, Nina was able to grow and succeed.

In this composition, how can a *main clause* be distinguished from a *dependent adverbial clause*?
A _____ clause contains a subject and a verb but can not stand alone as a sentence. A dependent clause must be attached to a _____ clause.

What kind of dependent clauses are in these sentences?
These sentences contain _____clauses.

What special type of word is used to begin adverbial clauses?
_____ are used to introduce adverbial clauses.

Can a dependent clause *stand alone* in a sentence?
_____ , a dependent clause must be connected to a _____clause.

When a dependent clause stands alone, what is it called?
A dependent clause which stands alone is called a _____ .

✔ Make the following fragmented dependent clauses into **complete sentences** by attaching a main clause.

1. Although I love to travel, _____ .
2. _____ even though she is thin.
3. When they saw the movie, _____ .
4. _____ while he studies.
5. If I were younger, _____ .
6. _____ when I was sleeping.
7. Even though I study very hard, _____.
8. Since they had already eaten, _____.
9. Because we love our parents, _____.
10. _____ after my English class ends.

✔ Make a list of subordinating conjunctions that are used to start adverbial clauses.

since	whenever	because	when
_____	_____	_____	_____
_____	_____	_____	_____
_____	_____	_____	_____

Rule

1

Adverbial clauses are **dependent clauses** that *can not* stand alone in a sentence and begin with a **subordinating conjunction**. An adverbial clause is not a complete sentence; it is a fragmented sentence.

complete sentence
example: Because I have a good education, I can write well.

fragmented sentence
*Because I have a good education.

Subordinating conjunctions include:

as	until	during	upon	since
even though	if	because of	while	so that
although	even if	when	whenever	providing that
inasmuch as	due to	because	whereas	till
as soon as	before	though	the first time	such as
after	once	so long as	in order to	

Punctuation of Adverbial Clauses . . . .

 Read the following sentences and underline the adverbial clause.

1. a. Nina was depressed and bored when she stayed home all day.
    b. When she stayed home all day, Nina was depressed and bored.
2. a. She worked in a department store while she went to college.
    b. While she went to college, she worked in a department store.
3. a. After they ate dinner, they took a nap.
    b. They took a nap after they ate dinner.

Where can a *dependent* adverbial clause be located in a sentence?
A dependent clause can be placed _____ or _____ the main clause.

Rule

2

An adverbial clause may be placed at the **beginning** or the **end** of a sentence. It can come before or after the main clause.

example: <u>After we called her</u>, we went out to dinner.
            We went out to dinner <u>after we called her</u>.

 Look at the two sentences listed in Rule Two.

When the adverbial clause is placed at the beginning of the sentence, what punctuation mark is placed between the two clauses?
When an adverbial clause is at the beginning of a sentence, a_____ is placed between the main clause and the adverbial clause.

When the adverbial clause is placed at the end of the sentence, what is punctuation mark is *omitted*?

When the adverbial clause is placed at the end of the sentence, the _____ is omitted.

R u l e

3

A. When an adverbial clause is at the **beginning of a sentence**, it is separated from the main clause by a **comma**.

B. However, when an adverbial clause is at the **end of the sentence**, it **is not** separated by a **comma**.

example: If I marry <u>him, I</u> will always be poor.
I will always be <u>poor if</u> I marry him.

 With a partner, punctuate the following sentences.

1. Because Don is rich he has a great deal of political influence.
2. I used to go swimming everyday when I was a child.
3. Although I am on a diet I have gained ten pounds!
4. She eats a lot of junk food even though she has high blood pressure.
5. After she returned from France she started college.

 With a partner if necessary, correct each of the sentences below. They may need a comma, or it may be a sentence that only contains a dependent clause and needs a main clause.

1. Even though she studied hard.
2. When the door bell rang she ignored it.
3. She worked a full day even though she was late.
4. After the dance. We went out to eat.
5. He will come. If Mary calls him.
6. If my parents were older.
7. I called her during the basketball game.
8. As soon as I heard the news, I told my parents.
9. Before, she left the house she called the doctor for an appointment.
10. When I'm tired. I usually go to bed early.

 With a partner or in a small group, read the following composition and make the necessary correction in order to eliminate any fragments.

In today's society, many parents hope their children will be successful in school, including my

parents. But, sometimes if they push their children too much their hope turns into pressure. If parents pressure their children. Their children will receive too many demands and might not be able to handle them.

My parents don't pressure my sister, brother or myself, but of course they would like to see us be successful in school. My parents don't burden me with unnecessary pressure, but they give me happiness and warmth. Both my parents were only able to attend high school, so they want their children to go to college. But, they also want us to be happy. Occasionally when I'm doing my homework in my room. They come in and ask me how I'm doing in school. They tell me not to pressure myself too much. Since they know I am doing my best. They tell me that I must also relax and rest.

My parents don't pressure me, but they give me the support I need to be successful. For instance, if my sister is watching TV. My mother will tell her to turn down the volume right away. So that I can concentrate and pay attention to my school work.

My parents have done a lot for me, but they haven't pressured me. I feel great without having anyone push me all the time. Because it tells me my parents are proud of what I am doing and value my happiness as much as my success. I have a friend whose mother always compares her daughter to other people. When my friend hears these comparisons. She gets angry and resentful. This is not good.

If the pressure is too much for the children. It can also create emotional problems for them. Moreover, if parents push their children too much. Sometimes their children won't do well, and they feel scared to tell their parents they are failing. Being scared makes children nervous. When the parents lean on the children too much. Sometimes children run away from home, because they can't take the pressure anymore. I read a newspaper article about a student who jumped off a very high building, because his parents pushed him to succeed. He killed himself.

Since he couldn't handle his parents demands. It was the only way to get out of the pressure. I felt very sorry and upset, after I finished reading this newspaper article.

In the end, I hope parents will not push their children too much, because pressure doesn't help anyone and will sometimes harm children. If parents hope their children will be successful in school. They shouldn't pressure them. They should let them be what they are.

 In small groups or with a partner, read the following composition and make any necessary corrections to eliminate fragments, comma splices and run on sentences.

In the United States older people are not appreciated by their families, they are viewed as a burden and a nuisance.

In this country the children of older people are often too busy to spend time with their parents. Many young people work and go to school every day. When the weekend comes. They want to relax. They want to go out with their friends who they believe are more interesting. Instead of spending time with their parents and grandparents. This is very sad. Because it means the young people have not learned to value or cherish their older family members.

Young people should pay more attention to older people. Since older people have a lot of knowledge and experience. The old people can use their wisdom to help the younger generation solve their problems. Because older relatives have gone through many hard times. They have many experiences they can share with us they can give us a lot of good advice too. I was surprised that my grandmother had the same problems with her friends that I have with mine. Although she was born many years ago in a different country.

I also believe children grow up to be decent adults if they learn to respect older people. My friends who spend time with their older relatives are more interested in getting a good education and want to please their families. Instead of hanging out on a corner until all hours of the night. However many of my other friends who have no relationships with their older relatives are more interested in drinking, smoking pot and using drugs.

Even though many American people don't like to be with their older relatives. I think children should learn to pay more attention to them. Because it will help the American youngsters to be good people and learn from the older people's experiences.

✔ **Writing:** Write a composition about either of the two topics listed below. Be sure to use at least ten adverbial clauses using the subordinating conjunctions: *because, since, when, while, instead of, after, during, before, if, whenever, despite, in spite of, although, even though, etc.*

✔ **Topic One:** Explain why parents should or shouldn't pressure their children to do well in school. Be sure to use examples from you personal experiences.

✔ **Topic Two:** Explain why you agree or disagree with the following statement. American people do not respect the elder members of society. They believe that once a person grows old they are no longer valuable or useful. Therefore, they are placed in nursing homes where they are ignored and die alone.

Adverbial Clauses of Reason and Contrast

The objective of this chapter is to teach students:

- *how to write and punctuate adverbial clauses of reason and,*

- *contrast using the subordinating conjunctions because, since, even though and although.*

Adverbial Clauses of Reason

 Read the following sentences and underline the adverbial clauses.

1. I left early because I felt sick.
2. She missed the bus because she had overslept.
3. I took this class because I want to improve my grammar.
4. Because we wanted a better life, we moved to the United States.

What subordinating conjunction begins each adverbial clause?
Each adverbial clause begins with the subordinating conjunction _____.

Explain the meaning the word because gives the adverbial clause.
The subordinating conjunction because expresses a _____. It explains why an event occurred.

What kind of adverbial clause begins with the subordinating conjunction *because*?
An adverbial clause of _____ begins with the subordinating conjunction because.

 Read the following sentences and underline the adverbial clause of reason.

1. a. Dana couldn't go on her class trip because she didn't save enough money.
   b. Dana couldn't go on her class trip since she didn't save enough money.
2. a. Because Milka is beautiful, she has a lot of boyfriends.
   b. Since Milka is beautiful, she has a lot of boyfriends.

What other subordinating conjunction can be used in an adverbial clause of reason?
An adverbial clause of reason can use the subordinating conjunction _____ or

_____.

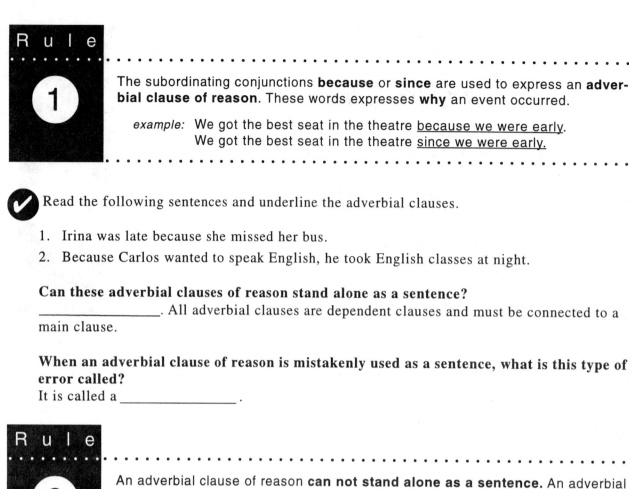

Rule 1

The subordinating conjunctions **because** or **since** are used to express an **adverbial clause of reason**. These words expresses **why** an event occurred.

example: We got the best seat in the theatre <u>because we were early</u>.
We got the best seat in the theatre <u>since we were early</u>.

Read the following sentences and underline the adverbial clauses.

1. Irina was late because she missed her bus.
2. Because Carlos wanted to speak English, he took English classes at night.

Can these adverbial clauses of reason stand alone as a sentence?
_____. All adverbial clauses are dependent clauses and must be connected to a main clause.

When an adverbial clause of reason is mistakenly used as a sentence, what is this type of error called?
It is called a _____ .

Rule 2

An adverbial clause of reason **can not stand alone as a sentence.** An adverbial clause of reason is not a complete sentence. It is a **dependent clause**. When used alone, it is a **fragment**.

> *fragment*
> *example:* *<u>Because Marco missed ten classes.</u> He didn't pass the course.

> *complete sentence*
> Because Marco missed ten classes, he didn't pass the course.

With a partner, combine each pair of sentences making them adverbial clauses of reason. Be sure to use the words *because* or *since* with the clause that gives the reason.

1. The children were hungry. There was no food in the house.

_____

2. The ferry is closed. We can't get to the other side of the river.

_____

3. My radio wouldn't work. The battery was dead.

_____

4. Ann woke up with a headache. She drank a lot of wine last night.

_____

5. The women went shopping. They were bored.

_____

6. The child screamed. She saw a ghost.

_____

7. I had an accident in my car. The streets were icy.

_____

8. The man had chest pains. He went to the emergency room to see a doctor.

_____

9. The students didn't study. They failed the course.

_____

10. The women were talking. They didn't see the child run in the street.

_____

✔ With a partner or in a small group, read each of the following statements. After discussing your opinion, *using adverbial clauses of reason* write a complete sentence stating why you agree or disagree with each statement. The first sentence is done for you.

1. An extremely jealous person has no control over these feelings.

   example: I agree that an extremely jealous person has no control over these feelings because such a person is usually in an irrational state of mind.

2. Extreme jealousy can be cured by seeking professional help from a skilled therapist.

   _____

   _____

3. Envy or jealousy are abnormal unhealthy emotions which can only create problems.

   _____

   _____

4. An obsessively envious person will sometimes seriously injure or kill the person he/she is trying to control.

   _____

   _____

5. If your mate is jealous of the relationship you have with other people, it demonstrates or proves his/her love.

   _____

   _____

6. If a man is traditional or macho, he's less likely to be envious than a man who is more modern.

   _____

   _____

7. Women with good careers are more jealous than housewives.

_____

_____

8. Sometimes jealousy can have positive results when it prompts the jealous person to make some positive changes in his/her life.

_____

_____

9. Every person experiences some level of jealousy at some point in his/her life.

_____

_____

Adverbial Clauses of Contrast ·

Read the following sentences and observe the subordinating conjunctions used to express an *adverbial clause of contrast* or an *unexpected result*.

1. a. Although cigarettes are bad for the heart and lungs, many people smoke them.
    b. Even though cigarettes are bad for the heart and lungs, many people smoke them.
2. a. Although a child may do bad things, his/her parents always love him/her.
    b. Even though a child may do bad things, his/her parents always love him/her.

What two subordinating conjunctions are used to introduce an adverbial clause of *contrast* which states an unexpected result?
An adverbial clause of contrast begins with the subordinating conjunctions_____
or_____ .

R u l e

3

The subordinating conjunctions **although** and **even though** are used to write **adverbial clauses** that express **a contrast** or an **unexpected result**.

example: Although I was hungry, I didn't eat.
Even though I was hungry, I didn't eat.

Read the following sentences and determine which word should be omitted from the sentence.

*1. Although Fred can't carry a tune, but, he sings anyway.
*2. Even though Peter doesn't cook well, however he calls himself a chef.

Explain what is being done incorrectly in each of these sentences.
When a person writes an adverbial clause of contrast, the subordinating conjunctions
_____ or_____ express the contrast in meaning. Therefore, a
_____of contrast such as but or however is *not used* with the main clause.

R u l e

4

When a person writes an **adverbial clause of contrast**, the main clause **should not contain a coordinating conjunction** such as **but** or **however** because the subordinating conjunction in the adverbial clause expresses the contrasting meaning.

example: Although Maria is engaged, she is dating two men.

✔ With a partner, complete each of the following sentences with either *because, since, even though,* or *although*.

Marta was a sweet young woman who was dating a man named Manuel. _____Manuel was a handsome guy, many women tried to catch his eye. _____Marta loved Manuel and wanted to trust him, she was always worried he would start dating another woman.

_____Marta loved Manuel, she gradually became uncertain of her relationship with him and began to argue with Manuel about what he did when he was away from her. She began to accuse him of seeing other women and started to follow him at night. _____ of Marta's hostile behavior, Manuel got annoyed and stopped dating her _____he still loved her deeply.

A year after Manuel ended the relationship, Marta saw him walking down the street with another woman. _____ Manuel was dating again, Marta was convinced that he had been seeing this girl while they were together. What Marta didn't realize was that her extreme jealousy turned Manuel off. _____Manuel was faithful to Marta while they were dating, by badgering him with false accusations, Marta destroyed their relationship.

✔ Write five sentences which contain adverbial clauses of contrast that express something illogical you once did. Be sure to use the subordinating conjunctions although or even though.
example: I bought an expensive new car even though I couldn't afford it.

✔ *Writing:* Write a composition describing a time you or someone you know was jealous or envious of another person. In order to explain your feelings, be sure to use at least six adverbial clauses of reason and contrast that use the subordinating conjunctions because, since, although and even though.

Adverbial Clauses of Reason and Contrast 27

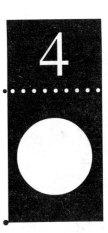

Conditional Clauses

The objective of this chapter is to teach students:

- *how to express conditional sentences in the present and past using the correct tenses and punctuation.*

Present Tense Conditional Clauses

 Read each set of sentences carefully.

1.
   a. If he <u>works</u> late, he <u>can meet</u> you.
   b. If he <u>worked</u> late, he <u>could meet</u> you.
2.
   a. If they <u>study</u> harder, they <u>can pass</u> the exam.
   b. If they <u>studied</u> , they <u>could pass</u> the exam.
3.
   a. If you <u>are</u> wise, you <u>will pay</u> cash.
   b. If you <u>were</u> wise, you <u>would pay</u> cash.
4.
   a. If I <u>go</u> on vacation, it <u>will cost</u> a lot of money.
   b. If I <u>went</u> on vacation, it <u>would cost</u> a lot of money.

Explain the difference in meaning in each of these sentence pairs.
Letter a in each example express a _____ conditional situation.
Letter b in each example expresses an _____ conditional situation.

Explain how the *tense of the verb* alters the meaning of the sentence.
The _____ tense is used with a <u>present true conditional</u> situation.
But, the _____ tense is used in a <u>present untrue conditional</u> situation.

When it is a true situation, what tense is used in the conditional if clause?
In a true situation, the _____ tense is used in the conditional if clause.

When it is a true situation, what modal(s) are used in the result clause?
In a true situation, the modals _____ or _____ are used in the result clause.

When it is an untrue situation, what tense is used in the conditional if clause?
In an untrue situation, the _____ tense is used in the conditional if clause.

When it is an untrue situation, what modal(s) are used in the result clause?
In an untrue situation, the modals _____ or _____ are used in the result clause.

1

PRESENT CONDITIONAL STATEMENTS

	If Clause	Result Clause
True situation	present tense	will or can + verb
Untrue/unreal situation	past tense	would or could + verb

example: (true situation)   If I <u>arrive</u> late, I <u>will call</u> you.
(untrue situation) If I <u>arrived</u> late, I <u>would call</u> you.

With a partner, read the given information, and complete the sentences with the words in parentheses.

1. I may need a new air conditioner next year.
   If I (need)_____a new air conditioner, I (buy) _____one.
2. I won't need a new air conditioner this year.
   If I (need)_____ a new air conditioner, I (buy) _____one.
3. I may go to Florida next year.
   If I (go)_____to Florida next year, I (see)_____my friend Ellen.
4. I won't go to Florida next year.
   If I (go)_____to Florida next year, I (see) _____my friend Ellen.
5. I may buy a new word processor.
   If I (have)_____a new word processor, I (write)_____a book.
6. I won't buy a new word processor.
   I (write) _____a book if I (have)_____a new word processor.
7. I don't have a ticket to the opera.
   If I (have)_____a ticket to the opera, I (give)_____it to you.
8. Ann needs new boots this winter. If Ann (need) _____new
   boots this winter, her mother (buy)_____them for her.
9. Maria can't sing well. Maria (join) _____the chorus if she (sing)
   _____well.
10. They dance very well. If they (dance)_____well, they (enter)
    _____the dance contest at the school.

Oral Exercise: Complete each of the following sentences with a partner. Be sure to use the correct tense depending on whether it is a true or untrue situation.

1. If I win the lottery, _____.
2. If my friend won the lottery, _____.
3. If my parents go on vacation this summer,_____.
4. If my parents went on vacation this summer, _____.
5. If they get married, _____.
6. If they got married, _____.

7. If the teacher is absent, _____.

8. If a student were absent, _____.

9. If we pass this course, _____.

10. If we passed this course, _____.

11. If my boy/girlfriend cheats on me, _____.

12. If the professor liked me, _____.

13. If you call me tonight, _____.

14. If I wrote well, _____.

15. If you studied harder, _____.

Oral Exercise: Complete each of the following sentences with a partner. Be sure to use the correct tense depending on whether it is a true or untrue situation.

1. I could visit my sister in South America if _____.

2. She can call you tonight if _____.

3. My mother would be wild if _____.

4. My husband/wife will kill me if _____.

5. They could write better if _____.

6. We would get home earlier if _____.

7. You could lose weight if _____.

8. You can pass this class if _____.

9. The professor will fail anyone if _____.

10. The doctor could cure him if _____.

Punctuation of Conditional Clauses ·

Read these sentences. Underline the dependent conditional clause in each sentence.

1. a. She can come if she calls.

   b. If she calls, she can come.

2. a. He would buy a car if he won the lottery.

   b. If he won the lottery, he would buy a car.

Explain when a comma is placed between the independant clause and the conditional adverbial clause.
When the conditional if clause is at the _____ of the sentence, a _____ is used after the conditional if clause and before the main clause.

Explain when a comma is not placed between the independant clause and the conditional adverbial clause.
When the conditional adverbial clause is at the _____ of the sentence, a _____ is not used between the main clause and the conditional if clause.

2

When the conditional **if clause** is at the beginning of the sentence, separate it from the main clause **with a comma**.

example: If I could <u>run, I</u> would enter the contest.

When the conditional **if clause** is at the end of the sentence, **do not** separate it from the main clause with a comma.

example: I would enter the <u>contest if</u> I could run.

✔ *Writing:*

1. a. Congratulations! You've completed your college degree. Write a sentence describing what you would do in this situation. (Remember: this is an **untrue** situation since you haven't graduated yet.)

   If I _____ , I _____ .

   b. You are doing well in this course. You expect to receive a passing grade. What will you do if you pass this course. (Remember: this is a **true** situation.)

   If I _____ , I _____ .

2. Write a composition describing what you would do if you won the lottery. Which conditional if statement would you use? Ask yourself is this a **true or untrue** situation?

✔ With a partner or in a small group, read the following paragraphs which contain a situation. Make any necessary corrections to the punctuation and the use of true and untrue conditional situations.

✔ *Situation One:* I am a forty year old woman with a lot of deep regrets about what I've done with my life. If I were twenty years younger I will go to college and study harder. I could get a good education if I was a lot younger. This will help me get a decent job and support my family. I can meet a man who will be reliable and not run away when there is trouble. I would do things very differently, if I was twenty years younger.

✔ *Situation Two:* Theresa is graduating from college this year. If she graduated from college, she could have a big party in honor of her accomplishment. If she wanted, she can go on a long vacation with her friends. Eventually, she will also have to get a job and help educate her younger brother and sister, if she finished her degree.

✔ *Situation Three:* Maria is a very disorganized woman. She can arrive at work by nine o'clock sharp if she got up on time. If she is well organized she could get her projects completed on time. Her boss will recommend her for a promotion if she does her work in a timely fashion. If Maria got her act together, she will be successful.

Past Conditional Situations ·

✔ Read the following sentences.

1. If he <u>had worked</u> late, he <u>could have met</u> you.
2. If she <u>had talked</u> to me, I <u>would have told</u> her.
3. If I <u>had heard</u> the weather report, I <u>would have dressed</u> properly.
4. If you <u>had been</u> in class, you <u>wouldn't have missed</u> the video tape.

Are these four conditional sentences discussing a present or a past situation?
These sentences are discussing a _____ situation.

Are these sentences true or untrue situations?
These sentences are _____ situations.

In a conditional past situation, what tense is used in the if clause?
In conditional past situations, the _____ tense is used in the conditional if clause.

In a conditional past situation, what verbs are used in the result clause?
In the conditional past situations, use the modal(s) _____ + _____ +
_____ in the result clause.

R u l e

3

· ·

PAST CONDITIONAL STATEMENTS

	If Clause	Result Clause		
Past Conditional	past perfect tense	would or could	+ have +	past participle

example: If she <u>had worked</u> harder, she <u>would have passed</u> the course.

· ·

✔ *Controlled Exercise:* With a partner, use the given information to complete the sentences with the words in parentheses.

1. I didn't go shopping this afternoon, so I didn't buy any food.
   If I (go) _____ shopping this afternoon, I
   (buy) _____ some food.
2. I didn't hear the door bell ring, so I didn't answer it. If I (hear)
   _____ the bell ring, I (answer) _____ it.
3. You didn't tell me about your problem, so I couldn't help you.
   I (help) _____ you if you (tell) _____ me
   about your problem.

4. Margaret didn't go to Japan, so she didn't see Tokyo. Margaret (see) _____ _____Tokyo if she (go) _____ to Japan.

5. Pat didn't study for his test, so he failed the course.
    If Pat (study)_____ for his test, he (pass) _____the course.

6. Sarah didn't wake up on time. Sarah (miss, not)_____her train if she (get)_____up on time.

7. Yvonne and Jean didn't go home for the holidays. If Yvonne and Jean (go) _____home for the holidays, they (attend)_____the wedding.

8. Silvia and I ate dinner before we visited Miriam. If Silvia and I (eat, not already) _____ dinner, we (eat)_____with you.

✔ Write a statement for the following situation.

1. You once had a course that you didn't do well in because you didn't study enough. Write a past conditional sentence.

    If I _____ , _____ .

2. A year ago your friend asked you to go in on a lottery ticket with him, but you said no. A week later you found out that your friend won four million dollars. You regret your decision. Write a conditional if statement to describe your situation.

    If I _____ , _____ .

✔ Correct the following paragraph. Be sure to use the correct conditional statement.

Anna and Hannah were best friends for many years until Anna became jealous of Hannah because she married a rich man and had a beautiful house. If Anna hadn't gotten jealous of Hannah, they would be good friends today. If Anna didn't call Hannah unkind names, Hannah would have been able to forgive her, and they would be friends today.

✔ *Oral Exercise:* With a partner complete the following sentences orally. Be sure to determine whether it is a present (true or untrue) or a past situation.

1. If I were thirsty during the class,_____.
2. If Peter and I had seen the child in the street,_____.
3. If you worked on Saturdays, _____.
4. If Frank knew how to fix a computer,_____.
5. If Ellen had known the truth, _____.
6. If Maria and Jose bought Peter's car, _____.
7. If Maria and Jose had bought Peter's car,_____.
8. If you complain to the teacher,_____.
9. If I hadn't warned you,_____.
10. If they went to the bank,_____.

 With a partner complete the following sentences orally. Be sure to determine whether it is a present or past situation.

1. If _____, you will pick me up at noon.
2. If _____, you would pick me up at noon.
3. If _____, you would have picked me up at noon.
4. If _____, she never would have lied to him.
5. If _____, she would have married him.
6. If _____, they can come for dinner.
7. If _____, we will end the class early.
8. If _____, they could have passed the test.
9. If _____, Anthony would learn English.
10. If _____, I can correct their papers.

Writing:

In life everyone has to make difficult choices and decisions. Sometimes a person makes a decision and later regrets it. Write a composition, telling about a time you made a decision and regretted it later. Be sure to use the Past Conditional Untrue to describe what should have been done.

example: When I was in college, I used to hang out in the student union building all the time. So, I eventually failed most of my courses and had to leave the college. Now I regret this behavior. If I <u>had attended</u> all my classes, I <u>would have passed</u> most of my courses. I <u>would have gotten</u> a college degree in computer science, and I would have had a good job.

Noun Clauses

5

The objective of this chapter is to teach students:

- *the formation and usage of dependent noun clauses in sentences,*

- *how a noun clause can be used as the subject, object, object of the preposition or to modify an adjective or a noun.*

Review of Nouns

What is a noun?
A noun is the name of a ___animal___, ___personal___ or ___thing___.

a. List five examples of a noun which functions as a <u>person</u>.
1. <u>Mr. Vasquez</u>   4. _____
2. _____   5. _____
3. _____

b. List five examples of a noun which functions as a <u>place</u>.
1. <u>the Statue of Liberty</u>   4. _____
2. _____   5. _____
3. _____

c. List five examples of a noun which functions as a <u>thing</u>.
1. <u>the book</u>   4. _____
2. the table   5. _____
3. the ball

Where can a noun be used in a sentence?
Read the following sentences and circle the nouns in each sentence.

a. The school was closed.

b. Maria is pretty.

Explain how these nouns function in these sentences.
These nouns function as the _____ of the sentence.

Read the following sentences and circle the nouns in them.

a. Shifra sang a song.

b. Yoni bought a car.

Explain how these nouns function in these sentences.

The noun that comes before the verb functions as the_____of the sentence.

The noun that comes after the verb functions as the_____ of the sentence.

Read the following sentences and circle the nouns in them.

a. Ada put the dog in the yard.

b. The school prepared the students for the exam.

Explain how these nouns function in these sentences.

The noun that comes before the verb functions as the_____of the sentence.

The noun that comes after the verb functions as the_____ of the sentence.

The noun that comes after the preposition is the _____ .

R u l e

1

A **noun** is the name of a **person**, **place** or **thing**.

 An example of a <u>person</u> is <u>Mrs. Abramova.</u>
 An example of a <u>place</u> is the <u>Golden Gate Bridge</u>.
 An example of a <u>thing</u> is <u>a book</u>.

A **noun** can function as the **subject of a sentence**.

 example: The <u>car</u> is very old.

A **noun** can function as the **object of a sentence**.

 example: I saw the <u>picture</u>.

A **noun** can function as the **object of a preposition**.
 example: They looked <u>into the backyard.</u>

Noun Clauses as the Subject and Object of a Sentence......

 Underline the subject in each of the following sentences.

1. a. Her statement was untrue.
   b. What she said was untrue.

2. a. The location is unknown.
   b. Where it is located is unknown.

3. a. Mary's behavior was odd.
   b. What Mary did was odd.

4. a. Her request was clear.
   b. What she requested was clear.

5. a. My knowledge has increased.
   b. What I know has increased.

6. a. Our salaries are private.
   b. What we earn is private.

In 1.a. the subject was *statement*. In 1.b. the subject was *what she said*.
What is different about the form of these two subjects?
In 1.a. the subject is a simple _____. However, in 1.b. the subject is a
_____ .

Is there a difference in meaning between 1.a. and 1.b ? _____

In general, in each sentence pair, the subject in letter a was a _____ .
However, the subject in letter b was a _____ .

These six examples demonstrate that a *noun clause* can function as the _____
of a sentence.

✔ Read the following sentences again.

Our salaries <u>are</u> private.

What we earn <u>is</u> private.

When a noun clause is the subject, is it singular or plural?
When a noun clause is the subject, it is _____ . There must be _____
between the subject and the verb.

✔ Read the following sentence pairs and circle the object in each pair.

1. a. You don't understand the question.
    b. You don't understand what is being asked.

2. a. She doesn't believe his story.
    b. She doesn't believe what he told her.

3. a. Jaime knows the answers.
    b. Jaime knows what he must say.

What form is the object in letter a of each pair?
The object in letter <u>a</u> of each pair is a _____ .

What form is the object in letter b of each pair?
The object in letter <u>b</u> of each pair is a _____ .

These three examples demonstrate that a noun clause can function as the _____
of a sentence.

✔ Read the following sentences and circle the object of the preposition in each pair.

1. a. I asked Maria about her vacation.
    b. I asked Maria about where she went on vacation.

2. a. Wei was interested in the story.
    b. Wei was interested in what she was saying.

3. a. Lise must deal with the problem.
    b. Lise must deal with what is happening.

What form is the object of the preposition in letter a of each pair.
The object in letter <u>a</u> of each pair is a _____.

What form is the object of the preposition in letter b of each pair.
The object is letter <u>b</u> of each pair is a _____.

These three examples demonstrate that a *noun clause* can function as the
_____.

Forming Noun Clauses

List some of the noun clauses used in the above examples.

1. _____   2. _____
3. _____   4. _____
5. _____   6. _____

The words that are used to introduce a noun clause are called _____.

What are some examples of a relative pronoun?

what   why   _____   _____
_____   _____   _____   _____
_____   _____   _____   _____

State the rule for forming a noun clause.

relative pronoun   + _____ + _____ +
    (optional object, or optional adjective or optional prepositional phrase)

R u l e

2

HOW ARE NOUN CLAUSES FORMED?

relative pronoun   +   subject   +   verb   +   (optional prepositional
                                                                      phrase, adjective or object)

example	what	she	knew	about the problem
	where	they	studied	

When a **noun clause** is the **subject**, it is **singular**. There must be **subject verb agreement** between the noun clause and the verb.

  example: Our requests <u>were</u> ignored.
         What we requested <u>was</u> ignored.

With a partner, read each of the following questions and write a response where a noun clause is used as the *subject* of the sentence. Be sure to have subject verb agreement between the noun clause and the verb.

  example: Where does our professor live?
         <u>*Where our professor lives* is a big secret</u>. (subject of sentence)

1. How many times has Mario failed Biology?
2. When will the final exam take place?
3. How much does a newspaper cost?
4. Where are the children?
5. How does Louisa pay the bills?
6. How long has Kaitlin been talking on phone?
7. How many courses is Ali taking?
8. Why does Santa bring gifts to children?
9. When does life begin?
10. Why don't the students proof read their papers?

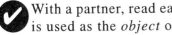 With a partner, read each of the following questions and write a response where a noun clause is used as the *object* of the sentence.

example: Where does our professor live?
              I don't know where our professor lives. (object of sentence)

1. How long will it take for a foreign student to graduate from this college?
2. How will we get the money to repair our car?
3. When will summer school begin?
4. What kind of gift will the students give the professor at the end of the term?
5. How much does a new car cost?
6. Where is the director of the ESL program?
7. Why is Carlota always late for class?
8. How far is it from New York to Florida?
9. What will you and your husband do after you complete your degrees?
10. How many stars are in the sky tonight?

Other Uses of Noun Clauses . . . .

 In numbers 1 and 2, read the following sentences. *Underline the noun clause* and answer the questions below them.

1. a. The reason why she failed the test is obvious.
   b. The times when I came to work late were recorded by the manager.

What part of speech are the words that precede the noun clause? _____
How are the noun clauses functioning in these sentences?
They are _____.

2. a. She is afraid that she is pregnant again.
   b. We were sure that she was stealing the money.
   c. They were delighted that she was safe.

What part of speech are the words that precede the noun clause? _____
How are the noun clauses functioning in these sentences?
They are modifying _____ .

Read the following letter. With a partner, complete the sentences with a noun clause.

Dear Andrea,

I am writing to ask your opinion about a problem my friend Sharon is having. Sharon is sixteen years old and six weeks pregnant. She is afraid and doesn't know what <u>she doing</u> .

When I heard about what _____ , my opinion was that _____ .

But, since I am only a seventeen year old young woman, I think that _____ if

you would recommend to us what _____ about what _____ .

Because her boyfriend, Carl, is only sixteen too and doesn't work, it is unlikely that

_____ . Moreover, he has said that _____ because

he wants to finish his education. But, I am fearful that _____ since he

hasn't called her since she told him about the pregnancy.

I believe you will know what _____. Please write back as soon as possible.

Love,
Carmela

Dear Carmela,

What _____ was quite a shock. I don't understand why

_____ , and I'm not sure about what _____.

I sense that _____ because he hasn't called Sharon since she told

him about the pregnancy. What _____ is not right, but he is probably

also frightened and unsure of what _____ . But, your friend can not depend

on what _____ . She must make some very serious decisions.

Are Sharon's parents aware of what _____? I suggest that

_____ . Her parents may be angry about this situation, but they are the

people who love and care about her. They will be interested in what _____ .

I am sure they won't be delighted about what _____ , but they are the

only ones who will really help her with this problem.

I hope that _____ . But, just remember every person is en-

titled to do whatever _____ ,and this is a very difficult decision.

Please let me know how_____ .

Love,
Andrea

Writing: Write a letter to Sharon. Tell her what you think she should do. Be sure to include at least eight noun clauses. Include at least one noun clause which is the *subject* of the sentence, one noun clause which is the *object of the sentence*, one noun clause which is the *object of the preposition* and one that *modifies an adjective*.

Yes/No Questions as Noun Clauses . . . .

 Read the following dialogs.

1. a: Is Tammy a college graduate?
   b: I don't know <u>if Tammy is a college graduate.</u>
   or b: I don't know <u>whether Tammy is a college graduate.</u>
   or b: I don't know <u>whether or not Tammy is a college graduate.</u>

2. a: Is Mary pregnant again?
   b: I'm not sure <u>if Mary is pregnant again.</u>
   or b: I'm not sure <u>whether Mary is pregnant again.</u>
   or b: I'm not sure <u>whether or not Mary is pregnant again.</u>

When a question can be answered by either *Yes* or *No* and the speaker wants to express uncertainty, what relative pronouns are used to introduce the noun clause?

_____ or _____ or _____

R u l e

4

When writing a noun clause that expresses **uncertainty**, the relative pronouns **if** or **whether** or **whether or not** are used to start the clause.

example: We aren't certain <u>if</u> she is married.
We aren't certain <u>whether</u> she is married.
We aren't certain <u>whether or not</u> she is married.

 With a partner, orally answer the following questions expressing *uncertainty*. Be sure to use the relative pronouns *if*, *whether* or *whether or not*.

example: Are you going on vacation this summer?
We're not sure <u>if we're going on vacation this summer.</u>

1. Does your teacher like apple pie?
2. Is the information that student gave us accurate?
3. Does this train go to Manhattan?
4. Is the library open on Sunday?
5. Does the book cost less than fifty dollars?
6. Does this class understand the lesson on noun clauses?
7. Is everyone in that class going to pass the writing exam?
8. Is the professor going to end the class early today?
9. Will the students give the instructor an expensive gift at the end of the term?
10. Can a student miss ten classes and still pass this course?

Other Noun Clauses ....

✔ Read the following sentences.

1. a. I don't know <u>when Macy's opens.</u>
    b. I'm not sure <u>when school begins.</u>
    c. <u>When to give a surprise test</u> is up to the teacher.

The relative pronoun <u>when</u> is used to write a noun clause of _____.

2. a. She doesn't know <u>where her coat is.</u>
    b. They are certain <u>of where he lives.</u>
    c. I wonder <u>where my husband is.</u>

The relative pronoun <u>where</u> is used to write a noun clause of_____.

3. a. She still wonders <u>why he never came home that night.</u>
    b. You have asked yourself <u>why she did that.</u>
    c. <u>Why she married him</u> is a good question.

The relative pronoun <u>why</u> is used to write a noun clause of_____.

4. a. <u>How much I paid for this dress</u> is my business.
    b. The mother told her son <u>how many shirts he should buy.</u>

The relative pronouns <u>how much</u> and <u>how many</u> are used to write noun clauses of

_____.

5. a. I don't know <u>how far we have traveled.</u>
    b. <u>How far we are from the lake</u> is anyone's guess.

The relative pronoun <u>how far</u> is used to write a noun clause of_____.

6. a. I am not sure <u>how long I can wait.</u>
    b. She wasn't aware of <u>how long she was out that night.</u>

The relative pronoun <u>how long</u> is used to write a noun clause which expresses a

_____.

5

A noun clause of **time** is introduced by the relative pronoun **when**.
example: I am sure of <u>when the party begins.</u>

A noun clause of **location** is introduced by the relative pronoun **where**.
example: I don't know <u>where I put my wallet.</u>

A noun clause of **reason** is introduced by the relative pronoun **why**.
example: I know <u>why I behaved so poorly.</u>

A noun clause of **quantity** is introduced by the relative pronouns **how much** or **how many**.
example: I am not sure <u>how much money I make.</u>
I know <u>how many students are absent.</u>

A noun clause of **distance** is introduced by the relative pronouns **how far**.
example: I am not sure <u>how far I walked </u>that day.

A noun clause which express the **duration of an amount of time** is introduced by the relative pronoun **how long**.
example: I don't know <u>how long the movie is.</u>

✔ With a partner, answer the following questions using the relative pronoun in parentheses to form a noun clause in the answer.

example: When will Abdul ever stop talking? (when)
We're not sure when Abdul will ever stop talking.
or
I wonder when Abdul will ever stop talking.
or
I don't know when Abdul will ever stop talking.

1. When was President Kennedy killed? (when)
2. Where was President Kennedy assassinated? (where)
3. Why was President Kennedy assassinated? (why)
4. How many bullets were fired at President Kennedy? (how many)
5. How much did President Kennedy change civil rights in this country? (how much)
6. How long was President Kennedy in office? (how long)

✔ *Writing:* With a partner, imagine that you are helping the person in charge of the ESL program at your school interview new ESL instructors. Create a list of questions to ask the candidates for the job. Then write the type of answers you would want to hear. Be sure each answer contains noun clauses that begin with the following relative pronouns: *what, if, whether or not, when, where, how many, how much, how long, why, who* etc.

example:
1. What is the teacher's name?
I would ask <u>what the teacher's name is.</u>

2. Where did you get your college degree?
I would want to know <u>where the teacher got his/her college degree.</u>

3. How long has he/she been teaching ESL?
I would ask <u>how long he/she has been teaching ESL.</u>

 Speaking: Ask your teacher or other teachers in the ESL program to answer your questions.

Noun Clauses Which Begin with the Relative Pronoun That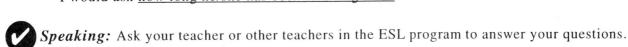

 Read the following sentences and underline the noun clause.

1. a. I think that she cooks well.
   b. I think she cooks well.
2. a. It is obvious that she is confused.
   b. It is obvious she is confused.

Is there a difference in meaning in these pairs of sentences?

_____

What is different in each of these sentence pairs?_____
The relative pronoun is_____ in letter b of each example.

Why isn't it necessary to use the word *that* in these noun clauses?

_____
When the relative pronoun _____introduces a noun clause, it (does, does not)
have any meaning. Therefore, it is_____.

R u l e

6

When the relative pronoun **that** introduces a noun clause, it has no meaning. It just marks the start of the noun clause. Therefore, it is **optional**.

example: I am sure <u>that she is lying.</u>
I am sure <u>she is lying.</u>

 With a partner, read the following letter. Locate the noun clauses and re-write the letter excluding the relative pronoun that from the noun clauses.

Dear Carl:

I received a letter from a friend of yours. It said that you and your girlfriend were expecting a

baby. I was very shocked when I heard this news, and I was wondering how you were feeling

about what has happened.

I am sure that you're feeling confused right now. But, don't think that it is the end of the world.

Sometimes it seems that there is no solution or good alternative. But, I believe that the two of

you will work this out carefully and responsibly.

Although I'm uncertain as to what you should do about this situation, I'm confident that you'll

do what is best for everyone concerned.

Take care.

Love,

Ali

Using the Subjunctive Mood in Noun Clauses . . . .

 Read the following sentences.

1. a. I suggested that she <u>study</u> harder.
   b. My husband insisted that he <u>pay</u> the bill.
   c. It is essential that young children <u>not use</u> drugs.

Why isn't there any subject verb agreement in these noun clauses?
The subjunctive mood is usually used in noun clauses after verbs that express
_____ . Therefore, the verb in the noun clause (is, is not) conjugated. It is
left in its simple form.

How was the verb made negative in this case?
When using the subjunctive mood in a noun clause, the verb is made negative by placing the
word _____before the unconjugated verb.

R u l e

7

The **subjunctive mood** is usually used in noun clauses after verbs that **express importance.** That is the verb is not conjugated. It is kept in the simple form.
   example: The doctor recommended that <u>he stay</u> in bed for a week.

The verb is made negative by placing the word **not** before the unconjugated verb.
   example: I advised that <u>she not do</u> the assignment.

✔ With a partner, complete the following sentences with an appropriate verb. Be sure to use the subjunctive mood or correct tense when necessary.

Dear Carl,

I heard your news the other day. Carmela requested that I (write)_____to you immediately. I suggest you (be)_____married immediately. You are responsible for what you (do)_____ and there is an innocent child involved in this situation. It is essential that you (not, ignore)_____your responsibility. It is also imperative that you (make) _____ plans to provide for your new family. You will have to get a full time job and continue your education at a later time.

It is also important that Sharon (see) _____a doctor in order to make sure that she (be)_____in good health. I advise that she (not, neglect) _____ her health or the baby's. Your mother is also insisting that she (help) _____out when the baby is born. I recommend that you (act)_____maturely since this is your family.

Love,

Your father

✔ With a partner write to Carl and tell him what to do. Be sure to sure to use some of the following verb noun clause combinations:

insist that	be important that	suggest that	be imperative that
demand that	advise that	propose that	be essential that
request that	recommend that		

✔ *Writing:* Read the following letter. Decide whether you agree or disagree with this young man. Then write a brief composition explaining your opinion. In this essay, be sure to include *ten noun clauses* and under line them. Be sure to include the following noun clause forms.

- One noun clause should be the <u>subject</u> of the sentence.
  example: <u>What this guy is doing</u> is immoral.
- One noun clause should be the <u>object</u> of the sentence.
  example: I don't understand <u>how he can act this way.</u>
- One noun clause should be the <u>object of the preposition</u>.
  example: This guy doesn't care <u>about what he's doing to his own child.</u>

- One noun clause should <u>modify an adjective</u>.
  example: I am certain <u>that this has affected his son badly.</u>
- One noun clause should use <u>the subjunctive mood</u>.
  example: The judge should have insisted <u>that he be put in jail for refusing to support his son.</u>

Dear Pedro:

I am 28 years old. A few years ago, I dated a girl named Maria who became pregnant during our short relationship. I was only 19 at that time and was not ready to have a family.

After Maria told me about the pregnancy, we split up, and I started college. Last year I married another girl, and two weeks later Maria filed for child support. The judge ordered me to pay 30 % of my income until this child is eighteen years old. I am really angry. I never wanted to have this child, so why should I have to pay for it?

Maria decided to have that child even though I told her to get an abortion or give the child up for adoption. She refused. Therefore, I think she should be completely responsible for supporting her child. Moreover, Maria has refused to work. Why must I shoulder all the financial burdens alone?

I can't afford all this child support. I have a lot of bills from my college loans, car, rent etc. I am barely able to pay my own bills.

I think this is extremely unfair! What do you think?

Forced to be a Father

Adjective Clauses

6

The objective of this chapter is to teach students:

- *how to form adjective clauses,*
- *how to use adjective clauses in order to enhance their writing.*

Review of Adjectives

 Read the following letter. Underline all the adjectives and draw an arrow to the noun that the adjectives describe.

Dear Manny,

I'm a single man. I am good looking. But, I can't seem to find a nice woman.

I've responded to personal ads. I've participated in singles groups. I've even gone to clubs.

The only interested women are not my type. They don't care about their appearance, or they are very religious and only want friendship. I'm sure you know about these women. It seems that all the beautiful professionals are already involved in relationships.

Are there any eligible, attractive women to date? Why are all the nice women tied down? I'd like some help.

Paolo

Purpose of Adjectives

What does an adjective do?
An adjective is a word that _____ a noun, pronoun or word groups that function as nouns.

How does using an adjective improve the meaning of a sentence?
An adjective makes a sentence more _____ .

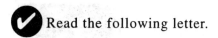 Read the following letter.

Dear Manny,

I'm a single man who wants to get married. I am good looking, but I can't seem to find a nice woman who is attractive to me.

I've responded to personal ads which never work out. I've participated in singles groups that are a bore. I've even gone to clubs which are just like a meat market.

The only women who are interested in me are not my type. They don't care about their appearance which is a big problem, or they are very religious and only want friendship. I'm sure you know about these women who don't understand the meaning of a healthy relationship. It seems that all the beautiful professionals to whom I'm attracted are already involved in relationships.

Are there any eligible, attractive women that are interested in dating? Why are all the nice women I like tied down? I'd like some help.

Paolo

Which letter is more interesting?
The_____ letter is more interesting.

Why was it more interesting?
The_____letter is more interesting because it contains_____.

What was added to this letter that made it more interesting?
_____were added to this letter to make it more interesting.

Where is an adjective clause located?
An adjective clause is located _____the noun it modifies.

Can an adjective clause stand alone as a sentence?
_____, an adjective clause is a _____clause and can not function as a sentence.

Rule

1

An **adjective** is a word that modifies or describes a **noun**, **pronoun** or a **group of words that take the place of a noun**.

> *example:* Maria and Jose bought a <u>beautiful</u> <u>red</u> car.

An **adjective clause** is positioned immediately after the **noun** it is modifying.

> noun
> modified   adjective clause
> *example:* Mary, <u>who is a wonderful cook</u>, is going to make the dinner.

An adjective clause is a **dependent clause** that can not stand alone as a sentence.

> *example:* Juana, <u>who works in the diner</u>, is in my class.

Creating Adjective Clauses

✓ Read each of the following sets of sentences.
Underline the adjective clause in each sentence.
Draw an arrow to the noun that the adjective clause is modifying.
Remember the sentences marked with * are incorrect.

1. a. The chair that he sat on is green.
   b. The chair he sat on is green.
   *c. The chair he sat on i̶t̶ is green.

2. a. The food that we ate was delicious.
   b. The food we ate was delicious.
   *c. The food that we ate i̶t̶ was delicious.

3. a. The car that we drove was red.
   b. The car we drove was red.
   *c. The car we drove i̶t̶ was red.

What word in the adjective clause must be omitted?
The word that refers to the _____ being modified must be omitted.

Why is the relative pronoun *that* optional?
The relative pronoun <u>that</u> may be omitted when the noun being modified is the _____ of the verb in the adjective clause.

Rule

2

The adjective clause must omit the word that refers to the **noun** it is modifying.

> *example:* The young woman who <u>(s̶h̶e̶)</u> cooks well is making the meal.

> *example:* The man that I will marry <u>(h̶i̶m̶)</u> must be rich.

Rule 3

The **relative pronoun** may be omitted only when the noun being modified is the object of the adjective clause.

> *example:* The statue <u>that</u> I put on the shelf is broken.
> The statue I put on the shelf is broken.

✔ Read the following pairs of sentences and answer the questions.

4. a. The clock which I bought is an antique.
   b. The clock that I bought is an antique.
5. a. The room which I cleaned is filthy again.
   b. The room that I cleaned is filthy again.

What relative pronouns are used to introduce the adjective clauses in numbers 4 and 5?
The relative pronouns_____ and _____ are used to introduce these two adjective clauses.

What *relative pronoun(s)* can be used when the noun is an *object* or a *thing*?
The relative pronouns_____ or_____ are used to introduce an adjective clause when the noun being modified is and *object* or a *thing*.

Rule 4

When the noun being modified is an **object** or a **thing**, use the relative pronouns **that** or **which**.

> *example:* The coat <u>that</u> I am wearing is old.
> The coat <u>which</u> I am wearing is old.

6. a. The book which is in the hall is mine.
   *b. The <u>book</u> which <u>are</u> in the hall is mine.
7. *a. The <u>toys</u> that <u>is</u> in the hall are my son's.
   b. The toys that are in the hall are my son's.

Why are 6.b and 7.a incorrect?
There must be subject verb agreement between the verb in the adjective clause and the _____ it modifies.

Rule 5

There must be **subject verb agreement** between the modified noun and the verb in the adjective clause.

| plural | plural |
| noun | verb |

> *example:* The <u>dogs that are gentle</u> make good house pets.

8. a. The women who arrived late got fired.
   b. The women that arrived late got fired.
   *c. The women arrived late got fired.
9. a. The children who are read to at home develop better reading skills.
   b. The children that are read to at home develop better reading skills.
   *c. The children are read to at home develop better reading skills.

What relative pronouns are used when the noun is a person?
The relative pronouns _____ or _____ are used when the noun being modified is a person.

Why can't the relative pronoun be omitted in 8.c and 9.c?
The relative pronoun <u>may not be omitted</u> when the noun being modified is the _____ of the adjective clause.

R u l e

6

When the noun being modified is a person, the relative pronouns **that** or **who** are used.
   example: The children <u>who</u> arrived late were sent to the office.
   The children <u>that</u> arrived late were sent to the office.

R u l e

7

The **relative pronoun** may not be omitted when the noun being modified is the **subject** of the adjective clause.
   example: The mothers <u>who</u> are in the PTA baked the cakes.

10. a. The women that I saw come in late got fired.
    b. The women whom I saw come in late got fired.
    ?c. The women who I saw come in late got fired.
11. a. The parents that the teacher saw were satisfied with the reports.
    b. The parents whom the teacher saw were satisfied with the reports.
    ?c. The parents who the teacher saw were satisfied with the reports.

Why is the relative pronoun *whom* used in 10.b and 11.b?
The relative pronoun <u>whom</u> is used when the noun being modified is a <u>person</u> and the _____ of the adjective clause.

Why are 10.c and 11.c correct or incorrect?
In <u>informal colloquial speech</u>, even though the noun being modified is the _____ of the adjective clause the relative pronoun <u>who</u> is sometimes used.

Rule 8

In formal writing or speech, the relative pronoun **whom** is used when the noun being modified is a **person** and the **object** of the adjective clause.

object

example: The girls <u>whom</u> I like t̶h̶e̶m̶ are all single.

Rule 9

When the noun being modified is the object of the adjective clause, the relative pronoun **who** is sometimes used in **informal colloquial speech**.

example: The girls who I like are all single.

✔ *Oral Exercise:* With a partner combine the following sentences making the second sentence an adjective clause.

example: I know the people. They are waiting at the corner for the bus.
I know the people who are waiting at the corner for the bus.

1. I met students at the restaurant. It also is a good place to go dancing.

_____

2. I met students at the restaurant. They are from my evening class.

_____

3. The child dove into the pool. She swims well.

_____

4. The teenagers saw the people. The people were waiting on line.

_____

5. The teenagers saw the people. The teenagers were very alert.

_____

6. The jewelry is very valuable. I found it in the attic.

_____

7. The eagle may become extinct someday. It is a beautiful bird.

_____

8. My friends never visit my house. They come from a different culture.

_____

9. The card shop sells newspapers. The shop is on the corner.

_____

10. The lady is reading a book. She is next on line.

_____

✔ *Oral Exercise:* With a partner, insert an adjective clause in each of the following sentences.

example: I had a date last night.
I had a date *which was a disaster* last night.

1. The class saw a movie last night.
2. The butcher shop sells meat.
3. The mosque was crowded with people on the holiday.
4. The picture of the baby is hanging on the wall.
5. The computer is broken.

✔ Read each of the following paragraphs and correct any mistakes in the use of adjective clauses.

1. I had a friend who he was twenty years old and handsome, but he never had a steady girl-friend because he was a selfish person. All the girls whom went out with him made negative comments about his egotistical personality. One of the girls who recently broke up with him told me that he was a real clown and always played mean jokes on her. Now she who hates him because he wasn't nice and never helped people whom needed a hand.

2. My friend Raul who he is a great guy is afraid to ask a girl out on a date because she might refuse him. He is a very sensitive person that get hurt very easily. He thinks he is an unattractive guy whom can't attract women, but some girls that I know them think he is really cute. One girl who asked him out on a date, but he turned her down because she was not his type. The girls that he like they don't ask him out, so he is a very lonely guy who sit alone at home every Saturday night. He is a very insecure person who should change if he wants to have a relationship with a woman.

3. My brother who is thirty-five years old has never had a girlfriend. The place which he work is very boring and there are no females whom are available. My mother is a very traditional woman who worries about why he doesn't associate with women. I believe he is the only guy who I know who never had a date by the time he was thirty-five. Now my mother who is looking for a girl for my brother, and she has located a twenty-eight year old woman who never

had a boyfriend either. My mother wants my brother to meet this woman who she work in a hospital and have a good job. I hope they will get married so that my mother will stop worrying.

✔ With a partner or in a small group, read the following letter written in response to the man who can't find an attractive woman. Whenever possible combine sentences in order to form an adjective clause, or add an adjective clause to make the letter more interesting.

example: I just finished reading your letter *which was quite interesting.* It reminds me of an incident *which happened many years ago.*

Dear Single Man:

I just finished reading your letter. It was quite interesting. It reminds me of an incident. It happened many years ago.

There was a young woman. Her name was Sarah. Sarah was very attractive, and many gentlemen wanted to date her. But, there was always something wrong with the men she met. One man was too fat. Another man didn't make enough money. Another had funny ears.

Sarah wasn't getting any younger. She wanted to get married and have a family. Year after year she hoped to meet a nice eligible guy. He had to be perfect. Since she always found fault with the fellows she met, Sarah never became serious with anyone.

Finally Sarah got desperate. She talked to some friends and told them about her problem. The discussions were long and painful. After several discussions, Sarah began to realize that she couldn't find a decent man because she was too dissatisfied with herself. Sarah got herself some professional help. It was very expensive. But, she learned to accept herself. She eventually met a very nice guy. He wasn't perfect. She married this guy. They now have two children and a lot of happiness.

Therefore, if none of the women you meet are good enough, maybe it is not the women. Maybe it is time to look within yourself.

Sincerely,
Imperfect Yet Married

Write a letter to Imperfect yet Married responding to her letter about this problem. Be sure to include five adjective clauses.

More on Adjective Clauses

 Read each sentence and underline the adjective clauses. Remember the * means a sentence is incorrect.

1. a. The teachers with whom I work are friendly.
   b   The teachers whom I work with are friendly.
   *c   The teachers with who I work are friendly.
   ?d. The teachers who I work with are friendly.
2. a. The children at whom I was looking are my nieces.
   b. The children whom I was looking at are my nieces.
   *c. The children at who I was looking are my nieces.
   ?d. The children who I was looking at are my nieces.

Why is whom used instead of who in 1.a and 2.a?
The relative pronoun <u>whom</u> is used because the adjective clause is the _____ of the preposition _____.

Why are the prepositions *in front of* the adjective clauses in 1.a. and 2.a. but in the end of the adjective clause in 1.b and 2b.?
When an adjective clause is the object of the preposition, the preposition may be placed at the _____ or the _____ of the adjective clause.

What is wrong in 1.c and 2.c?
When an adjective clause is the object of the preposition and the preposition is placed <u>in the front of the clause</u>, the relative pronoun _____ must be used.

Why can 1.d and 2.d be correct and incorrect?
In _____English, the relative pronoun <u>who</u> can be used if the preposition is at the _____ of the adjective clause.

Writing: Write a personal ad to meet a boy/girlfriend using adjective clauses.

example: A single woman who is a tall attractive professional is seeking a serious relationship with a tall rich man who is an intelligent professional who knows how to cook, clean and have fun.

10

1. An **adjective clause** can be the **object of a preposition**.

   example: I am the person <u>to whom you must speak</u>.

2. The **preposition** can be in the **front** or the **end** of the adjective clause.

   example: The child <u>to whom I spoke</u> is very sick.
   The child <u>whom I spoke to</u> is very sick.

3. When the **preposition** is in the **front** of the adjective clause and the modified noun is a person, the relative pronoun **whom** must be used because whom is the object of the preposition.

   example: The man <u>for whom I work</u> is very fair.

4. When the **preposition** is at the end of the adjective clause, in casual or colloquial English, the relative pronoun **who** can be used.

   example: This is the student <u>who you asked me about</u> yesterday.

   But, in formal written English, it is correct to use the relative pronoun **whom**.

   example: This is the student <u>whom you asked me about</u> yesterday.

 Read each sentence and underline the adjective clauses.
Remember the * means a sentence is incorrect.

3. a. I like the man that I talked to.

    b. I like the man I talked to.

    *c. I like the man t̸o whom I talked <u>to</u>.

4. a. They enjoyed the women with whom they dined.

    b. They enjoyed the women they dined with.

    *c. They enjoyed the women <u>with</u> whom they dined w̸th.

What is omitted in 3.b and 4.b?
When the preposition is placed at the end of the adjective clause, the _____ can be omitted.

What is wrong with 3c and 4c?
The preposition may be placed at either the <u>beginning</u> or the <u>end</u> of the adjective clause but _____ in both the beginning and the end of the adjective clause.

Rule 11

1. When the preposition is at the end of the adjective clause, the **relative pronoun may be omitted**.

   example: The girl <u>all the men are looking at</u> is beautiful.
   Note the relative pronoun is omitted.

2. When an adjective clause is the object of the preposition, the **preposition** should be placed either in the **beginning** or the **end** of the clause. It **should not be in both the front and the back**.

   example: The boy <u>to</u> whom the teacher spoke is brilliant.
   The boy whom the teacher spoke <u>to</u> is brilliant.

5. *a.   They who are late will be fired.
   b.   Anyone who is late will be fired.

6. *a.   He who fails the final must repeat the course.
   b.   Everyone who fails the final must repeat the course.

Why are 5.a and 6.a incorrect?
A subject or object _____ can not take an adjective clause.

Why are 5.b and 6.b correct?
An indefinite _____ can take an adjective clause.

Rule 12

1. A subject or object pronoun **can not** take an adjective clause.

2. An indefinite pronoun **can** take an adjective clause.

   example: <u>Someone who was sitting at my desk</u> made a mess.

✔ *Oral Exercise:* With a partner combine the following sentences making the second sentence an adjective clause which is the object of the preposition.

1. The vacation was great. We went on it.
2. Here is the book. Mary asked me for it.
3. The doctor is not available. You should talk to him.
4. The bed was very uncomfortable. I slept on it.
5. That woman is not too nice. He is crazy about her.
6. The person is annoying me. I am angry at her.
7. The students are lazy. She studies with them.
8. The child is frightened. I spoke to him.
9. The gifts are nice. I am interested in them.

Read each paragraph carefully and make corrections in the use of adjective clauses.

1. The man to who Maria is married to is kind of weird. He is forty-five years old, but he still wants to live with his mother whom he lived with until he got married six months ago. His mother who is extremely selfish and enjoys breaking up his relationships she wants to end his marriage to which she objected to it from the beginning.

2. Caesar is an irresponsible person who is always asking for more money which it is hard to get these days. He wants cash because he has a girlfriend with who he has been going out she likes to go to expensive places. Caesar has a cousin who he is rich and is trying to get Caesar's girl to date him. I wonder what will happen with this relationship in which there are a lot of problems in it.

3. My parents who I have been living with in this country are very strict. They won't let me go on dates because dating which it is permitted in this country is not part of our customs in which my folks are immersed in. My older relatives who I love them very much they don't understand that this is a very different culture in which I must learn to survive in it.

4. Back home I had a friend with whom I was very close with, and he had a great personality. He was like my brother. We always hung around and had lots of fun together. His face who was badly scared and wasn't too attractive, and he was rather skinny too. Even though he wasn't great looking, his character and personality were the best. Therefore, he had a lot of girlfriends that were also really pretty. This proves to me that there are a lot of people who understands the importance of a good person.

With a partner or in a small group, use the following list of preposition combinations or the list in Appendix B to add adjective clauses which are the object of the preposition to the following letter. You may also add appropriate sentences which contain adjective clauses.

speak to	tired of	wait for	discuss with	different from
prepared for	take care of	arrived at	believe in	compared to
depend on	devoted to	aware of	accustomed to	ready for
sure of	proud of	hear about	introduce to	insist on
satisfied with	listen to	familiar with	interested in	dissatisfied with
engaged to	feel for	get rid of	kind to	responsible for

example: I just read your letter *which I would like to respond to,* and I can't help but pity you and your shallow attitude *which you are suffering from.*

Dear Single Man:

I just read your letter, and it made me angry. You want to date a perfect woman. She must be of high intelligence, attractive and willing to have an intimate relationship. Why would a substantial woman find this kind of relationship appealing?

You said nothing seems to work for you. You've answered personal ads, joined singles groups and gone to night clubs. But, you never meet any suitable women. All the available women are either obese, deeply religious or already committed. It appears that no woman is good enough for you.

Are you a perfect individual? Is it possible that there are unpleasant sides to your appearance or personality? Just because a woman isn't extremely beautiful, it doesn't mean she isn't worthwhile.

I suggest you take a good look at yourself instead of complaining about the women you attract.

Single Girl Who Isn't Perfect

Writing: Write a response to *Single Girl Who Isn't Perfect.* Be sure to include three adjective clause which are the object of the preposition.
or
Write a composition comparing dating in your country to dating in the United States.

Restrictive Adjective Clauses································

 Read the following sentences and underline the adjective clauses.

1. a. The doctor who performed the surgery was a very skilled surgeon.
    b. Dr. Bush, who performed the surgery, was a very skilled surgeon.

Why is the adjective clause in 1.b separated by commas, yet 1.a is not separated by commas?
In 1.a the adjective clause is＿＿＿＿＿＿＿to identify who the doctor is. This is known as
a＿＿＿＿＿＿adjective clause. However in 1.b, the adjective clause is not＿＿＿＿＿＿＿
since we already know who the doctor is, so commas are inserted. This is known as a ＿＿＿＿＿
＿＿＿＿＿＿ adjective clause.

R u l e

13

When an adjective clause is **not separated by commas**, it is a **restrictive** adjective clause which is needed to identify the noun being modified.

example: The teacher who the students like is on maternity leave this semester.

This clause is needed in order to determine which teacher the students like. Therefore, it is a restrictive clause.

When an adjective clause **is separated by commas**, it is a **nonrestrictive** adjective clause which is not needed to determine the identity of the noun being modified.

example: Mrs. Delia, who the students like, is on maternity leave this semester.

This adjective clause is not needed to identify the noun being modified. Therefore, it is a nonrestrictive adjective clause.

 Read the following sentences and underline the adjective clauses.

2. a. The students who passed the final exam celebrated.
    b. The students, who passed the final exam, celebrated.
3. a. The parents who wanted to speak to the principal waited for him after the meeting.
    b. The parents, who wanted to speak to the principal, waited for him after the meeting.

What is different in each pair of sentences?
The adjective clause in letter <u>a</u> of each sentence pair is not separated by＿＿＿＿＿＿＿＿＿.

How does the use of commas to separate the adjective clause alter the meaning of these sentence?
Letter <u>a</u> of each sentence pair contains a ＿＿＿＿＿＿＿＿＿adjective clause, but letter <u>b</u> contains a ＿＿＿＿＿＿＿ adjective clause. When the adjective clause is made restrictive (the commas are omitted), it limits the meaning. In this case, it means that only some of the students passed the test or only some of the parents spoke to the principal. However, when the adjective clause is made nonrestrictive (the commas are included), it does not limit the meaning. In these examples, it means＿＿＿＿＿＿＿＿ of the students passed, or ＿＿＿＿＿＿＿＿＿ of the parents wanted to speak to the principal.

Rule 14

A **restrictive** adjective clause **is not separated by commas** and it limits the meaning of the clause.

> *example:* The women who are laughing are my aunts.

This restrictive adjective clause limits the group of women to just those who are laughing.

A **nonrestrictive** adjective clause **is separated by commas** and does not limit the meaning.

> *example:* The women, who are laughing, are my aunts.

This nonrestrictive adjective clause does not limit the meaning of the word women since all the women in the group are laughing.

 Read the following sentences.

4. a. Mrs. Korfski, who is my neighbor, will drive me to class.
    *b. Mrs. Korfski, that is my neighbor, will drive me to class.
5. a. The friends, whom I like the best, always mind their own business.
    *b. The friends, that I like the best, always mind their own business.

Both of the above sentences contain nonrestrictive adjective clauses. But what is wrong in 4.b and 5.b?
In nonrestrictive adjective clauses, which are separated by commas, the relative pronoun _____ is never used.

Rule 15

Nonrestrictive adjective clauses never use the relative pronoun **that**.
> *example:* The books, which are on the table, are mine.

 Add restrictive and nonrestrictive adjectives to the following sentences.

Maria is my neighbor. She has become one of my best friends because of her willingness to help my children and me survive in this new country. When I first arrived in New York City, I didn't know how to speak English. Therefore, when I had to enroll Carla in kindergarten, I didn't know how to communicate or where to go. But, Maria asked her husband Diego to escort me to the school and translate the information for me. Another time, I was called to the Office of Immigration for an interview. Since I didn't know much about the subways, Maria drove me to the office so that I would be safe. Maria has also helped me when my children were sick and I had to work at the hospital. In general, Maria has always been there for me, and that's why she has become my best friend in the United States.

 Read each paragraph carefully and make any corrections necessary to the adjective clauses.

1. Jose who work in a grocery store wants his boss to increase his salary, but Jose is a young person who doesn't do much work and expect his boss to pay him well. His boss said he would increase his salary if he worked harder. Jose who the boss really likes him even though he is lazy didn't like the idea of working harder, so he left his job. Which paid him well for what he did and was located in a nice neighborhood. Now he has no job. He makes no money and hangs out on the street where he does nothing productive.

2. My friend, Mike whom is a very dependent guy would like to marry an independent woman which could take care of him. He always makes negative comments about the girls whom he dates. Mike who is not faultless wants to find a perfect woman. He always tells his friends that women who has a lot of money want to be friends with him, but nobody believes what he says. Everyone who know Mike knows the sad truth.

 Writing: The following is a very simple composition. Re-write the composition to make it more interesting by inserting adjective clauses that include:

- the relative pronouns who/whom, that, which,
- omit the relative pronoun at least one time,
- use the relative pronoun with the object of the preposition in the front and end of two different clauses,
- use restrictive and nonrestrictive adjective clauses correctly.

A man lived in a house. His name was Paul. Paul didn't work. Paul didn't have any friends. He never took a bath. His house was old and dirty. Paul didn't clean himself or his house.

Once a week Paul's sister would visit him. His sister would bring him food and spending money. But, Paul never left the house, and he never spent the money. His sister would try to clean up the house. But, it was impossible. The house was just too dirty.

When Paul knew his sister was coming, he would wait at the front door. One week Paul's sister didn't arrive. Paul waited and waited by the door. Finally, he stepped outside into the front garden. When he looked down the block, he saw an ambulance. Paul's heart pounded. His mind began to race. He was afraid that something had happened to his sister.

✔ Complete this story. Describe why Paul's sister was either late or hurt in an accident. Be sure to use at least six adjective clauses.

····Review of the Present Tense····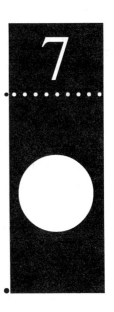

The objective of this chapter is to teach students the meaning and form of:

- *present tense affirmative,*
- *negative,*
- *interrogative.*

Review of Subject Verb Agreement in the Present Tense. . . . .

 Read the following sentences.

a. I **walk** to school everyday.
b. You **walk** to school everyday.
c. He **walks** to school everyday.
d. She **walks** to school everyday.

e. It **walks** to school everyday.
f. We **walk** to school everyday.
g. You **walk** to school everyday.
h. They **walk** to school everyday.

How is the verb formed in the present tense?
In the present tense, use the _____ when the subject is the first person singular or plural (I or we), the second person plural (you) or the third person plural (they). However, add an ___s___ to the simple verb when the *subject is in the third person singular* (he, she, it).

R u l e

1

In the first person singular and plural (I and we), the second person plural (you) and the third person plural (they), use the **simple form of the verb** . **Do not** add the letter **s**.

example: I <u>speak</u> French fluently.   We <u>speak</u> French fluently.
You <u>speak</u> French fluently.   They <u>speak</u> French fluently.

When the subject of a present tense verb is **in the third person singular** (he, she, or it), the letter **s** is added to the end of the simple form of the verb.

example: Marla speak<u>s</u> French.   Carlo like<u>s</u> ice cream.
The dog bark<u>s</u> loudly at night.   A car run<u>s</u> on gasoline.

✔ Complete each of the following sentences with the present tense of the verb in parenthesis.

1. I (take)___take___a shower everyday.
2. She (take)___takes___a bath in the evening.
3. You (get)___get___up very early.
4. Chris (get)___gets___up at noon.
5. Patrick and Michael (sleep)___sleep___in the same room.
6. Liam (sleep)_____in a crib.
7. My husband and I (drive)_____to work together in the morning.
8. Cristafano (shave)_____before he goes to work.
9. Mario and Luigi (drink)_____coffee with their breakfast.
10. Theresa (talk)_____too much.

✔ Complete each sentence using the present tense of the verb in parenthesis.

Dear Yelena,

You'll never believe what I did this year for the holidays. Let me fill you in on the details.

Every year I (receive)_____hundreds of holiday greeting cards. Some people just (sign)_____their names. Other cards (contain)_____small personal notes from the sender. These notes (detail)_____the major events that have taken place in the sender's life. Some of these notes (hold)_____very happy news while others are sometimes sad. However, the cards that (drive)_____me crazy are the ones that have generic news letters.

These generic letters (describe)_____the perfect lives of the people who send them. Each letter usually (include)_____a laundry list of accomplishments that are sometimes outrageous. Moreover, the senders of some of these newsletters frequently (ignore)_____any tragedy or difficulty the recipient of the letter has had during the year by saying something trite such as, "We're all doing very well, and we're certain you are, too." The irony is that you've already sent this person a card telling them about the death of a close relative and a major illness you have had.

On a lighter side, some folks (send)_____ newsletters that (attempt) _____to discretely brag about their financial worth or other accomplishments. For instance, my mother received one card where a friend described her son's new home. Instead of saying that he'd bought a big expensive house, his mother stated, "I can't wait until John David (get)_____the heating bill for this house." In another newsletter, we received the male writer stated, " I finally acquired my dream car which is a Jaguar. I absolutely (love)_____this car But, my wife (make) _____me keep the baby's car seat in the back so that women (know)_____I'm not available."

Well when it came time to send my Christmas cards, I decided I would write a generic letter too, but mine contained a list of tragedies and problems we'd endured during the year. I (wonder) _____what the recipients of my letter thought when they read it. My husband and I also (wonder) _____if anyone caught the humor in it, too

Love,
Rina

✔ Read each of the following sentences.

   a. Mary rarely **brushes** her hair.
   b. John never **teaches** the children bad things.
   c. Peter rarely **watches** television.
   d. Ann usually **kisses** me good night.
   e. Peter never **fixes** his own cars.

What is done differently when the verb ends in *sh, ch, ss* or *x*?
When a verb <u>ends</u> in the consonants <u>sh</u>, <u>ch</u>, <u>ss</u>, or <u>x</u>, add the letters_____ to the simple verb in the third person singular (he, she, or it) of the present tense.

R u l e

2

When the subject of a **present tense** verb is in the **third person singular** (he, she or it) and the verb ends in **sh, ch, ss**, or **x**, the letters **es** are added to the simple form of the verb.

   example: He teach<u>es</u> well.
            The baby kiss<u>es</u> his dolls.
            She mix<u>es</u> the cake batter.

✔ Read both of the following sentences which contain verbs which end in *y*.

1. a. I **study** Italian.   We **study** a lot.
    b. You **study** French.   You **study** a lot.
    c. She **stud<u>ies</u>** a lot.
    d. He **stud<u>ies</u>** a lot.
    e. It **stud<u>ies</u>** a lot.   They **study** a lot.

2. a. I always **pay** in cash.   We always **pay** in cash.
    b. You **buy** candy.   You always **pay** in cash.
    c. He always **pay<u>s</u>** in cash.
    d. She always **pay<u>s</u>** in cash.   They always **pay** in cash.
    e. The ATM always **pay<u>s</u>** in cash.

In the third person singular, what happens when the verb ends in *y* and a consonant precedes the *y*?
When a verb in the third person singular of the present tense (he, she or it) ends in a <u>consonant</u> <u>+ y</u>, ___<u>los</u>___ the letter <u>y</u> to the letter ___<u>ic</u>___ and add the letters ___<u>s</u>___.

In the third person singular, what happens when the verb ends in a *vowel + y* ?
When a verb in the third person singular of the present tense (he, she, it) ends in a <u>vowel + y</u>, the letter _____is added.

R u l e

3

When the subject of a present tense sentence is in the third person singular (he, she or it) and ends in a **consonant** plus the letter **y**, the **y** is changed to an **i** and **es** is added.

example: The word <u>worry</u> becomes <u>worries</u> in the third person singular.
Ann worries about her children.

But, when verb ends in a **vowel** and the letter **y**, the letter **s** is added to the simple form of the verb in the third person singular (he, she or it).

example: The word <u>buy</u> becomes <u>buys</u>.
He always buy<u>s</u> too much meat.

✔ Complete each of the sentences with the word in parenthesis.

1. I (wash)_____the dishes after dinner.
2. Rina (wash)_____the clothes in the washing machine.
3. Elena (brush)___<u>brushes</u>___ her teeth after dinner.
4. Elena and I (brush)_____ our teeth before dinner.
5. After I (wake)_____up, I (stretch)_____ my arms.
6. After Sven (wake)_____up, he (stretch)_____his arms.
7. They (kiss)_____ their mother as they (leave)_____ .
8. The baby (kiss)_____ her mother at bedtime.

9. The repair man (fix)_____ my refrigerator for a small fee.
10. They (fix)_____ my tire at the gas station while I wait in the office.
11. You (mix)_____ the fruit in a large container.
12. Franco (mix)_____ the cake by hand.
13. That child (watch)_____ television all day.
14. Each mother (worry)_____ about her child's health.
15. I (buy)_____ a new car every year.
16. Pete (buy)_____ a new car every two years.
17. Maria and I (study)_____ together after class.
18. Jose (study)_____ in his bedroom after work.
19. The class (enjoy)_____ doing homework.
20. Marco and Chris (enjoy)_____ playing soccer.

✔ *Oral and Written Exercise:* With a partner make a list of some activities you perform every day. Be sure to include the following list of verbs and any others that may be applicable to you.

wake up	drink	ride	speak	wash
sleep	fix	buy	worry	eat
brush	walk	listen	annoy	kiss
rest	pay	study	enjoy	

Next write a paragraph describing what your partner does every day. Try to keep the paragraph in chronological order.

example: Every day Shawnia *wakes* up at seven o'clock and *brushes* her hair.

Irregular Present Tense Verbs ·

✔ Read the following sentences and determine how each verb is used.

I <u>have</u> a red car.   We <u>have</u> four classes on Friday.
You <u>have</u> a test every Monday.   They <u>have</u> two assignments.
He <u>has</u> four brothers.
She <u>has</u> a big brown dog.
It <u>has</u> a big tail.

What verb is used in each of these sentences?
The verb_____ is used in each sentence.

What tense is used in each sentence?
The _____ tense is used in each sentence.

When the subject is *he*, *she* or *it*, what happens?
When the subject is <u>he</u>, <u>she</u> or <u>it</u>, the irregular verb_____ is used.

What is the rule for using the irregular verb *to have* in the present tense?

I _____   we _____
you _____
he _____
she _____   they _____
it _____

R u l e

4

The verb **to have** is an **irregular** verb in the present tense. In the third person singular when the subject is he, she or it, the verb takes the irregular form of **has**.

I	have	we	have
you	have		
he	<u>has</u>		
she	<u>has</u>	they	have
it	<u>has</u>		

✔ Read the following sentences and determine how each verb is used.

I <u>go</u> to college everyday.   We <u>go</u> to the pool on weekends.
You <u>go</u> shopping once a week.
He <u>goes</u> to work at six o'clock.
She <u>goes</u> home by train.   They <u>go</u> to the park to play ball at night.
The dog <u>goes</u> on a walk at night.

What verb is used in each of these sentences?
The verb _____ is used in each sentence.

What tense is used in each sentence?
The _____ tense is used in each sentence.

When the subject is *he*, *she* or *it*, what happens?
When the subject is <u>he</u>, <u>she</u> or <u>it</u> the irregular verb _____ is used.

What is the rule for using the irregular verb *to go* in the present tense?

I _____   we _____
you _____
he _____
she _____   they _____
it _____

5

The verb **to go** is an **irregular** verb in the present tense. In the third person singular when the subject is **he, she or it**, the verb takes the irregular form of **goes**.

I	<u>go</u>	we	<u>go</u>
you	<u>go</u>		
he	<u>goes</u>		
she	<u>goes</u>	they	<u>go</u>
it	<u>goes</u>		

✔ Read the following sentences and determine how each verb is formed.

I <u>do</u> well in school.
You <u>do</u> your homework at night.
He <u>does</u> well on his tests.
She <u>does</u> exercises in the book.
A cat <u>does</u> whatever he wants.

We <u>do</u> our homework in the library.

They <u>do</u> their assignments quickly.

What verb is used in each of these sentences?
The verb _____ is used in each sentence.

What tense is used in each sentence?
The _____ tense is used in each sentence.

When the subject is _he_, _she_ or _it_, what happens?
When the subject is <u>he</u>, <u>she</u> or <u>it</u>, the irregular verb _____ is used.

What is the rule for using the irregular verb _to do_ in the present tense?

I _____	we _____
you _____	
he _____	
she _____	they _____
it _____	

6

The verb **to do** is an **irregular** verb in the present tense. In the third person singular when the subject is **he, she or it**, the verb takes the irregular form of **does**.

I	<u>do</u>	we	<u>do</u>
you	<u>do</u>		
he	<u>does</u>		
she	<u>does</u>	they	<u>do</u>
it	<u>does</u>		

✔ Read the following sentences and determine how each verb is used.

I <u>am</u> a student.   We <u>are</u> at the pool.
You <u>are</u> too young to get married.
He <u>is</u> at work by six o'clock.
She <u>is</u> beautiful.   They <u>are</u> too young to see that movie.
The dog <u>is</u> in the yard.

What verb is used in each of these sentences?
The verb _____ is used in each sentence.

What tense is used in each sentence?
The _____ tense is used in each sentence.

What is the rule for using the irregular verb *to be* in the present tense?

I _____   we _____
you _____
he _____
she _____   they _____
it _____

Rule

7

The verb **to be** is an **irregular** verb in the present tense and uses the following forms:

I	<u>am</u>	we	<u>are</u>
you	<u>are</u>		
he	<u>is</u>		
she	<u>is</u>	they	<u>are</u>
it	<u>is</u>		

✔ Complete each of the following sentences with the word in parenthesis.

1. Maria and Paolo (have)_____two cats and one dog.

2. Claude and I (go)_____to work every morning.

3. Antonio (have)_____ no pets.

4. We (do)_____ our assignments carefully.

5. I (be)_____ a student at the college.

6. Sonia and Pablo (be)_____best friends.

7. Sean (be)_____ always late for class.

8. Jean Louis (go)_____to basketball practice on Saturday morning.

9. Juan (do)_____his piano practice in the evenings.

10. Francois and Joseph (go)_____ swimming on Tuesdays.

11. You (have)_____to study for your exam every day.

12. Alfanso (have)_____to work tonight.

13. They (be)_____very interesting people.

14. She (be)_____too thin.

15. You (be) _____friends with Chris.

Negation in the Present Tense..............................

Read the following sentences.

a. I walk to work everyday.
   I <u>do not</u> walk to school everyday.

   We walk to school everyday.
   We <u>do not</u> walk to school everyday.

b. You walk to school every day.
   You <u>do not</u> walk to school everyday.

c. She walks to school everyday.
   She <u>does not</u> walk to school everyday.

d. He walks to school everyday.
   He <u>does not</u> walk to school everyday.

   They walk to school everyday.
   They <u>do not walk</u> to school everyday.

e. The dog walks to school everyday.
   The dog <u>does not walk</u> to school everyday.

How are verbs in the present tense made negative?
Present tense verbs are made negative by inserting the present tense of the verb _____
after the subject. Next insert the word_____and then the _____ of
the verb. But, note in the third person singular, the verb <u>do</u> takes the form of _____ .

A **present tense** verb is made **negative** by using the following rule.

subject	+	use the present tense of the verb to do	+	not	+	the simple form of the verb	
example:							
Mary		does		not		smoke.	
·I		do		not		drink	beer.

With a partner, orally make the following sentences negative.

1. Some people send newsletters each year.

2. I enjoy receiving generic news letters.

3. Maria makes Steve keep the baby's seat in the car.
4. Their newsletters make me happy.
5. You know what the letter will say.

 Read the following sentences carefully.

a. I am pretty.   We are friends.
   I <u>am not</u> pretty.   We <u>are not</u> friends.
b. You are pretty.
   You <u>are not</u> pretty.
c. She is home.   They are young.
   She <u>is not</u> home.   They <u>are not</u> young.
d. He is home.
   He <u>is not</u> home.

Why don't the following sentences use the verb *do* to make them negative?
When making the verb <u>to be</u> (am, is or are) negative, the word_____is inserted immediately after the words: am, is or are. The verb _____is not used.

Rule

9

In the present tense the verb **to be** (am, is or are) is made negative by inserting the word **not** immediately **after** the verb.

   example: I <u>am not</u> a student anymore.
             She <u>is not</u> in class today.
             They <u>are not</u> happy about the test results.

 Orally make the following sentences negative.

1. The holiday newsletter is enjoyable.
2. We are tired of receiving generic newsletters.
3. You are annoyed when you receive such letters.
4. I am interested in your ideas about my newsletter.
5. Generic newsletters are a way for people to boast about their lives.

 With a partner make the following underlined verbs negative.

Too all,

This <u>is</u> a typical holiday newsletter where I will write about all my accomplishments and those

of my family. I <u>want</u> to tell you what a wonderful year we had. Instead, I want you to know that

my life <u>is</u> a bowl of cherries. I <u>am</u> extremely happy since I've had some serious financial, physi-

cal and family problems.

Our lives <u>are</u> as easy as they were years ago. I <u>work</u> at a job I enjoy. I work for a company that <u>pays</u> me well. I <u>get</u> insurance benefits; therefore, I have to pay over eight thousand dollars a year for decent health coverage. This means that we <u>take</u> any kind of decent vacation each year, and we <u>are</u> on easy street. Our lives <u>are</u> so great anymore.

My husband <u>worries</u> about the bills anymore because he is too busy holding down two jobs. He <u>likes</u> to work two jobs, but he <u>has</u> a choice.

My child <u>is</u> happy in high school. She <u>is</u> interested in getting any kind of education right now. She <u>is</u> very satisfied with her life either.

In summary, our lives <u>are</u> very merry, but I hope yours are!

Seasons Greetings!

The Gasper Family

✔ With a partner, re-read the holiday newsletter in letter D. Write a paragraph explaining why this letter is or is not an appropriate holiday greeting. Be sure to use the present tense in the affirmative and the negative to express your opinion.

example: This is a terrible letter because it does not express any pleasant feelings which are supposed to be expressed during this season.

Forming Questions in the Present Tense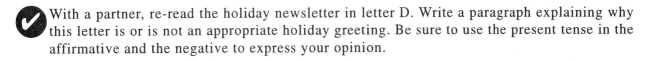

✔ Read the following sentences paying careful attention to the way that the questions are formed.

1. I call my parents every month.
   <u>Do you call</u> your parents every month?

2. You write letters everyday.
   <u>Do you write</u> letters everyday?

3. He studies everyday.
   <u>Does he study</u> everyday?

4. She speaks Chinese.
   <u>Does she speak</u> Chinese?

We listen to music at night.
<u>Do you listen</u> to music at night?

They work on Sundays.
<u>Do they work</u> on Sundays?

How are questions formed in the present tense?

In the present tense, a question is formed by using the present tense of the verb _____ plus the _____ plus the simple form of the _____. Note: in the third person singular (he, she or it) the verb <u>do</u> takes the form of _____ .

R u l e

10

A question is formed in the present tense by using the following rule.

Use the present tense of the verb <u>do</u>	+	the subject of the sentence	+	simple form of the verb	
example:					
Does		Peter		smoke?	
Do		you		study	at night?
Does		Maria		like	pizza?

✔ With a partner, write a list of seven questions you'd like to ask the teacher and the students about their everyday lives. Then ask them the questions, and write down their responses.

example: Does Sonia live in a house or an apartment?
Sonia lives in a house with her aunt and uncle.

✔ Read the following sentences carefully.

1. a. Mary is a teacher.
    b. <u>Is Mary</u> a teacher.

2. a. You are smart.
    b. <u>Are you</u> smart?

3. a. They are friends.
    b. <u>Are they</u> friends?

4. a. I am a student.
    b. <u>Are you</u> a student?

5. a. We are friends.
    b. <u>Are you</u> friends?

6. a. He is handy.
    b. <u>Is he</u> handy?

Why isn't the verb *do* used to form these present tense questions?

When a sentence is written in the present tense and the verb is_____ , a question is formed by_____the subject and the verb.

R u l e

11

When a sentence is in the present tense and the verb in the sentence is **to be** (am, is or are), a question is formed by inverting **the subject** and **the verb** in the sentence.

example: Are they students?   Are we late?
Is she out of her mind?   Am I a student at the college?

✔ With a partner write a list of seven personal questions which contain the present tense of the verb *to be*. Ask some students in the class the questions, then write down their response.

example:
Is that Mary's real hair color?
Yes, it *is* Mary's natural hair color. or
No, it *is not* Mary's natural hair color.

Summary Writing..

✔ On a piece of paper write a sentence which describes two things:

- you do everyday,
- a classmate does everyday,
- a classmate never does,
- you never do.

✔ Complete each task with a partner.

1. Write a question asking someone two things he/she does everyday.
2. Write a question asking someone in the class about two things another person in the class does everyday.
3. Write a question asking two people two things they do not do everyday.

✔ Ask the questions to a classmate or friend.

✔ Write down all the questions and answers received.

✔ *Writing:* With a partner, write a class newsletter describing everything that routinely happens in your class.

example: Everyday the professor arrives ten minutes early, but some of the students don't arrive on time.

Using the Present Tense................................

✔ Read the following essay and complete each sentence with the present tense of the verb in parentheses. If it is an irregular verb, turn to Appendix C for the correct form.

Each country (have)_____its own ritual ceremonies for weddings, births and even

death. In my country, Haiti, there (be)_____special customs which are followed

when a person (die)_____ .

When somebody (die) _____ , the deceased (be) _____ immediately taken to the undertaker's until the day before the funeral. The night before the funeral service, family, friends and neighbors (go)_____ to view the dead person. Then they (get)_____ together to drink, sing and remember the person who has died. The women (make)_____ coffee and tea, and they even (serve)_____ alcoholic beverages. The men (play)_____ cards or dominoes while the others (tell)_____ stories about the deceased. This (sound)_____ and (look) _____ like fun, but it (be)_____ not. After that night, all the sadness, tears and pain (resurface)_____ and (not, go)_____ away for a long time.

The day of the funeral, the body of the dead person is taken to the church for a religious service. After the church service, everybody (go)_____ to the cemetery where the family and friends (weep) _____ , (yell) _____ and (scream)_____ in order to express their grief. If the mother of the person who died (be) _____ still alive, she can not go to the cemetery and is excluded from this part of the ritual since we (believe)_____ the burial is too painful for her to endure. After the burial, everybody (have)_____ to return to the deceased person's home to wash their hands, but I (not, know)_____ the meaning behind this rite.

Many Haitian people in the United States (not, like)_____ the rules that must be followed when a person (die) _____ , but I (prefer)_____ to continue these traditions since they (make) _____ the process of burying a loved one seem complete to me.

✔ Write a composition describing a ritual or ceremony that occurs in your culture. The ritual can relate to birth, marriage or death.

Read the following sentences. Underline the subject and determine what form of the verb is used in the present tense.

1. Traveling to other counties is interesting.
2. Teaching ESL students requires special skills.
3. Writing good books involves months of work.
4. Listening to music relieves stress.
5. Starting a business costs a lot of money.

What is unique about each of the subjects in these five sentences?
The subject of each of these sentences contains a ——————.

When the subject of a sentence contains a gerund, what form of the verb is used in the present tense?
When the subject of the sentence contains a gerund, the—————— is used.

R u l e

12

When the subject of the sentence contains a gerund, the <u>third person singular</u> is used in the present tense.

example: <u>Watching television</u> is relaxing.
<u>Painting a picture</u> takes many hours.
<u>Raising children</u> involves many years of sacrifices.

 Complete each of the following sentence using the present tense.

1. Experts say that reading to young children (help) —————— them develop good listing skills.
2. Listening to a friend's problems (be)—————— not always easy to do.
3. Correcting students' compositions (entail)—————— many hours of work.
4. Wearing old shoes (ruin)——————your feet.
5. Falling in love (create)——————many problems for some people.
6. Walking in the snow (be)—————— fun.
7. Getting married (cost)—————— a lot of money these days.
8. Learning to use a computer (require)——————time and patience.
9. Driving a car while under the influence of alcohol (cause)——————life threatening injuries.
10. Being rich (make)—————— life easy.

 Write five different sentences where a gerund is used as the subject of the sentence and be sure there is subject verb agreement.

example: Learning to use gerunds correctly allows students to write well.

Read the following sentences. Underline the subject and determine what form of the verb is used in the present tense.

1. Love conquers all.
2. Knowledge is a dangerous thing.
3. Sugar costs twenty-five cents per pound.
4. Air pollution increases during the summer.
5. Patience comes easily for some people.

What type of noun is used as the subject of each of these sentences?
The _____ of each of these sentences contains a non-count noun.

When the subject of a sentence contains a non-count noun, what form of the verb is used in the present tense?
When the subject of the sentence contains a non-count noun, the_____ is used.

R u l e

When the subject of the sentence is a non-count noun, the <u>third person singular</u> is used in the present tense.

example: Good furniture cost**s** a lot of money.
Wisdom come**s** with age.

 Complete each of the following sentence using the present tense.

1. Noise in a classroom (be)_____ disruptive.
2. My hair (get)_____ washed everyday.
3. His bravery (show)_____ how courageous he is.
4. All the excitement (make)_____the children behave poorly.
5. Her honesty (create)_____ a trusting environment.
6. Ignorance (be)_____ bliss.
7. Beauty (originate)_____ from within a person.
8. Too much pride (destroy)_____relationships.
9. Love (bring)_____ out the best and the worst in people.
10. Her modesty (be)_____seen in many situations.

 Read the following sentences. Underline the subject and determine what form of the verb is used in the present tense.

1. Everyone asks a lot of questions in that class.
2. Nobody ever arrives late for her dinner parties.
3. Someone wants to ask a question.
4. Somebody is born every ten seconds.

What type of pronoun is the subject of each of the four sentences listed above?

The subject of these sentences contain an _____ pronoun.

What are some examples of indefinite pronouns?

Some examples of indefinite pronouns are: _____

When an indefinite pronoun is the subject, what form of the verb is used in the present tense?

When the subject of a sentence is an _____ and the verb is in the present tense, the third person singular (he, she or it) is used.

R u l e

14

When the subject of the sentence is an indefinite pronoun such as **someone**, **anyone**, **everyone**, **no one**, the <u>third person singular</u> is used in the present tense.

example: Someone drinks coffee at my desk everyday.
              Everyone wants to win the lottery.
              No one likes to be sick.

✔ Complete each of the following sentence using the present tense.

1.   No one (want) _____ to help her with her assignment.

2.   Somebody in my apartment building (enjoy)_____ playing their stereo all night.

3.   Everyone who (be)_____ born in the United States automatically (become) _____ a citizen.

4.   Anyone who (require)_____ extra help (ask) _____ our instructor for a tutor.

5.   Nobody (have) _____ an extra pencil.

6.   No one (require)_____ three thousand calories a day.

7.   Anybody who (threaten)_____ a teacher should not be allowed to attend classes at the college.

8.   Anybody who (buy)_____ the instructor a gift at the end of the term will automatically pass the course.

9.   Somebody (hope)_____ to win the game.

10. Everybody who (learn)_____ to read and write in English can enter the college level courses next semester.

✔ *Writing:* Write a composition describing something you or a person in your class do habitually everyday. Be sure to use the following types of subjects at least two times each.

•   Gerunds
     example: Swimming is an excellent form of exercise.

•   Non-count nouns
     example: Wisdom takes time to develop.

•   Indefinite pronouns
     example: Somebody in my class doesn't want to write this paper.

Review of the Past Tense

The objective of this chapter is to:

- *instruct students in determining whether to use the past or present tense of a verb,*

- *instruct students in determining how the past tense is formed in the affirmative, negative and interrogative,*

- *develop the concept of irregular past tense verbs.*

Difference Between the Past and Present Tenses

 Read and observe the changes in the following pairs of sentences.

1. a. I <u>walk</u> to school everyday.
   b. I <u>walked</u> school yesterday.
2. a. Mary <u>talks</u> to John every morning.
   b. Mary <u>talked</u> to John this morning.
3. a. We <u>study</u> at home.
   b. We <u>studied</u> at home.
4. a. That country <u>produces</u> wine.
   b. That country <u>produced</u> wine.

5. a. You <u>cook</u> dinner at night.
   b. You <u>cooked</u> dinner last night.
6. a. He <u>locks</u> the door every evening.
   b. He <u>locked</u> the door last night.
7. a. They <u>help</u> them everyday.
   b. They <u>helped</u> them yesterday.
8. a. The sun <u>rises</u> in the east.
   b. The sun <u>rose</u> at 6:45 yesterday.

What tense is used in letter a of each sentence pair?
The _____ tense is used in letter <u>a</u> each sentence pair.

What type of action does the present tense describe?
The present tense describes usual activities that occur _____

How is the present tense used in numbers 4.a and 8.a ?
The present tense is used to state a _____.

What tense is used in letter b of each sentence pair?
The _____ tense is used in letter <u>b</u> of each sentence pair.

Besides the tense of the verb, what other word(s) in each sentence signal which tense to use?
Each sentence contains an adverb of _____ which indicates whether the situation occurred in the past or the present.

Make a list of adverbs of time which indicate whether to use the past or present tense.

Present Tense Adverbs	Past Tense Adverbs
today	yesterday

Rule 1

The **present tense** is used to describe **usual habits** or **activities** that occur daily.

example: We <u>study</u> in the library after class.

The **present tense** is also used to **state a fact.**

example: Grass is green.

The **past tense** is used to describe an action that has been **completed.**

example: You cooked dinner <u>last night</u>.
I walked to school <u>the other day.</u>

Adverbs of time are frequently used along with the present and past tenses and clearly indicate whether an event is happening in the present or has already happened in the past.

example: Tomas <u>jogs</u> to work <u>everyday.</u>
Tomas <u>jogged</u> to work <u>yesterday.</u>

How is the past tense formed?
The past tense is formed by adding _____ to the simple form of the verb.

In number 3.b, how is the past tense formed when a verb ends in a consonant + y?
When forming the past tense and the verb ends in a <u>consonant + y,</u> change the letter <u>y</u> to the letter _____ and add the letters _____ .

The **past tense** of a verb is formed by adding **ed** to the simple form of the verb.

example:

I walk<u>ed</u>	We walk<u>ed</u>
You walk<u>ed</u>	You walk<u>ed</u>
He walk<u>ed</u>	
She walk<u>ed</u>	They walk<u>ed</u>
It walk<u>ed</u>	

When the past tense is used with a verb that ends in a **consonant and the letter y**, change the letter **y** to **i** and add **ed**.

example: The word stud<u>y</u> becomes stud<u>ied</u>.
Mary stud<u>ied</u> Italian for five years.

✔ Complete each of the following sentences with the present or past tense.

Every night I (have)_____a hard time sleeping because the people who live above

me are very noisy. At about midnight, they (get)_____home from work and

(turn) _____on their stereo as loud as it can go. Then they (laugh)_____

and (scream) _____until about three o'clock in the morning. I (guess)_____

about this time, they finally go to bed and sleep until noon the following day. Well last night

was the worst night yet.

When they (arrive)_____home, they immediately (turn)_____on

the stereo full blast. Then some friends (stop)_____by at about one in the morning

for a few drinks. The two couples (dance) _____and (party) _____

until five o'clock in the morning. When they finally went to bed, my alarm clock rang, and I

had to get up for work. I was so exhausted I couldn't face the morning sun. At about eight

o'clock while I was drinking my coffee, I (decide)_____to turn on my ste-

reo at a normal volume to enjoy some music. Five minutes later, I heard someone knocking at

my door. I couldn't imagine who it could be. When I (open)_____ the door, I was

shocked to see it was my upstairs neighbor complaining about the noise I was making!

The Past Tense in the Negative Form

Read the following sentences and observe how they are made negative.

1. a. I <u>walked</u> to school.
    b. I <u>did not walk</u> to school.
2. a. We <u>called</u> the doctor.
    b. We <u>didn't call</u> the doctor.

3. a. They <u>cooked</u> the dinner.
    b. They <u>didn't cook</u> the dinner.
4. a. He <u>turned</u> on the music.
    b. He <u>did not turn</u> on the music.

How was each of these sentences made negative?
The past tense is made negative by placing the past tense of the auxiliary verb _____
immediately after the subject. Next the word _____ is placed after the auxiliary verb.
Last insert the simple form of the _____ .

R u l e

3

The **past tense** is made negative by using the following rule.

	subject	+	the past tense of the verb do	+	not	+	the simple form of the verb
example:	I		did		not		talk.
	We		did		not		study.
	They		did		not		call us.

With a partner, make the following past tense sentences negative.

1. The woman listened to her noisy neighbors all night.
2. The girl refused to answer the telephone.
3. They asked Mario to speak to the young couple.
4. She opened the door.
5. Their neighbors played music all night.

With a partner, write five sentences describing what the woman with the noisy neighbors *did not do* in the above story.

   example: The woman who lived downstairs did not call up her neighbors.

Read the following sentences, and observe how the verb to be is formed in the past tense.

1. I <u>was</u> at school.
2. You <u>were</u> absent.
3. He <u>was</u> late.

4. We <u>were</u> home.

5. They <u>were</u> early.

How is the verb *to be* formed in the past tense?
When the subject is in the first person singular (I) or the third person singular (he, she or it),
use the verb_____. When the subject is in the second person singular or plural (you), the
first person plural (we) or the third person plural (they), use the verb_____.

 Read the following sentences and observe how the past tense of to be is made negative.

1. a. I was late for work.
    b. I <u>was no</u>t late for work.

2. a. You were early.
    b. You <u>were not</u> early.

3. a. Carlos was hungry.
    b. Carlos <u>was not</u> hungry.

4. a. We were late for work.
    b. We <u>were no</u>t late for work.

5. a. Tomas and Juan were bored.
    b. Tomas and Juan <u>were no</u>t bored.

How were these sentences made negative?
The past tense of the verb _____is made negative by placing the word _____
immediately after the words _____ or _____.

R u l e

4

In the past tense, the irregular verb t**o be** is conjugated as follows.

I <u>was</u> tired.
You <u>were</u> interested.
He <u>was</u> sick.
She <u>was</u> funny.
It <u>was</u> a rainy day.

We <u>were</u> late.

They <u>were</u> awake.

The past tense of the verb **to be** is made **negative** by placing the word **not** immediately after the words **was** or **were**.

example:

I <u>was not</u> at work.
You <u>were not</u> here.
Mary <u>was not</u> occupied.

We <u>were not</u> busy.

They <u>were not</u> annoyed.

 Make each of the following sentences negative.

1. Sandra was at work today.
2. Franco and I were late yesterday.
3. Raul and Cristafano were in the living room watching television.
4. You were very busy at that time.
5. I was annoyed that day.

With a partner or in a small group, read the following composition and complete each sentence in either the past or present tense.

When a new immigrant first (arrive)_____in the United States, he/she (need)

_____to become acquainted with the laws of this country and his/her city. A new im-

migrant usually (understand) _____ and (respect) _____the laws of basic

human rights but (lack)_____knowledge regarding laws surrounding motor vehicle

requirements and many other local nuances.

When I first (arrive)_____ in this country, I (purchase) _____a car from

an acquaintance of mine. My friend (inform)_____me that I could not drive a car

without a set of license plates, so I (borrow) _____an old pair of plates from him.

Since I was busy with my family, job and classes, I (not, go)_____to the Department of

Motor Vehicles for several weeks, but I still drove the car because it was such a convenience

and I (not, think)_____ it was illegal.

One day while I was driving on the highway, a police car (signal) _____for me to pull

over. When I (stop)_____the car and (pull)_____ it over to the

shoulder of the road, the police officer asked for my driver's license, registration and insurance

identification card. Naturally I (have, not)_____any of these required documents

since I hadn't yet gone to the Department of Motor Vehicles. I (try) _____to explain

this to the police officer, but he was extremely angry. He kept shouting something about how

foreigners did not obey the laws in this country. I became so frightened and nervous I couldn't

understand a thing the police officer was saying to me.

Finally the police officer (call)_____for a tow truck and had my car impounded be-

cause I (not, have)_____the required documents. I (receive)_____

about nine different summons for every little infraction of the law that I had committed.

Three weeks later I had to appear before a judge in a local court. The judge (lecture)_____

me on the laws of operating a motor vehicle in his municipality, and he (fine) _____

me almost three hundred and fifty dollars for the violations and the towing of my car. Worse

yet, I wasn't allowed to get a driver's license for at least six more months, so I (end)_____

up paying for a car I couldn't even use.

This unfortunate event (happen) _____ seven years ago when I first (arrive)

_____ in this country. Since that time, I have become familiar with the laws of this

land, and I (know)_____what I must do to survive without getting in trouble

with the law. Now whenever I (meet)_____a new immigrant, I (warn)_____

him/her about these potential problems so that they will not have the problems I had with the

law.

The Formation of Questions in the Past Tense . . . .

✔ Read the following sentence pairs.

1. a. Ann <u>talked</u> to John.
   b. <u>Did</u> Ann <u>talk</u> to John?
2. a. We <u>helped</u> the old woman.
   b. <u>Did</u> you <u>help</u> the old woman?
3. a. You <u>kissed</u> the baby.
   b. <u>Did</u> you <u>kiss</u> the baby?
4. a. They <u>called</u> the doctor immediately.
   b. <u>Did</u> they <u>call</u> the doctor immediately.

How are questions formed in the past tense?
Questions are formed in the past tense by using the past tense of the auxiliary verb _____
plus the _____ of the sentence and the _____ .

R u l e

5

A **past tense** question is formed by using the following rule.

the past tense of the verb do	+	the subject	+	the simple form of the verb	
example:					
Did		he		call	immediately?
Did		we		study?	
Did		you		dance?	

With a partner, make the following sentences into questions.

1. Boris yelled at his friends.
2. The young man and woman worked all night.
3. The child didn't arrive late for school.
4. The judge listened to the case.
5. Alicia cleaned the house.

With a partner, write five past tense questions about the two narratives in this chapter. After completing the questions, write the answers.

example: Did the woman lower the volume on the stereo?
The author didn't tell us if the woman lowered the volume on the stereo.

Read the following sentence pairs.

1. a. Ann <u>was</u> angry.
    b. <u>Was</u> Ann angry?

2. a. We <u>were</u> too young to drink wine.
    b. <u>Were</u> you too young to drink wine?

3. a. You <u>were</u> a child.
    b. <u>Were</u> you a chile?

4. a. They <u>were</u> at home.
    b. <u>Were</u> they at home?

How are questions formed in the past tense when the verb *to be* is used?
Questions are formed in the past tense with the verb <u>to be</u> (was or were) by inverting the _____ and the words <u>was</u> or <u>were</u>.

R u l e

6

Questions are formed in the past tense with the verb **to be** (was or were) by inverting the **subject** and the words **was** or **were**.

example:

I <u>was</u> early for class.   They <u>were</u> in the kitchen.
<u>Were</u> you early for class?   <u>Were</u> they in the kitchen?

Make each of the following sentences into questions.

1. Pietro and Ali were in the yard working.
2. Ana and I were not at home.
3. You were outside the house.
4. She was young and beautiful.
5. He was very unhappy about the assignment.

Irregular Verbs in the Past Tense . . . .

✔ Read the following sentences and observe the change in spelling of the past tense verbs.

1. a. I <u>buy</u> milk everyday.
   b. I <u>bought</u> milk yesterday.
2. a. She <u>teaches</u> Spanish.
   b. She <u>taught</u> Spanish ten years ago.
3. a. We <u>drink</u> coffee everyday.
   b. We <u>drank</u> coffee yesterday.

4. a. The boy always <u>catches</u> the ball.
   b. The boy <u>caught</u> the ball last night.
5. a. I <u>go</u> to work by train.
   b. I <u>went</u> to work by train yesterday.
6. a. I <u>see</u> her on the bus everyday.
   b. I <u>saw</u> her on the bus yesterday.

Why isn't the past tense formed by adding *ed* to these verbs?
These are _____ verbs. _____ verbs do not follow the rules and must be memorized.

R u l e

7

Some past tense verbs are **irregular verbs**. That is they do not follow the typical rules for forming the past tense.

example:

I <u>was</u> sick. (to be)   They <u>were</u> bored. (to be)
Elena <u>had</u> a baby. (to have)   Paulette <u>went</u> to work late. (to go)

A complete list of irregular past tense verbs can be found in Appendix C.

✔ With a partner, complete each sentence with the irregular verb in parenthesis. After completing this exercise, check Appendix C to see if the answer is correct.

1. I _____(ride) a bike yesterday.
2. You_____(think) about the answer before you wrote it.
3. Chang_____(go) to school last week.
4. Jose and I_____(teach) them how to drive.
5. Pietro and Mario_____(see) the bird this morning.
6. I_____(be) at home last night, but you _____(be) out.
7. We _____(be) in the back yard.
8. You _____(drive) to school this morning.
9. The bird_____(fly) over the house.
10. I _____(meet) my wife at a party.
11. Regina_____(feel) badly when her father died.
12. The leaves_____(fall) from the trees early this year.
13. I_____(pay) the rent last week.
14. Peter_____(hear) the baby crying yesterday.
15. The phone_____(ring) at midnight last night.
16. Chris_____(speak) to the boy's parents.
17. The old man_____(take) a hot bath this morning.

18. Her boyfriend _____(send) her flowers last month.

19. Sarah _____(put) her bag in the car before leaving.

20. This morning I_____ (cut) myself with a knife.

✔ Write a list of 8 questions that you will ask a partner about events he/she *did* or *did not* do in his/her homeland.

example:

1. Did you study English in your home land?

2. Did you go to college in your country?

3. Did you get married before you came here?

4. _____ ?

5. _____ ?

6. _____ ?

7. _____ ?

8. _____ ?

✔ Using the questions and answers you received from your partner, write a paragraph describing what your partner did and did not do in his/her country.

✔ Complete each of the following sentences with the word in parentheses and refer to Appendix C for the spelling of irregular verbs.

Before graduating from the eighth grade, I (do)_____something I (regret)_____

later on. This (be)_____an unforgettable experience which (occur)_____

when I (cheat)_____on a test.

During my last year of elementary school, all the courses I (take)_____were in preparation for the admission to high school. This (be)_____the most difficult year for me because if a student (not, get)_____into the best high school, he/she would never get into a college in my country. Therefore, everyone (have)_____to study very hard. English (be)_____the most difficult part of the test which many of my classmates were afraid they would fail. In preparation for the exam, many students (use)_____different study methods to succeed. In fact, my favorite teacher even (tutor)_____us after school during her own free time.

The week before the test, everyone (become)_____very anxious. One day I (hear)_____ a rumor that the answers to the English section of the test (be) _____for sale. At first, I (refuse) _____ to purchase them because I (feel) _____cheating was wrong, but I finally (buy)_____ them since I was afraid I wouldn't do as well as the students who had the answers.

The week after we (take)_____the test, the principal (announce)_____the exam had been thrown out because too many of the answers were identical, so we all had to take another exam which was even harder than the first. Fortunately, I (do)_____well and was admitted to a good high school. However, I (feel)_____ extremely guilty and could hardly even look at the teacher who had tutored us for so many months.

The last week of school, I (go) _____to that teacher's classroom to ask her to sign my autograph book, but I (not, look) _____ at her note in front of her because I (be) _____afraid of what she had written to me.

When I (get) _____home, I (open)_____ up my autograph book and (see) _____this teacher's note. It (say)_____ , "Whatever you attempt to do in life, just do your best so that you will succeed by your own merit." I (shake)_____as I (read) _____those words, but I (know)_____ she was right.

I now realize there are many obstacles in life we must overcome, but we always feel better when we accomplish our goals through our own hard work and effort. When we cheat, we only deceive ourselves and will never enjoy the pride associated with real success.

Write a composition telling about a time you or a friend of yours got in trouble with the law. Include examples in the story about situations that already occurred and be sure to use the past tense to describe these incidents. However, use the present tense to describe any present time habitual behavior or facts that are relevant to the story.

 Write a composition describing what would happen to a student in your country if he/she were caught cheating on a test.

··*The Present Progressive Tense*··

The objective of this chapter is to teach students:

- *the difference in meaning and form between the present and present progressive tense and,*

- *how to form the affirmative, negative and interrogative forms of the present progressive tense using present participles.*

Present Tense versus the Present Progressive Tense·········

 Observe the difference in meaning in each pair of sentences.

1. a. They <u>eat</u> breakfast at work.
   b. They <u>are eating</u> breakfast now.

2. a. We <u>walk</u> to school everyday.
   b. We <u>are walking</u> to school now.

3. a. I <u>work</u> in a store.
   b. I <u>am working</u> in a store now.

4. a. She <u>smokes</u> cigarettes.
   b. She <u>is smoking</u> a cigarette.

What tense is used in letter a in these pairs of sentences?
The ——————————tense is used in letter <u>a</u> of each example.

What tense is used in letter b in these pairs of sentences?
The——————————tense is used in letter <u>b</u> of these examples.

What tense is used to describe an action that takes place everyday on a regular basis or states a fact?
The ——————————tense is used to describe a habitual action or to state a fact.

What tense is used to describe an action that is occurring right now?
The——————————— tense is used to describe an action that is occurring at the present time.

Rule

1

The **present tense** is used to describe an action that takes place habitually. It is also used to make general statements about a fact.

> *example:* I wash my hair every day.
> Birds fly in the sky.

The **present progressive tense** is used to describe an action that is occurring or actually happening right now or at that the moment.

> *example:* I am writing a book at the moment.
> I am cleaning my house right now.

✔ Read the following sentences and observe how to form this tense.

I <u>am typing</u> this paper.   We <u>are watching</u> a movie.
You <u>are reading</u> a book.   You <u>are eating</u> lunch.
He <u>is talking</u> to me.
She <u>is walking</u> home.   They <u>are talking</u> to the children.
It <u>is raining</u>.

How is the present progressive tense formed?
The *present progressive tense* is formed by using the present tense of the auxiliary verb
_____plus the_____of the verb.

Rule

2

The **present progressive tense** is formed by using the following rule.

Subject	+	the present tense of the verb to be	+	the present participle of the verb	
example:					
I		am		writing	a book.
Frank		is		working.	
We		are		cooking	dinner.

Observe the above examples and state how a *present participle is formed*?
A *present participle* is formed by placing the letters _____at the end of the_____.

Rule

3

The **present participle** of a verb is formed by adding the letters **ing** to the end of a verb.

example: want<u>ing</u>   listen<u>ing</u>   learn<u>ing</u>   go<u>ing</u>   see<u>ing</u>

✔ Write the present participle of the following verbs:

1. sleep _____   4. watch _____   7. drink _____
2. look _____   5. turn _____   8. touch _____
3. think _____   6. cook _____   9. hear _____

✔ With a partner, complete each of the following sentences with either the present tense or the present progressive. Remember to look for words in the sentence which indicate if the action occurs everyday (in this case use the present tense) or if it is occurring right now (in this case use the present progressive tense).

1. Mary (buy) _____ a coat right now.

2. Every year Mary (buy) _____ a new coat.

3. We (go) _____ out to eat on Sundays.

4. We (go) _____ out to eat now.

5. They (dance) _____ in the disco on Friday nights.

6. At this moment, they (dance) _____ in a disco while I am home studying.

7. I (write) _____ to my mother once a week.

8. I (write) _____ a letter to my mother right now.

9. You (smoke) _____ cigarettes.

10. At this time, you (smoke) _____ two cigarettes at once!

11. After a movie, I always (clap) _____ my hands.

12. She (push) _____ the baby in the carriage now.

13. She (run) _____ 10 miles everyday.

14. At the moment, she (run) _____ down the block.

15. By this time, she (sit) _____ in a chair reading a book.

16. Keep Quiet. The baby (sleep) _____ . The baby (sleep) _____ for eight hours every night.

17. Right now I (sit) _____ at my desk. I usually (sit) _____ at my desk and study every morning.

18. Coco (speak) _____ French. French is her first language, but at the moment she (speak) _____ English.

19. My husband (stand) _____ up right now. He (look) _____ at all the pretty girls.

20. It (snow) _____ right now. But, the sun (shine) _____ .

21. It (rain) _____ a lot in Seattle.

22. It is a beautiful day. The sun (shine) _____ .

23. It's 5 PM and the Rushs are in their kitchen. Mrs. Rush (cook) _____ their dinner and (drink) _____ soda.

✔ *Oral Activity:* With a partner, state five things you are doing *right now.*

example: I am getting hungry waiting for lunch to be served.

✔ With a partner, state five things you do habitually.

example: Before class begins, I buy coffee every day.

Negation of the Present Progressive Tense· · · · · · · · · · · · · · · · ·

✔ Read the following sentences and observe how the present progressive tense is made negative.

1. a. I <u>am working</u> right now.
   b. I am <u>not</u> working right now.

2. a. We <u>are eating</u> at the moment.
   b. We are <u>not</u> eating at the moment.

3. a. You <u>are studying</u>.
   b. You are <u>not</u> studying.

4. a. They <u>are wasting</u> their time talking.
   b. Thy are <u>not</u> wasting their time talking.

How is the present progressive tense made negative?
The present progressive tense is made negative by inserting the word _____
between the auxiliary verb and the _____.

R u l e

4

To make a present progressive sentence negative, insert the word **not** between the **auxiliary verb** (am, is, are) and the **present participle**.

Subject	+	Present Tense of To Be	+	Not	+	Present Participle
example:						
Ann		is		not		sleeping.
We		are		not		working.

✔ With a partner, write a list of five things you *are not doing* right now.

example: I am not watching the television right now.

1. _____
2. _____
3. _____
4. _____
5. _____

✔ With a partner, complete each of the following sentences with either the present or the present progressive tense. Remember to look for words in the sentence that indicate if the action occurs everyday (in this case use the present tense) or if it is happening right now (in this case use the present progressive tense).

Everyday in my ESL writing and reading class, we (read) _____ and (write) _____

about human interests topics in American society. Today we (read) _____ about a

man who got in trouble with the law because he didn't know he had to register his car and get insurance before he could operate it. I (know)_____many new immigrants who have similar problems because they (be, not)_____ familiar with the laws in this country. Unfortunately, these types of problems always (happen)_____to people who have just recently arrived.

Even though we (study, not)_____ chapter five, I (read)_____ the short stories, letters and composition topics which (be)_____in this chapter. They (be)_____ quite interesting. There is a young woman whose name (be)_____ Sharon. Sharon (expect)_____ a baby, but she (be, not)_____ married. Sharon has told her boyfriend, but he has become cool and distant. Sharon (know, not)_____ what to do. Therefore, she (ask) _____ her girlfriends for advice. I (think) _____ it is odd a woman would become pregnant without being married. This never (happen)_____ in my country. Our women (remain)_____ untouched until they are married. That is if a woman (have)_____a baby, she is expected to be married. If she (be, not)_____married and (become)_____pregnant, she is not respected in our society. In my country, this is something that (change not)_____; however, in some European and South American urban areas, this (change)_____ . I (be not)_____sure if this (be)_____ good because I (see)_____ a lot of young single American mothers who (starve) _____and poor. They (beg) _____for food and (live)_____ in the streets. I (wonder)_____ if these women were married if it would make a difference in the quality of their lives.

Another topic I (read)_____ about in this book is about a single guy who can't meet an attractive woman. In his letter, he (complain)_____about the type of women that are available. He (say)_____ that all the attractive women (be)_____either attached to someone or too busy to date. In my country, a man (select, not)_____

dates for himself. The parents of a young man and woman (get)_____together

and (arrange)_____a meeting of the two young people so that they can see if they

(be)_____compatible. The meeting (take)_____ place in the young

man's home. While the young couple (get)_____acquainted, the parents (super-

vise)_____them. This (be)_____how a man and woman (meet)

_____ and (decide)_____to marry. It is done under the close supervision

and permission of the parents. In my country, young men and women (hang, not) _____

around bars trying to meet people. You never see a woman who (sit)_____around a

bar. This (seem)_____sad and depressing to me. I (like)_____the ar-

ranged meetings much better.

This country (be)_____very different from mine. Things (change, always)_____

here. This (frighten) _____me because I never (know)_____what to expect

or how to live. But, when I (read)_____these little excerpts about American situations,

I (feel)_____safe since I (be, not)_____the person with these problems.

Questions in the Present Progressive Tense . . . .

✔ Read the following sentences.

1. a. Mary is cooking dinner.
    b. Is Mary cooking dinner?
2. a. We are studying English.
    b. Are we studying English?
3. a. The student is reading the stories.
    b. Is the student reading the stories?

4. a. You are doing your homework.
    b. Are you doing your homework?
5. a. I am eating dinner.
    b. Are you eating dinner?
6. a. They are discussing the movie.
    b. Are they discussing the movie?

How are questions formed in the present progressive tense?
In the present progressive tense, questions are formed by_____ the subject and
the auxiliary verb.

5

When a **question** is formed in the **present progressive tense**, the subject and the auxiliary verb are **inverted.** That is the auxiliary verb (be) comes first, and the subject is second.

Present Tense of To Be	+	Subject	+	Present Participle	
example:					
Is		Mary		eating	dinner?
Are		we		learning	to write well?

✔ With a partner, write five present progressive questions that you would like to ask the teacher or the people in your class.

example: Student: Are you wearing perfume today?
Teacher: Yes, I am wearing an inexpensive perfume today.

✔ Writing assignment with a partner or small group.

Cut five pictures out of a magazine or newspaper. For each picture, write a paragraph describing exactly what is occurring.

example:
If a student cuts out a picture of a group of people marching outside of City Hall, the student could write a paragraph explaining why these people are marching.

These men and women are marching outside of City Hall because they want to receive better health benefits from their city jobs. The are trying to get the mayor to listen to their concerns. etc.

The Past Progressive Tense

The objective of this chapter is to teach students:

- *the difference in meaning and form between the past and past progressive tense,*

- *how to form the affirmative, negative and interrogative forms of the past progressive tense.*

Simple Past Tense Versus the Past Progressive Tense

✔ Read each of the following sentence pairs and specify the tenses being used in the underlined verbs.

1. Tim <u>was typing</u> his paper while Janet <u>was studying</u> for her test.
2. When Alicia <u>opened</u> the door, the children <u>were playing</u> soccer.

What tense is used in number 1?
The_____tense is used.

In the adverbial clause in 2, what tense is used?
The _____tense is used.

What is the difference in meaning between the *past tense* and the *past progressive tense*?
The <u>past tense</u> describes an activity that is_____ . The <u>past progressive tense</u> is used to describe an activity that was_____ at some point in time in the past.

✔ Read each pair of sentences and determine the difference in meaning.

1. a. When I walked in the door, the alarm <u>sounded</u>.
   b. When I walked in the door, the alarm <u>was sounding</u>.
2. a. When Chris won the race, everyone <u>cheered.</u>
   b. When Chris won the race, everyone <u>was cheering</u>.

In letter a of each pair, which action occurred first?
In letter <u>a</u> of each pair, the action in the_____clause occurred first. Then the action in the _____ clause occurred second.

In letter b of each pair, what action occurred first?
The action in the _____clause was already occurring when the action in the adverbial clause occurred.

1

The **past tense** expresses a different meaning from the past progressive tense. The **past tense** describes an action that is **completed** in the **past.**
The **past progressive tense** describes an activity that was **in progress** at a certain time in the past. It stresses the duration or continuance of the action and is only used to **emphasize** that an event was in progress in the past.

> *example:* Ali <u>was reading</u> a book when the clock <u>struck</u> twelve.
> This example stresses what Ali was doing when the clock struck twelve.

The past progressive tense can also be used to demonstrate that a second event was already in progress when another event happened.

> *example:* a. When the school bell <u>rang</u>, the children <u>screamed</u> with joy.
> b. When the school bell <u>rang</u>, the children <u>were screaming</u> with joy.

In letter **a**, the school bell rang. After it rang, the children screamed with joy. However, in letter **b**, the children were already screaming with joy when the bell rang.

 Read the following sentences and observe the tenses used in each part of the sentence.

1. While we <u>were drinking</u> coffee, the children <u>were playing</u> checkers.
2. While the class <u>was taking</u> a test, the teacher <u>was reading</u> a book.
3. While the professor <u>was teaching</u> the class, Paolo and Jorge <u>were eating</u> sandwiches.
4. While you <u>were reading</u> that murder mystery, I <u>was cleaning</u> up the kitchen.

Why is the past progressive tense used in both parts of this sentence?
The *past progressive* tense can be used to describe _____ actions or events that were _____ at the same time or simultaneously in the past.

2

The **past progressive** tense is used to **describe two actions** that were <u>in</u> **progress at the same time** or **occurring simultaneously** in the past. Therefore, it is used in both parts of the sentence.

> *example:* While <u>Paula was working</u>, her husband <u>was resting</u>.

Formation of the Past Progressive Tense....................

 Read the following sentences and observe how the past progressive tense is formed.

I <u>was typing</u> this paper.
You <u>were reading</u> a book.
He <u>was talking</u> to me.
She <u>was walking</u> home.
It <u>was raining</u>.

We <u>were watching</u> a movie.
You <u>were eating</u> lunch.

They <u>were talking</u> to the children.

How is the past progressive tense formed?

The past progressive tense is formed by using the subject plus _____ of the verb _____ and the _____ of the main verb.

Rule

3

The **past progressive tense** is formed by using the following rule.

subject	+	the past tense of the verb to be	+	the present participle of the verb	
example:					
I		was		writing	a book.
Frank and I		were		working.	
He		was		cooking	dinner.

✔ With a partner, complete each of the following sentences with either the *past tense* or the *past progressive tense.*

1. Mario and Louisa (eat) _____their breakfast when their neighbor (walk) _____in the back door.

2. While I (take)_____ a bath, the baby (sleep)_____in his room.

3. The students arrived ten minutes before the class began. When the professor (walk) _____ in the door, the students (discuss)_____the homework assignment.

4. This morning I (go)_____to Chinatown to buy some fresh vegetables. While I (travel)_____on the train, I (run)_____into my cousin and his wife. When we (get)_____to Chinatown, it (be)_____about noon time. While my cousin and his wife (eat)_____lunch, I (buy)_____my vegetables. On the way home, I (meet)_____my cousin again, so we traveled back home together. While my cousin's wife and I (chat)_____, my cousin (sleep) _____.

5. Yesterday there was a cultural festival at the college. While some students (eat)_____ foods from different countries, others (watch)_____students performing ethnic dances.

✔ With a partner or in a small group, read the following paragraph and complete each sentence with either the simple past or the past progressive tense.

Many years ago when Sonia first_____(come) to this country, she used to go to

work by bus every morning. One morning, it _____ (rain) very hard. While she

_____(wait) for the bus, a man _____(pull) up in a car

and _____ (offer) Sonia a lift to work. Sonia _____(think)

she ——————————(know) the man and ——————————(decide) to take the lift

since it ——————————(rain) so hard. Besides in her homeland, this ——————————

(be) what any gentleman would do in such weather, so Sonia ——————————(jump) in the car.

While Sonia —————————— (ride) in the car, the man ——————————(begin) to act

strangely. Because her English wasn't too good yet, she wasn't sure what he——————————

(say). But eventually, Sonia ——————————————(realize) he had called her names and

—————————————— (threaten) her. Sonia ——————————(become) frightened and

——————————(begin) to yell and scream for help. While she ——————————(yell), a police

officer ——————————(hear) her cries and——————— (order) the man to release her at once.

After this incident, Sonia ——————————(understand) that she had to be more careful

since she ——————————(live) in a big city in a new country.

✔ Write a paragraph explaining why Sonia's behavior was dangerous. Be sure to use the past progressive for actions that were occurring.

✔ With a partner, write five sentences describing something you, the teacher or another student was doing while the teacher *was explaining* a lesson.

> *example:* While the teacher <u>was filling</u> out the chart on the board, Marco was drawing a funny picture of Davida.
> When the teacher <u>was speaking to Marco</u>, the other students <u>were doing</u> their work.

1. ————————————————————————————————
2. ————————————————————————————————
3. ————————————————————————————————
4. ————————————————————————————————
5. ————————————————————————————————

Negation of the Past Progressive Tense · · · · · · · · · · · · · · · · ·

✔ Read the following sentences and observe how they are made *negative*.

1. a. I <u>was sewing</u> when he called.
   b. I was <u>not</u> sewing when he called.

2. a. She <u>was dialing</u> the telephone when he walked in the room.
   b. She was <u>not</u> dialing the telephone when he walked in the room.
3. a. We <u>were running</u> around trying to get our work done.
   b. We were <u>not</u> running around trying to get our work done.
4. a. You <u>were listening</u> carefully while the professor was speaking.
   b. You were <u>not</u> listening while the professor was speaking.

How is the past progressive tense made negative?
The past progressive tense is <u>made negative</u> by placing the word _____ b e t w e e n
the past tense of the auxiliary verb _____ and the _____.

R u l e

4

To make a **past progressive sentence negative**, insert the word **not** between the past tense auxiliary verb (be) and the present participle.

Subject	+	Past Tense of To Be	+	Not	+	Present Participle	
example:							
Alana		was		not		cleaning	the house.
Douglas and I		were		not		telling	a lie.

 Oral Exercise: With a partner, make the following sentences negative.

1. We were baking a cake for the party when he called.
2. I was reading my English book while he was telling jokes.
3. When I stopped by his house, he was swimming in the pool.
4. When the children played in the yard, she was preparing dinner.
5. The students were sleeping while the teacher was lecturing them on grammar.

With a partner, write a list of five things you *were doing* last year and five things you *were not doing* last year.

example: I was attending college last year.
         I was not driving a fancy sports car.

1. _____
   _____
2. _____
   _____
3. _____
   _____
4. _____
   _____
5. _____
   _____

Forming Questions in the Past Progressive Tense..........

 Read the following sentences and observe how a *question* is formed in the *past progressive tense*.

1. a. Mary <u>was yelling</u>.
    b. <u>Was Mary yelling</u>?

2. a. You <u>were studying</u> English.
    b. <u>Were you studying</u> English?

3. a. We <u>were studying</u> English
    b. <u>Were we studying</u> English?

4. a. They <u>were eating</u> bacon and eggs.
    b. <u>Were they eating</u> bacon and eggs?

How are questions formed in the past progressive tense?
Questions are formed in the past progressive tense by_____ the subject and the _____.

R u l e

5

When a **question** is formed in the **past progressive tense**, the subject and the auxiliary verb (to be) are **inverted.** That is the auxiliary verb is first, and the subject is second.

Past Tense of To Be	+	Subject	+	Present Participle

example:

Was   Mary   smiling at that man?
Were   we   looking at him?

 With a partner, convert the following present progressive sentences into questions.

1. Inez and Martina were driving to the store.
2. Frank and I were washing the car when the phone rang.
3. Theresa was yelling.
4. Rose was playing when her mother left the school yard.
5. I was waiting for Mr. Right to come along at that time.

 Writing: Pretend you and a partner are writing an dialogue for a play. In this act, a police officer is interviewing a murder suspect and is trying to find out where the suspect was and what he was doing at the time the murder occurred. Be sure to use the *past progressive tense* to describe events that *were occurring* in the past.

example: Police: What <u>were you doing</u> on December 18, 1987?
               Suspect: I'm not sure what <u>I was doing</u>. Let me think.
               Uh.... <u>I was living</u> in Mexico.
               Police: Who <u>were you living</u> with in Mexico?

Writing: You were in a car accident, and your insurance company wants you to write out a report describing what happened. Be sure to use the *past progressive tense* to describe actions that were going on during the accident.

example: I <u>was sitting</u> in my car waiting for the light to turn green. All of a sudden, I saw a big yellow taxi cab. It <u>was heading</u> directly toward my car. When the taxi cab struck me, a woman who <u>was watching</u> the accident started screaming and yelling.

The Present Perfect Tense ····

The objective of this chapter is to teach students:

- *the difference in meaning and form between the present perfect and the past tenses,*

- *to form the present perfect in the affirmative, negative and interrogative forms,*

- *to practice the use of irregular past participles.*

The Simple Past Tense Versus the Present Perfect Tense ····

✔ Read the following sentences and observe the difference in tense and meaning in each pair of sentences.

1. a. I <u>have eaten</u> at that restaurant.
    b. I <u>ate</u> at that restaurant last year.

2. a. Ali <u>has gone</u> to Europe before.
    b. Ali <u>went</u> to Disney World in June.

3. a. I <u>have seen</u> that movie before.
    b. I <u>saw</u> that movie ten years ago.

4. a. We <u>have tried</u> Japanese food in the past.
    b. We <u>tried</u> Japanese food last week.

What tense is used in letter a of each sentence pair?
The _____tense is used in letter a of each sentence pair.

What tense is used in letter b of each sentence pair?
The _____tense is used in letter b of each sentence pair.

What tense is used to describe an activity that occurred at a specific time in the past?
The _____tense is used to describe an action that occurred at a <u>specific time in the past</u>.

What tense is used to describe an activity that occurred at *an indefinite time in the past*?
The _____tense is used to describe an action that occurred at <u>an indefinite time in the past.</u>

115

1

- The **Present Perfect Tense** is used to describe an activity that occurred at an **indefinite** or **unspecified** time in the past.
- The **Simple Past Tense** is used to describe an activity that occurred at a **specific** time in the past.

example: I <u>have done</u> my homework.

This sentence suggests that the homework was completed at some **unspecified** time in the past. But, read the following sentence.

example: I <u>did</u> my homework this afternoon.

This sentence suggests that the homework was completed at a **specific** or exact time in the past.

 Read the following sentences and observe the difference in tense and meaning in each pair of sentences.

1. a. She <u>has lived</u> in New York <u>since</u> 1979.
   b. She <u>lived</u> in New York for fifteen years.
2. a. Angela <u>has worked</u> at the bank <u>since</u> she graduated from school.
   b. Angela <u>worked</u> at the bank from the time she graduated from school.
3. a. I <u>have loved</u> you <u>for</u> many years.
   b. I <u>loved</u> you for many years.
4. a. They <u>have been</u> on vacation <u>for</u> an entire week.
   b. They <u>were</u> on vacation last week.

In letter a of each pair, is the action completed or still in progress?
In letter a of each pair, the action _____ .

In letter b of each pair, is the action completed or still in progress?
In letter b of each pair, the action _____ .

What tense is used to describe an action that is completed?
The _____ tense is used to describe an <u>action that has been completed.</u>

What tense is used to describe an action that began in the past and continues in the present?
The _____ tense is used to describe an action that <u>began in the past and</u> <u>continues in the present</u>.

What words are used along with the present perfect tense in order to describe an activity that began in the past and continues in the present?
The words _____ or _____ are frequently used along with the present perfect tense to describe an activity that began in the past and continues in the present.

Rule

2

- The present perfect tense is used along with the words **for** or **since** in order to describe an activity that **began in the past and continues in the present**.

    example: Agnes <u>has studied</u> accounting <u>for</u> three years.
    Nina <u>has taught</u> kindergarten <u>since</u> she graduated from college.

 Read the following sentences and observe the difference in tense and meaning in each pair of sentences.

1. a. We <u>have gone</u> to Italy several times.
    b. We <u>went</u> to Italy two times.
2. a. They <u>have been</u> late many times.
    b. They <u>were</u> late yesterday.
3. a. He <u>has purchased</u> several new cars.
    b. He <u>purchased</u> a new car two times.
4. a. You <u>have called</u> me several times.
    b. You <u>called</u> me five times.

What tense is used to express an activity that has been repeated an *indefinite number of times*?
The _____ tense is used to express that an event has occurred an <u>indefinite number of times</u>.

What tense is used to express an activity that was completed an exact number of times?
The _____ tense is used to express that an event has occurred <u>a definite or exact number of times</u>.

Rule

3

- The **present perfect** describes an activity that has been repeated an **indefinite number of times**.
- The **past tense** describes an activity that was performed a **specific number of times** in the past.

    example: Jane **has called** Noreen many times.

This sentence suggests that Jane has called Noreen several times in the past, but the exact number of times is unknown. However, read the following sentence.

    example: Jane **called** Noreen two times.

This sentence states Jane called Noreen exactly two times.

Formation of the Present Perfect Tense

 Read the following sentences.

<u>I have eaten</u> at that restaurant many times.
<u>You have eaten</u> at that restaurant many times.

She <u>has eaten</u> at that restaurant many times.
We <u>have eaten</u> at that restaurant many times.
They <u>have eaten</u> at that restaurant many times.

How is the present perfect tense formed?
The present perfect tense is formed by using the subject plus _____ plus the _____.

R u l e

4

The **present perfect tense** is formed by using the following rule.

Subject	+	Present Tense of the verb have	+	Past Participle of the verb	
I		have		worked	late many times.
You		have		called	her for days.
He/She		has		gone	home early before.
We		have		done	our homework well.
They		have		seen	E.T. several times.

✔ Read the following sentences and observe what is placed between the auxiliary verb *have* and the past participle.

a. I have <u>already</u> called my mother.

b. She has <u>never</u> cooked anything!

c. I have <u>just</u> finished my work.

d. They have <u>never</u> told me this.

What part of speech are the words that are *underlined* in the above examples?
These words are called _____ , and they are frequently used to add clarity to a sentence written in the present perfect tense.

Where is the adverb placed when using the present perfect tense?
The adverb is placed _____ the <u>auxiliary verb have</u> and the <u>past participle</u>.

R u l e

5

When an adverb is used in the present perfect tense, it must placed **between** the **auxiliary verb (have)** and the **past participle**.

example: She has rarely gone to see her mother.
We have frequently called her up.

✔ With a partner or in a small group, orally complete the following exercise with either the simple past or the present perfect.

1. a: When are you going to telephone Jose?
   b: I (telephone, already)_____ him. I (telephone)_____ him a half an hour ago.

2. a: When are you going to start writing your paper?
   b: I (start, already) _____ writing it. I (start) _____ writing it last Saturday.

3. a: Are you going to eat dinner soon?
   b: I (eat, just) _____ it. I (eat) _____ it a few minutes ago.

4. a: When are you going to buy a new car?
   b: I (buy, already) _____ one. I (buy) _____ it last week.

5. a: When is Stephen going to learn to drive?
   b: He (learn, just) _____. He (learn) _____ to drive this year.

6. a: Will you please lock the car door?
   b: I (lock, already) _____ it. I (lock) _____ it when I came home.

7. a: Will you please carry down the dirty laundry to the washer?
   b: I (carry, already) _____ it down. I (carry) _____ it down as soon as you asked me to.

8. a: When is Marta going to finish college?
   b: She (finish, just) _____ college. She (finish) _____ college last June.

✔ Read the following letter. With a partner, complete the sentences with either the present perfect tense or the past tense.

Dear Khalid:

I (be, always) _____ a generous mother. Whenever one of our children (have)

_____ a problem, my husband and I (help) _____ them.

Since we (assist, always) _____ them, a recent incident (be) _____ a

shock to me.

Last year, I (inherit) _____ more than $20,000 and (use) _____ the

money to renovate our home. I (have) _____ an unforeseen health problem and (have)

_____ to have surgery which wasn't covered by my insurance, so I (take) _____ a

loan out on our home. Well, you wouldn't believe the way my children (react) _____.

When our son and daughter (learn) _____ of this, they (become) _____ ir-

ritated. One (yell) _____ , "This is our inheritance! Did you really have to have

this operation?" I (be) _____ very hurt and angry and (say) _____ so to

them.

It makes me sad to think my children are more concerned about my money than my health. My feelings toward my children (change)_____. What do you think? Am I being unreasonable?

Sincerely,
Ahmed

 With partner write two sentences for each of the following situation.

- Describe something you or someone else did at an unspecific time in the past.
  example: Simon and Jaktar have already done their homework.
- Describe an activity that began in the past and continues in the present.
  example: We have been at this college since 1999.
- Describe an activity that has been performed several times in the past.
  example: We have discussed this tense many times before.

 Read the following sentences and observe how they are made negative.

1. a. Mary has <u>not</u> done her homework yet.
   b. François has <u>not</u> called his father since last month.
   c. We have <u>not</u> eaten there since they changed chefs.
   d. You have <u>not</u> written to me for almost two months.

How is the present perfect tense made negative?
The present perfect is made <u>negative</u> by placing the word_____after the auxiliary verb (have) and before the _____.

R u l e

6

The present perfect tense is made **negative** by using the following rule.

Subject +	Present Tense + of the verb have	Not +	Past Participle of the verb
example:			
I	have	not	worked.
You	have	not	called.
He/She/It	has	not	gone.
We	have	not	studied.
They	have	not	seen.

Oral Exercise: With a partner, make the following sentences negative.

1. My daughters have lost their interest in TV.
2. Mary Ellen has asked her parents for financial assistance.
3. You have expressed anger about this situation.
4. My parents have always been generous with me.
5. Brian and Kate have had some difficult times financially.

 Read the following sentences and observe how a question is formed in the present perfect tense.

1. a. Carlos <u>has eaten</u>.
   b. <u>Has Carlos eaten</u>?
2. a. We <u>have finished</u> our work.
   b. <u>Have you finished</u> your work?

3. a. You <u>have talked</u> to him.
   b. <u>Have you talked</u> to him?
4. a. I <u>have heard</u> these stories.
   b. <u>Have you heard</u> these stories?

How are questions formed in the present perfect tense?
In the present perfect tense a question is formed by _____ the subject and the _____ verb.

Rule

7

When a **question** is formed in the present perfect tense, the **subject** and the **auxiliary verb** (have/has) are **inverted**. That is the auxiliary verb comes first, and the subject is second.

Present Tense of have	+	Subject	+	Past Participle	
example:					
Has		Mary		arrived	home yet?
Have		the girls		finished	their assignment?

 Oral Exercise: With a partner, convert the following present perfect sentences into questions.

1. My parents have saved their money for a vacation.
2. I have been in Paris several times.
3. Theresa has complained about the amount of homework she gets.
4. We have been offended by them many times.
5. You have expressed your feelings about this situation in the past.

 Complete each of the following sentences with either the *present perfect tense* or the *past tense*.

1. I (come) _____ from a small farm community where the buildings (be) _____

very low to the ground, and there (be)_____ plenty of greenery. In my homeland, I (see)_____urban areas, but (never, see)_____anything like the buildings in New York City.

2. Enos (visit) _____ her homeland many times, but she (never visit)_____ Europe. She (leave)_____for England last week, and she (be) _____there since. Yesterday, she (call)_____and (say)_____she was going on a tour of London. For ages, Enos (want)_____to meet the Queen of England, but I don't think she will see her from her tour bus.

3. Yvette is ready to go to France. She (be) _____to England, but she (be, not) _____ to Paris before. She (study) _____French since she (start) _____high school, so she hopes to be able to communicate easily. She (pack, already)_____ her suitcase. The last time she (go)_____on a vacation, she (telephone)_____me collect five times. When I (receive)_____the telephone bill, I (tell)_____ her that she wasn't to call collect on her next trip.

4. Paulina and Pietro (live)_____in Boston since they (arrive)_____ in the United States ten years ago. They (rent) _____ an apartment for seven years until they had saved enough money to buy a small house.

Pietro (work)_____ for a small computer company for several years now, but he also goes to college at night. He (attend)_____college for a few years and plans to graduate soon.

✔ Write a paragraph describing something you have seen or done several times in the past.

✔ Write a paragraph describing activities you have engaged in since you arrived at this school.

✔ Write a response to Ahmed telling him what you think of his children's behavior. Back up your opinion with short stories or examples from your experiences in this country and yours. Be certain to use the present perfect tense to describe events that:

- occurred at unspecified times in the past,
- began in the past and continue in the present, or
- were repeated several times.

✔ **Writing:** Reread the letter written by Ahmed and write three present perfect tense questions about the letter.

The Present Perfect Progressive Tense

12

The objective of this chapter is to teach students:

- *the difference in meaning and form between the following tenses: the present progressive, the present perfect and present perfect progressive,*

- *the formation of the present perfect progressive in the affirmative, negative and interrogative forms.*

The Meaning

 Read the following sentences and observe the difference in meaning in each pair.

1. a. I <u>am writing</u> a paper right now.
    b. I <u>have been writing</u> a paper <u>since</u> I got up this morning.
2. a. Sharon <u>is running</u> at the park now.
    b. Sharon <u>has been running for</u> ten years.
3. a. You <u>are studying</u> English now.
    b. You <u>have been studying</u> English <u>since</u> you arrived here.
4. a. Shifra and Yoni <u>are studying</u> English now.
    b. Shifra and Yoni <u>have been studying</u> English <u>for</u> a few years.

What tense is used in letter a in these pairs of sentences?
The _____ tense is used in letter a.

What tense is used in letter b in these pairs of sentences?
The _____ tense is used in letter b.

What is the difference in meaning between the present progressive tense and the present perfect progressive tense?
The <u>present progressive tense</u> expresses an activity that _____.
The <u>present perfect progressive tense</u> expresses the _____ of time an activity has been in progress. It stresses that the activity began in the _____ and _____ in the present.

125

What *time expressions* are frequently used with the present perfect progressive tense?
The time expressions _____ or _____ are frequently used with the present perfect progressive tense.

Rule

1

The **present progressive tense** expresses an activity that is **in progress now**. However, the **present perfect progressive tense** expresses the **amount of time** an activity has been in progress. It stresses that an activity **began in the past** and **continues in the present**. Time expressions such as **for** and **since** are frequently used with the present perfect progressive tense.

> *example:* Patrick <u>has been smoking</u> since he started high school.

This sentence suggests that Patrick began smoking in high school and still continues to smoke today. However, read the following sentence.

> *example:* Patrick <u>is smoking</u>.

It suggests that Patrick is smoking right now. This sentence doesn't explain when he began to smoke or how long he has been smoking. It simply states he is smoking now.

Read the following sentences and observe the difference in meaning in each pair.

1. a. Barbara <u>has watched</u> that movie many times.
   b. Barbara <u>has been watching</u> that movie since seven o'clock.
2. a. We <u>have traveled</u> to Brazil on several occasions.
   b. We <u>have been traveling</u> to Brazil for six and a half hours.
3. a. You <u>have slept late</u> in the past.
   b. You <u>have been sleeping</u> late for the past six years.
4. a. I <u>have sat</u> in many ESL classrooms.
   b. I <u>have been sitting</u> in this ESL class since ten o'clock this morning.

What tense is used in letter a in these pairs of sentences?
The _____tense is used in letter a of each sentence pair.

What tense is used in letter b in these pairs of sentences?
The _____tense is used in letter b of each sentence pair.

What is the *difference in meaning* between the *present perfect tense* and the *present perfect progressive tense*?
The present perfect progressive tense is used to express an activity that began in the_____
_____and continues in the _____. It expresses the _____
of an activity. However, the present perfect tense expresses an action that was_____
many times or performed an_____ number of times in the past.

2

The **present perfect progressive tense** is used to express the duration of an activity that **began in the past and continues in the present**. However, the **present perfect tense** expresses an action that was **repeated many times** or was **performed at indefinite times** in the past.

> *example:* Henrick <u>has fixed</u> that old car on many occasions.
> This sentence shows that Henrick has had to repair his car many times.

However, if you read the following sentence, it indicates that Henrick started to repair his car at six o'clock this morning and is still repairing it now.

> *example:* Henrick <u>has been fixing</u> that old car since six o'clock this morning.

Forming the Present Perfect Progressive

 Read the following sentences and observe how the present perfect progressive tense is formed.

1. I <u>have been studying</u> for five hours.
2. You <u>have been studying</u> for five hours.
3. She <u>has been studying</u> for five hours.
4. We <u>have been studying</u> for five hours.
5. They <u>have been studying</u> for five hours.

How is the *present perfect progressive tense* formed in the above sentences?
The <u>present perfect progressive tense</u> is formed by using the <u>subject</u> plus the _____ plus the_____ plus the_____ .

3

Form the **present perfect tense** by using the following rule.

Subject +	Present tense of verb have	+	Past Participle to be	+	Present Participle of the verb	
example:						
We	have		been		working	since noon.
He	has		been		talking	for two hours.

✔ ***Controlled Exercise:*** Complete the following exercise with the *present progressive* or the *present perfect progressive* tense.

1. Tina and Kaur (talk)_____on the telephone now. They (talk)_____since seven o'clock.

2. You (listen)_____to music right now. You (listen)_____to music since you got up.

3. Rina and Rafaela (exercise)_____ at this very moment. They (exercise) _____ for over an hour.

4. I (write)_____ a composition for my class now. I (try) _____ to write it for two hours.

5. Marco (work)_____ at the factory now. He (work)_____at the factory for six months now.

✔ Complete the following exercise with the *present perfect* or the *present perfect progressive* tense.

1. The college is only a mile from my house; therefore, I (walk)_____t o the college many times.

2. The college is several miles from my house, but today I decided to walk. I (walk)_____ to the college since seven o'clock this morning.

3. Chris (watch) _____ the news since five o'clock hoping to see himself on television.

4. I (watch)_____the five o'clock news many times.

5. We (practice)_____our English since we started our language classes in our country.

6. Jean Baptiste is tired. He (clean) _____up the garden since he got up this morning.

7. The students (read)_____that paper many times, but they still don't understand it.

8. The students (read)_____that paper since they arrived this morning.

✔ Complete each of the blanks in this letter with either the *present progressive* tense, the *present perfect* tense or the *present perfect progressive* tense.

Dear Ben:

I (write)_____to you because I am worried and afraid. I (date)_____a

woman named Joan for about a year, and we (find) _____that we are quite com-

patible. This woman is only 22 and (be)_____married a couple of times. She also has

a four year old son. As you know, I am a 31 years old and have never been married.

Two months ago, I bought a house. Since Joan and her son have no place to live, they (live)

_____ with me. Now I (support, also) _____them financially.

The problem is that Joan (demand) _____ that we get married for the last couple of weeks. She (insist) _____ on my marrying her now even though I (date, not) _____ anyone else for a long time.

She (tell) _____ me that other men (ask) _____ her to date them. I (get) _____ envious, but I'm not ready for marriage yet. I don't care for the way she (pressure) _____ me. Yet I'm afraid she'll dump me if I don't marry her soon.

I (wonder) _____ what I should do to maintain this relationship but not be rushed into a marriage. I know you once had a similar problem so I thought you could give me some suggestions.

I (await, anxiously) _____ your response.

Ramon

✔ *Writing:* With a partner, list three activities you have been doing during the past couple of years.

   example: I have been studying English since 1999.

✔ Ask a partner to tell you three activities he/she has been doing during the past couple of years and write them down.

   example: Thomas has been working as a waiter since January.

✔ Read the following sentences and observe how they are made negative.

   1. I <u>have not been studying</u> for five hours.
   2. You <u>have not been studying</u> for five hours.
   3. She <u>has not been studying</u> for five hours.
   4. We <u>haven't been studying</u> for five hours.
   5. They <u>haven't been studying</u> for five hours.

How is the *present perfect progressive* tense made *negative* in the above sentences?
The present perfect progressive tense is made negative by inserting the word _____ between the auxiliary verb _____ and the _____.

4

The present perfect progressive tense is made **negative** by doing the following.

Subject	Present tense of verb have	+ not +	Past Participle of be (been)	Present Participle of main verb	
We	have	**not**	been	working	since noon.
He	has	**not**	been	talking	for two hours.

✔ *Controlled Exercise:* With a partner, make the following present perfect progressive sentences negative.

1. Ramon has been living with Joan for three years.
2. Joan has been complaining about not being married.
3. We have been telling Ramon to stay single.
4. Joan and Ramon have been dating for a year.
5. I have been reading about Ramon's problem.

✔ *Writing:* List three activities that have *not* been happening during the past couple of years.

example: I have <u>not</u> been studying hard enough to pass the exam.

✔ Ask a partner to tell you three activities he/she has not been doing during the past couple of years and write them down.

example: Tanya has <u>not</u> been listening to the professor.

✔ Read the following sentences and observe how *questions* are formed in the *present perfect progressive* tense.

1. a: <u>Have you been eating</u> all my candy?
   b: No, I haven't been eating all your candy.
2. a: <u>Have they been doing</u> well in school?
   b: Yes, they have been doing very well.
3. a: <u>Has Ramon been</u> dating other women?
   b: No, he has not been dating other women.
4. a: <u>Have you been studying</u> for the final exam?
   b: Yes, we have been studying for the final exam.
5. a: <u>Has the dog been going</u> out for a run everyday?
   b: Yes, the dog has been going out for a run everyday since I arrived here.

How is the present perfect progressive tense made into a question in the above sentences?
A question is formed in the <u>present perfect progressive tense</u> by _____the subject and the _____ .

Rule

5

A question is formed in the **present perfect progressive** tense by **inverting** the subject and the verb has or have.

Present tense of verb have	+	subject	+	Past Participle of be (been)	+	Present Participle of main verb

example:

Has   Peter   been   smoking all his life?

✔ ***Controlled Exercise:*** Convert the following present perfect progressive sentences into questions.

1. We have been supporting ourselves since we graduated from school.
2. Joan has been living in Ramon's house for two months.
3. Joan and Ramon have been arguing for several weeks.
4. I have been eating for almost two hours.
5. You has been threatening to punish your child for over two hours.

✔ ***Writing:*** Write three questions asking your partner if he/she has been doing certain activities during the past few years.

example: Have you been working part time for the last year?

✔ Write three questions asking what another person in your class has been doing during the past few years.

example: Has the professor been teaching English during the last ten years?

✔ ***Writing:*** Write a letter to Ramon telling him what he should do about his girlfriend's demanding they be married. Be sure to summarize the problems Ramon has been facing and to use the correct tenses.

✔ Write a letter to a friend and tell him/her what you've been doing during the past year. Be sure to use the *present perfect progressive* to express activities that you were doing a year ago and continue to do now. However, be certain to use the *past tense* for activities that are completed and the *present perfect* for actions that were repeated in the past or completed at some indefinite time before now.

The Future Tense

The objective of this chapter is to teach students:

- *the form and meaning of the future tense,*

- *to distinguish between the use of the modal will and to be going to,*

- *the formation of the future tense in the affirmative, negative and interrogative forms.*

The Future Tense

 Read the following sentences and observe how the future tense is expressed.

1. a. Tomorrow I <u>will clean</u> the house.
   b. Tomorrow I <u>am going to clean</u> the house.
2. a. We <u>will buy</u> a new car next year.
   b. We <u>are going to buy</u> a new car next year.
3. a. They <u>will study</u> for the test after school.
   b. The <u>are going to study</u> for the test after school.

How many ways can the future tense be expressed?
The future tense can be expressed in _____ different ways.

What is the first method used to express the future?
The first method used to express the future tense is use the modal_____plus the _____.

What is the second method used to express the future?
The second method used to express the future tense is to use _____plus the _____.

1

The future tense can be expressed in **two ways**. Observe the first method.

Subject	+	**Will**	+	**Simple Form of the verb**	

example:

She	will	study	after dinner.
We	will	meet	you at ten o'clock.

Observe the second method used to express the future.

Subject	+	**to be going to**	+	**Simple Form of the verb**	

example:

Patrick	is going to	visit	us next week.
I	am going to	go	on a diet tomorrow.
You	are going to	study	French in school.

 Read the following sentences.

1. a. I <u>am going to go</u> to school because I want to get a good job.
   b. Joan and Tom <u>are going to sell</u> their house because it is too large.

2. a. My mother <u>will help</u> you with the baking for the party.
   b. I <u>will assist</u> you with your project.
   c. They <u>will help</u> Steve set up the pool.

3. a. He <u>will win</u> the game because he is the best player.
   b. He <u>is going to win</u> the game because he is the best player.

In numbers 1 and 2, what is the difference in the way that *will* and *be going to* are used in these sentences?
The word <u>will</u> is used to_____or express willingness to do something
or _____ someone. However, the words <u>to be going to</u> are used to express a _____ .

In number 3, why isn't there any difference in meaning between the sentences in letters a and b?
There is no difference in meaning since both the terms <u>will</u> and <u>to be going to</u> are used to make _____about the future.

R u l e

2

The word **will** is used to **volunteer** or **express willingness** to do something or **help** someone.

example: We will help you pay your college expenses.

The words **to be going to** are used to express a **preconceived plan**.

example: I am going to travel around Europe for two months.

Both the terms **will** and **to be going** are used to make **predictions about the future**.

example: I will become a millionaire before the age of thirty.
I am going to become a millionaire before the age of thirty.

✔ With a partner, complete the following composition with either the *present tense* or the future tense of *will* or *to be going to*.

Dear Stephanie,

In two months, I (graduate) _____from college. Because I had to learn and improve my English, it took me seven years, but I (be)_____proud of myself for accomplishing this goal.

After I (graduate) _____ , I (take)_____a long vacation. I (plan) _____ to go to Europe with a few of my friends. We (go)_____to London, Paris, Rome, Madrid and Lisbon. We (take)_____the Concord to Europe. Once we arrive, we (travel)_____around Europe by train. It (be)_____ the best way to see the continent.

When I (come)_____back from my trip, I (begin)_____to look for a job. Since my college degree (be) _____ in Economics, I (look) _____ for a job doing research either in a bank or a brokerage house.

Once I (get) _____a job, I (start)_____to look for my own apartment.

My parents (be, not) _____happy about this because in my country children (be

The Future Tense 135

supposed to) _____ live with their parents until they (get) _____ married. However, I've explained to them that here in the United States, it (be) _____ different. Children (be) _____ encouraged to be independent. Once a child has completed his/her education, he/she (move)_____ out of his/her parents home. I (know) _____ that is not acceptable in our homeland, but I (like)_____ the idea of living by myself and having privacy. It (seem)_____ that our culture (believe, not)_____ that individual privacy (be)_____ important. Instead it (stress)_____ the importance of family. My family (be) _____ very important to me, but I (guess)_____ I've become Americanized because I really (want)_____ to have some autonomy and privacy.

I (have)_____ the feeling that you would like to take your own place someday, too. I (think) _____ our parents (feel) _____ much better if we share an apartment together. They (feel) _____ more comfortable if they know that we (live) _____ together.

I (hope) _____ I can afford to do all these things. It (be)_____ so exciting.

Take care and write soon.

Love,
Rebecca

✔ With a partner, orally complete each of the following sentences using *will* or *to be going to*.

1. She _____ (invite) Stephanie to live with her.
2. I _____ (go) on a trip after graduation.
3. We _____ (visit) Paris first.
4. They _____ (travel) by train.
5. We _____ (send) postcards to our parents.
6. Stephanie and Rebecca _____ (rent) an apartment.
7. Rebecca _____ (respond) soon.
8. They_____ (look) for an apartment.
9. Rebecca _____ (help) me if I ask her.

10. I _____(get) my own place if it is the last thing that I do.

11. My parents_____(find) a solution to this problem.

12. My friends and I _____(visit) Germany during this trip.

13. Rebecca and Stephanie_____(rent) a house.

14. My mother _____(help) me fix up my apartment.

15. My friend _____(be) successful if he tries harder.

✔ Complete each of the following sentences with either the *future tense* or the *present tense*. Be sure to look for context clues in order to determine the tense.

Stephanie (have) _____a roommate at her college who (go)_____to see the

college doctor at least once a week. Her name (be)_____Melissa. Every Monday

or Tuesday, Melissa (wake)_____up with some sort of illness. Then she (tele-

phone)_____the campus doctor and says, "I (have to)_____to see

you this morning because I (think) _____ I have a ..." Then she (tell)

_____ the doctor about some psychosomatic illness she (have)

_____ . The doctor usually (tell)_____her to come in after her

classes. Then Melissa states, "By that time, I (be) _____near death. You (have to)

_____ see me immediately." Sometimes the doctor (give)_____ in

and (let)_____her come in. Other times, when the doctor (be)_____

too busy, he (tell) _____her, "You told me the same thing last week, and you

survived that illness. I (be)_____sure you (make)_____it this

time, too. I (see) _____ you later today."

I (wonder)_____why Melissa (think, always)_____she (be)

_____ sick even though she (be) _____perfectly healthy.

✔ *Writing:*

1. Write a composition explaining what you will do when you graduate from college.

2. Each person in the class should pick another student's name. With a partner, write five sentences making predictions about the future of that person. Be sure to use both <u>will</u> and <u>be going to</u> in these sentences.

3. Write five sentences expressing a plan that you have. Be sure to use <u>be going to</u> in these sentences.

4. Write three sentences expressing willingness to volunteer or help. Be sure to use <u>will</u> in these sentences.

Negation of the Future Tense......................................

 Read the following sentences and observe how the future tense is made negative.

1. a. I <u>am going to cook</u> dinner.
   b. I am <u>not</u> going to cook dinner.

2. a. We <u>are going to clean</u> up.
   b. We are <u>not</u> going to clean up.

3. a. Ann <u>is going to go</u> to Italy.
   b. Ann is <u>not</u> going to go to Italy.

1. a. I <u>will cook</u> dinner.
   b. I will <u>not</u> cook dinner.

2. a. We <u>will clean</u> up.
   b. We will <u>not</u> clean up.

3. a. Ann <u>will go</u> to Italy.
   b. Ann will <u>not</u> go to Italy.

When the word *will* is used to express the future tense, how is it made negative?
When the modal <u>will</u> is used to express the future, it is made negative by placing the word
_____ between the word <u>will</u> and the _____.

When the words *to be going to* are used to express the future tense, how are they made negative?
When the expression <u>to be going to</u> is used to express the future, it is made negative by placing the word _____ after the verb _____.

R u l e

To make the future tense negative with the modal **will**, the word **not** is placed after the word will.

Subject	+	**will**	+	**not**	+	**simple verb form**

example:

Sarah	will	not	call	her.
We	will	not	eat	with you.

To make the future tense negative with the expression **to be going to**, the word **not** is placed after the verb **to be** (is, am, are).

Subject	+ to be +	not +	going to +	**simple verb form**

example:

Mary	is	not	going to	live	forever.
We	are	not	going to	buy	a new car.

✔ With a partner, make the following sentences negative.

1. Melissa will be sick again next Monday.
2. She is going to fail her classes if she keeps getting sick.
3. Stephanie will write to you when she makes her decision.
4. Rebecca is going to graduate in a few months.
5. Rebecca's parents will continue to love her even if she moves out of their house.
6. Rebecca and Stephanie are going to rent an apartment.
7. I am going to call the doctor.
8. She is going to get sick if she drinks spoiled milk.
9. Rebecca and I will need your help when we move into our apartment.

✔ *Oral Exercise:* Tell a partner two things *you will not do* and two things *they will not do* in the future.

We will not write your term paper for you.
They will not move out of their parents' houses.

Questions in the Future Tense . . . .

✔ Read the following sentences and observe how questions are formed in the future tense.

1. a. She will be late tonight.
   b. <u>Will she be</u> late tonight?

2. a. I will cook dinner someday.
   b. <u>Will you cook</u> dinner someday?

3. a. She is going to be late tonight.
   b. <u>Is she going to be</u> late tonight?

4. a. I am going to cook dinner someday.
   b. <u>Are you going to cook</u> dinner someday?

When the future tense uses the word *will*, how is a question formed?
A question is formed in the future tense by _____ the modal will and the _____ of the sentence.

When the future tense uses the words *to be going to*, how is a question formed?
A question is formed in the future tense by _____ the _____ and the verb to be (am, is or are).

4

When the **future tense** is formed with the word **will**, a question is formed by **inverting** the subject and the verb.

Will + **subject** + **verb**

example:

| Will | you | visit | me tonight? |
| Will | she | drive | you home? |

When the **future tense** is formed with the words **to be going to**, a question is formed by **inverting the subject** and the verb **to be** (am, is or are).

To be + **subject** + **going to** + **verb**

example:

| Are | you | going to | read | this book? |
| Is | he | going to | call | her? |

 Make the following sentences questions.

1. Stephanie and her friends are going to go to Europe on vacation.
2. Rebecca's parents will always care about their child.
3. I am going to buy furniture for my new apartment next week.
4. She will need some money to pay the deposit on the apartment.
5. Rebecca is going to write to Stephanie this afternoon.
6. We will improve our French in Paris.
7. We are going to study Spanish in Madrid.
8. Melissa is going to make a fool out of herself.
9. You will help Stephanie learn English.
10. I am going to scream the next time Melissa goes to see the campus doctor.

 Oral Exercise: Prepare a list of five questions which attempt to guess what your partner will do this weekend. Ask your partner the questions and have them respond in a complete sentence.

example:
a: Will you visit the Empire State Building on Saturday?
b: No, I am going to visit my Aunt Jane.

 Writing:

1. Pretend you are preparing to interview a well known celebrity for a television talk show. Decide what celebrity you will interview and write five questions to ask this person about his/her future plans. Then write answers to these question as you believe this person would respond.

2. Write five sentences predicting what will happen to you and some of your classmates in the next five years.

.... *The Past Perfect Tense* ....

The objective of this chapter is to teach students:

- *the difference in meaning and form between the past and past perfect tenses,*

- *the formation of the past perfect in the affirmative, negative and interrogative forms.*

The Past Perfect Tense versus the Simple Past Tense........

Read the following sentences and observe the *two different tenses* used.

1. a. John <u>said</u> that Ann <u>cooked</u> dinner.
   b. John <u>said</u> that Ann <u>had cooked</u> dinner.
2. a. You <u>knew</u> that her husband <u>worked</u> in a factory.
   b. You <u>knew</u> that her husband <u>had worked</u> in a factory.
3. a. I <u>told</u> Francois that Jean <u>called</u> twice.
   b. I <u>told</u> Francois that Jean <u>had called</u> twice.

What tense is used in letter a in each of the sentence pairs?
The _____ tense is used in letter <u>a</u> of all three examples.

What two tenses are used in letter b in each of the sentence pairs?
The _____ and _____ tenses are used in letter <u>b</u>.

The Past Perfect Tense

Read the following sentences. *Underline the verb* and state the tense being used. Next determine which action was completed first and which action was completed second. Place a number 1 above the verb whose action was completed first and a number 2 above the verb whose action was completed second.

1. I had just finished studying when the telephone rang.
2. When the police arrived, the burglar had already left.
3. He had hung up the phone before I picked it up.
4. The mother had just started to sleep when the baby cried for a bottle.
5. We had been in the class for ten minutes when the professor arrived.

In each of these sentences, what tense is used to describe the first action that took place?
The _____tense is used to describe the action that occurred <u>first</u>.

What tense is used to describe the second or most recent action that took place?
The _____tense is used to describe the <u>second or most recent action</u> that occurred.

Rule

1

The **past perfect tense** is used when discussing **two different points in the past**. The **past perfect tense** is used to describe an activity that **occurred first** or before a particular time in the past. The **past tense** is used with the more recent activity.

                  1   2

example: At 8:30 PM, Mary was asleep. At 8:45 PM, her husband came home.

                 1   2

Mary <u>had been</u> asleep for 15 minutes when her husband <u>came</u> home.

✔ Read the following sentences and observe the way the past perfect is used.

1. We had never been in such a mess <u>before</u>.
2. <u>By that time</u>, I had already called her ten times.
3. We had only studied written English in my country <u>at that time</u>.

If there is only one verb in the sentence, why is only the past perfect tense used?
The past perfect tense can be used in a sentence where a past time is _____by the use of time expressions such as _____ or _____ .

✔ Read the following sentences. Underline the adverbial clause and observe the use of the past perfect in the main clause.

1. She had lived alone before getting married.
2. Prior to her returning home, I had straightened up the house.
3. She had worked in supermarket until completing her college education.

Why can the past perfect tense be used in these sentences when there is only one verb?
The past perfect tense can be used in a sentence where the second or more recent activity is referenced in a _____adverbial clause.

2

- The past perfect can be used in a sentence where a past time is **implied** by the use of time expressions such as **before, by that time, until** etc.

  example: Until that time, she had never had a drink.

- The past perfect can also be used in a sentence where the **adverbial clause** has been **reduced**.

  example: Before receiving the promotion, she had looked for another job.

Forming the Past Perfect Tense

Reread the examples in the previous section and state how the past perfect tense is formed.
The <u>past perfect tense</u> is formed by using a subject plus the _____ o f
the verb _____ plus the _____ of the main verb.

R u l e

3

The **past perfect tense** is formed using the following rule.

Subject	+	Past tense of the verb have (had)	+	Past Participle of verb
example:				
Mary		had		called.
We		had		eaten.

✔ Read the following sentences and observe what kind of words are used along with the past perfect tense.

1. I had <u>already</u> eaten when he called.
2. We had <u>just</u> left when she arrived.
3. They hadn't <u>yet</u> finished cleaning when their parents came home.
4. We had <u>never</u> met such an interesting person before.

What part of speech are the underlined words?
The underlined words are _____. An <u>adverb</u> is a word that modifies a verb, an adjective or another adverb.

Where are adverbs placed when using the past perfect tense?
An adverb is placed between the _____ and the _____.

Why are these adverbs used in conjunction with the past perfect tense?
These adverbs are used to _____or _____to the meaning of the sentence.

4

The adverbs **already**, **just**, **yet**, and **never** can be used with the past perfect tense. These words are placed **between** the auxiliary verb **had** and the **past participle.** They are used to **give emphasis** or **clarity** to the meaning of the sentence.

example: Filipo had <u>never</u> taken drugs before this time.
Anna Maria and her boyfriend said that Sarah had <u>already</u> returned.

✔ With a partner, read the following story and complete each blank with either the simple past tense or the past perfect tense.

Several years ago before I (come)_____to this country, I (decide)_____I'd better start to learn English. Until that time, I (have)_____no interest in learning English, but I (know)_____, when I (decide)_____to come here, English was essential. Therefore, I (begin)_____to study English in my homeland. I (think) _____ this program would prepare me for life in my new country, but I (have)_____ no idea just how much time, dedication and motivation it takes to master a new language.

I (arrive)_____on a plane from China all by myself. When I (exit)_____the plane, I (have)_____to pass through customs. I (assume) _____ there would be someone there to translate for me, but for some reason, there wasn't anyone who could speak my dialect. Since I (anticipate) _____having a translator, I (be)_____ completely flustered and embarrassed when I had to communicate. Fortunately, a businessman who (see)_____what was going on came over to the counter and facilitated our conversation.

After I (finish) _____ with customs, I (have)_____to get myself to my cousin's apartment by taxi-cab. This (be)_____another catastrophe since the taxi-cab driver (be)_____also a foreigner and hardly (speak)_____any English either. The two of us (struggle)_____for almost twenty minutes trying to interpret my destination. Finally, after an exhaustive conversation, the driver (understand) _____my request and (drive)_____me to my cousin's place.

By the time I (arrive)_____at the apartment, it (be) _____ almost two o'clock in the morning. My cousin was waiting for me anxiously. We (talk)_____about my trip and the problems I had at the airport. My cousin said the language was only one of the many adjustments I would have to make. Yet I told her what (scare)_____me the most (be)_____my inability to communicate. My cousin indicated that many new immigrants (have)_____the same type of experience when they first (ar-rive)_____ here, but that I would gradually improve my English and be able to survive in my new world.

That night as I (sit)_____on a new bed in a strange country where I didn't really speak the language and had very few friends and relatives, I (wonder)_____ if I would ever be able to succeed in this new environment. At that late hour of the night, it (seem) _____ like an impossibility, but finally I (just, close)_____my eyes and (decide)_____to deal with it one day at a time.

✔ *Oral Exercise:* With a partner instruct the students to recall some event that impressed them greatly. Then the partner should be prepared to report back their partner's experience to the class.

   example: My husband and I had never felt such joy before this time.
   Until that time, Marie and her husband had never felt such joy.

✔ Read the following sentences and observe how they are made negative.

Marla had **not** cooked dinner she said.
Kathryn had **not** called before that time.
We had **not** done our assignments by that time.

How is the past perfect tense made negative?
The past perfect is made <u>negative</u> by placing the word _____ between the auxiliary verb and the _____.

R u l e

5

The **past perfect tense** is made negative by using the following rule.

Subject	+	Past Tense of the verb **have**	+	Not	+	Past Participle of the verb
I		had		not		worked.
You		had		not		called.
He/She/It		had		not		gone.
We		had		not		done.
They		had		not		seen.

 Make the following sentences negative.

1. I had been unhappy in my homeland before this time.
2. She had taught home economics during those years.
3. We had studied endlessly at that time.
4. They had given us a lot of work before.
5. You had complained about the problem previously.

 Oral Exercise: Tell a partner or members of a small group about something you had not done before this time.

example: I had not studied English before this time.
I had not lived in a big city until moving to the United States.

 Read the following sentences and observe *how questions are formed* in the past perfect tense.

1. a. Carl <u>had already eaten</u>.
   b. <u>Had Carl already eaten</u>?

2. a. They <u>had just called</u> me.
   b. <u>Had they just called</u> me?

3. a. We <u>had finished</u> the test earlier.
   b. <u>Had you finished</u> the test earlier?

4. a. You <u>had not eaten</u> meat before.
   b. <u>Hadn't you eaten</u> meat before?

How are questions formed in the past perfect tense?
A <u>question</u> is formed in the <u>past perfect tense</u> by_____ the_____ and the auxiliary verb.

R u l e

6

A **question is formed** in the past perfect tense by **inverting** the **subject** and the **auxiliary verb** (had). That is the auxiliary verb is first, and the subject is second.

example:

Past Tense of have	+	Subject	+	Past Participle	
Had		Mary		arrived	home yet?
Had		the girls		finished	before going home?

 Make the following past perfect sentences into questions.

1. The teacher had worked as a clerk before graduating.
2. I had just received the bad news.
3. You had worked for the government until that time.
4. We had already finished the classes by the time she arrived.
5. The instructor had asked Lydia to speak in English.

 Oral Exercise: Ask a partner or a member of your group a question about something he/she had done before this time.

example: Had you lived in a big city before you came to the United States?
Had he studied English before he move here?

 Controlled Exercise: With a partner, write the following two sentences as one sentence using the past and past perfect tenses. Add or re-arrange words to clarify the sentence, or make one sentence an adverbial clause using an appropriate subordinating conjunction.

example: At midnight Jane was sound asleep. At 2:00 AM a dog barked and woke her up.
Jane had already been sound asleep when a dog barked and woke her up.

1. Mrs. Smith left for work. An hour later, her daughter tried to call.

   _____

2. The class began at 10 o'clock. John arrived at 10:10.

   _____

3. She ate dinner at 6:30. She told me the news at 7:30.

   _____

4. We called our parents at 11:30 PM. They went to sleep at 10:00 PM.

   _____

5. He left at 5 o'clock. She arrived at 5:30.

   _____

6. She lived in France for two years. Then she moved to England.

   _____

7. The teacher asked the class a question. The student knew the answer right away.

   _____

8. Susan got up at 11:30. I went shopping at 9:00.

   _____

9. I studied Spanish for 10 years. I went to Spain after this time.

   _____

10. Dana walked to the bus. At the bus stop, Peter picked her up.

   _____

✔ Complete the following chart describing what activities you performed yesterday at each specific time of the day. Be sure to use the simple past to state each individual event on the chart.

Time		Activity
7:00	AM	_____
8:00	AM	_____
9:00	AM	_____
10:00	AM	_____
11:00	AM	_____
12:00	PM	_____
1:00	PM	_____
2:00	PM	_____
3:00	PM	_____
4:00	PM	_____
5:00	PM	_____
6:00	PM	_____
7:00	PM	_____
8:00	PM	_____
9:00	PM	_____
10:00	PM	_____

✔ Using the *past perfect tense* and the *simple past*, write five sentences describing the activities that you had completed by specific times of the day.

example: By the time I **left** for work, I **had already cleaned** up the breakfast dishes.

1. _____

2. _____

3. _____

4. _____

5. _____

The Past Perfect Progressive · *Tense*

The objective of this chapter is to teach students:

- *the difference in meaning and form between the past perfect and the past perfect progressive tenses,*

- *the formation of the past perfect progressive in the affirmative, negative and interrogative forms.*

The Meaning of the Past Perfect Progressive Tense·········

Read the following sentences and observe the difference in the two tenses used.

1. a. I <u>had been studying</u> for two hours when my sister called.
   b. I <u>had studied</u> for two hours when my sister called.

2. a. By that time, we <u>had been working</u> on the project for two hours.
   b. By that time, we <u>had worked</u> on the project for two hours.

3. a. Before graduating, he <u>had been studying</u> for three hours each day.
   b. Before graduating, he <u>had studied</u> for three hours each day.

What tense is used in letter a in these pairs of sentences?
The _____ tense is used in letter a of each example.

What tense is used in letter b in these pairs of sentences?
The _____ tense is used in letter b of each example.

What is the difference in meaning between the *past perfect tense* and the *past perfect progressive* tense?
The <u>past perfect progressive tense</u> stresses the _____ or the _____ of an activity that was in progress before another activity in the past. The <u>past perfect tense</u> stresses the _____ of an act before another activity in the _____ .

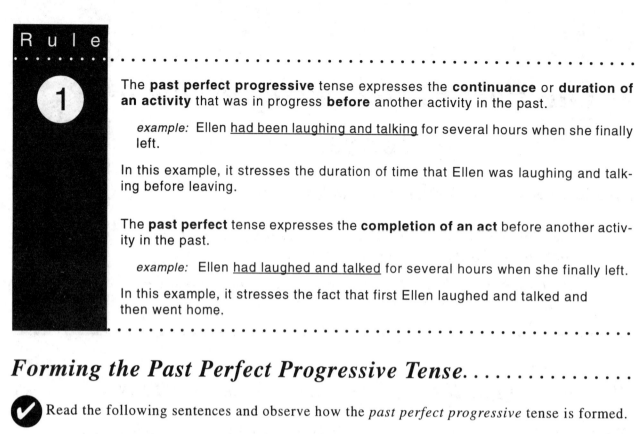

1

The **past perfect progressive** tense expresses the **continuance** or **duration of an activity** that was in progress **before** another activity in the past.

> *example:* Ellen <u>had been laughing and talking</u> for several hours when she finally left.

In this example, it stresses the duration of time that Ellen was laughing and talking before leaving.

The **past perfect** tense expresses the **completion of an act** before another activity in the past.

> *example:* Ellen <u>had laughed and talked</u> for several hours when she finally left.

In this example, it stresses the fact that first Ellen laughed and talked and then went home.

Forming the Past Perfect Progressive Tense. . . . .

✓ Read the following sentences and observe how the *past perfect progressive* tense is formed.

1. I <u>had been reading</u> for more than an hour when they called me.
2. You <u>had been studying</u> English for five years when you moved here.
3. She <u>had been trying</u> to solve a problem for two hours when she finally asked for help.

How is the past perfect progressive tense formed in the above sentences?
The <u>past perfect progressive</u> tense is formed by using a subject plus the _____
plus the _____ of to be and the _____ of the main verb.

R u l e

2

The **past perfect progressive** tense if formed by using the following rule.

Subject +	Past tense of verb have	+	Past Participle to be	+ Present Participle	
We	had		been	working	all night.
He	had		been	cooking	for days.

Oral Exercise: With a partner, orally complete the following sentences in the past perfect progressive tense.

> *example:* She (feel) _____ sick for several hours when she decided to go to the hospital.
> She <u>had been feeling</u> sick for several hours when she decided to go to the hospital.

1. I (wash)_____the windows for five hours when I slipped on a wet rag.

_____

2. We (learn)_____French for over two years when we went to Paris.

_____

3. They (talk)_____on the phone for over two hours when her husband got home.

_____

4. You (complain)_____about that problem for months when you finally found a solution.

_____

5. I (drive)_____ to Florida for over fifteen hours when I finally decided to pull over and sleep.

_____

✔ With a partner complete the following exercise with either the past perfect or the past perfect progressive tense.

Marco: I was recently reading a newspaper article that said almost everyone in this country who was alive at the time of the assassination of President John F. Kennedy could remember vividly what they were doing when they heard the terrible news. (*Marco asks the teacher.*) Do you remember what you were doing when President Kennedy was killed?

Prof.: I was in fourth grade. We (returned, just)_____from lunch when an announcement came over the loud speaker. Ironically, we (learn, just)_____ about the process of electing a president. When we heard the announcement, our teacher (just tell) _____us that President Kennedy (be, already)_____ president for almost three years and that he was probably going to run for office next November again.

Marco: When President Kennedy was killed, I was still living in Panama, but I was at home that day because I had a virus. I (attend) _____a small Catholic school in Panama where the nuns were from the United States and proudly told us about the first Catholic president. They informed us that many people (be)_____ afraid to elect a Catholic to the office of the presidency since they (fear) _____ a Catholic President would take orders from the pope whom the Catholics believed was infallible.

Prof.: That is an interesting point since at that time many people in this country (debate)

_____ whether or not prayers should be said in the public schools. However,

President Kennedy's religion didn't seem to play a major role in his decision making. In

fact, before his election, he (claim)_____ to be a practicing Catholic, but there

were all sorts of rumors about his having affairs with different women and having ties to

organized crime.

Marco: Professor, is it true the school prayer issue is popping up again in certain sections of

this country?

Prof.: Yes, this is true. I also believe it is a major concern for many of you who come from

diverse religious backgrounds. In fact, many of the issues President Kennedy (address)

_____ at that time are resurfacing again today. I imagine that is why so many

of you are so interested in President Kennedy. What else do you know about his term as

president?

Claude: Actually what many of President Kennedy's constituents (realize, not)_____

when they elected him was his strong commitment to civil rights. In fact, the day he was

killed, he (try)_____ to get political support in Dallas since he (lose)_____ a

lot of his constituents because of his firm position on the civil rights.

Tanya: That's right! My high school social studies teacher said that day Kennedy (attempt)

_____ to get more support in the South since he (lose)_____ a

lot of it because of his stand on civil rights. Moreover, she said those civil rights laws

which were aimed at giving equal rights to the African American community have also

helped many new immigrants protect themselves from discrimination.

Marco: Until recently I (realize, not)_____ that it was also President Kennedy

who was a Democrat who committed the first military troops to the War in Vietnam. For

some reason, I (think, always) _____ the Republicans (commit)

_____ the first troops to Vietnam.

Prof.: At that time, many people felt that this country didn't belong in that war. In the end, this war had an unusual ending since the United States (fight)_____ it for almost a decade when it finally ended without any real sense of completion. Today many historians believe one of the basic flaws in the military strategy was the inability to understand the cultural thinking of the people in Vietnam.

Irina: That's interesting since many new immigrants also have problems in their new homeland because they have difficulty understanding the culture, too.

✔ Recall two very important events (personal or historical) in your life. Tell a partner what you had been doing when this important event took place.

example: I had been writing an essay when my mother called me to say my grandfather had died.
or
We had been watching our favorite television show, when she began to scream for help.

✔ Read the following sentences and observe how they are made negative.

1. I <u>had not been sleeping</u> since this afternoon when Juan called me.
2. You <u>had not been dancing</u> for hours when he interrupted you.
3. They <u>had not been listening</u> at the door when you saw them.

How is the past perfect progressive tense made negative in the above sentences?
The <u>past perfect progressive tense</u> is made <u>negative</u> by placing the word _____ after <u>had</u> and before the_____ of <u>to be</u>.

R u l e

3

The **past perfect progressive tense** is made negative by using the following rule.

Subject	+	Past tense of have	+	not	+	Past Participle of to be	+	Present Participle of verb	
We		had		not		been		driving	for days.
He		had		not		been		reading	for two hours.

✔ Make the following past perfect progressive sentences negative.

1. President Kennedy had been trying to get votes the day he was assassinated.
2. The teachers had been telling the students about the president at that time.
3. The students had been learning about President Kennedy in Panama.

4. President Kennedy had been losing support in the South because of his stand on civil rights.

5. The pupils had been hearing a lot about the war in Vietnam.

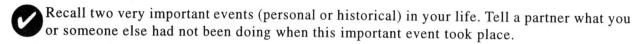Recall two very important events (personal or historical) in your life. Tell a partner what you or someone else had not been doing when this important event took place.

example: I had not been drinking alcohol when the car spun out of control.
   or
   The child had not been calling her friend names when the teacher arrived.

Read the following sentences and observe how questions are formed.

1. a: <u>Had you been studying</u> enough when you failed your class?
   b: No, I hadn't been studying enough when I failed my class.

2. a: <u>Had he been doing</u> well in school when he applied for medical schools?
   b: Yes, he had been doing very well when he applied for medical schools.

3. a: <u>Had you been following</u> your diet when you had this problem?
   b: No, I had not been following my diet when I had this problem.

How is the past perfect progressive tense made into a question in the above sentences?
The <u>past perfect progressive tense</u> is made a question by _____ the subject and the auxiliary verb_____ .

R u l e

4

The **past perfect progressive tense** is made negative by **inverting** the subject and the auxiliary verb **had**.

Past tense of verb have	+	subject	+	Past Participle to be	+	Present Participle
Had		Peter		been		smoking all his life?

Make the following past perfect progressive sentences into questions.

1. We had been hearing a lot about the war in that class.
2. The union had been trying to get an increase in pay.
3. The children had been learning about foreign affairs.
4. Our social studies teacher had been telling us about Abe Lincoln.
5. Katrina had been planning to have a party until that time.

Recall two very important historical events in your life or someone else's life. Ask a partner what he/she or you had been doing when this important event took place.

example: Had you been working at the college when you heard about the Gulf War?
   Had the children been reading about the revolution when you walked in the room?

Writing: Write a composition describing what you had been doing in your life when you started this class or arrived in this country. Be sure to use the *past perfect progressive* tense to express activities that were in progress before another event that took place in the past.

example: Before I moved to this country, I had been dating a man named Jean. He had been trying to get me to marry him for several years. But, I had been resisting since he was too possessive.

·········· *The Passive Voice* ··········

The objective of this chapter is to teach students:

- *the difference in meaning and form between the active and passive voices and,*

- *the formation of the passive voice in the following tenses: present, past, present progressive, past progressive, present perfect, past perfect and with modals.*

The Form of the Passive Voice. . . . .

 With a partner read the following sentences and answer the questions below.

1. a. Ann <u>teaches</u> English.
    b. English <u>is taught</u> by Ann.

2. a. I <u>speak</u> two languages.
    b. Two languages <u>are spoken</u> by me.

3. a. You <u>wash</u> the dishes.
    b. The dishes <u>are washed</u>.

4. a. We <u>bake</u> cookies.
    b. Cookies <u>are baked</u> by us.

5. a. They <u>clean</u> the garden.
    b. The garden <u>is cleaned</u> by them.

6. a. A person <u>makes</u> fine wine in France.
    b. Fine wine is made in France.

What tense is used in letter a of each of these sentence pairs?
The _____ tense is used in each sentence.

Who performs the action in letter a of each sentence pair?
The _____ performs the action in letter a of each sentence pair.

What *voice* is used in letter a of these sentence pairs?
The _____ voice is used in letter a of each sentence pair.

What tense is used in letter b of each of these sentence pairs?
The _____ tense is used in letter b of each sentence pair.

Who performs the action in letter b of each sentence pair?
In letter b of each sentence pair, the action is performed by _____ .

What *voice* is used in letter b of these sentence pairs?
The _____ voice is used in letter b of each sentence pair.

In letter b of numbers 3 and 6, what has been omitted from the passive voice sentences?
In 3.b and 6.b, the _____ has been omitted.

Is it always necessary to know who performs the action?_____

Read the following sentence pairs and observe how many objects are contained in each active voice sentence.

1. a. Santa gives children gifts.
    b. <u>Gifts</u> are given to children by Santa.
    c. <u>Children</u> are given gifts by Santa.

2. a. We buy Sandra new clothes each summer.
    b. <u>Sandra</u> is bought new clothes by us each summer.
    c. <u>New clothes</u> are bought for Sandra by us each summer.

How many objects are there in these two sentences?
There are _____ objects in each sentence.

What are these objects called?
These objects are called _____ or _____ objects.

Therefore, what can the subject in the passive voice be?
When a verb takes two objects, in the passive voice, the subject can be either the _____ or the _____ object.

Rule

1

The passive voice is created by using the following steps.

*   The **object** of the active voice sentence becomes the **subject** of the passive voice sentence. If there are **two objects**, either of the objects can become the subject of the passive voice.
*   The **subject** of the active voice sentence is either **omitted**, or it is placed after the preposition **by**.
*   The verb in the **present tense of the passive voice** is formed by using the present tense of the verb **to be** and the **past participle** of the **main verb**.

	sub.	pres. tense verb in active voice	object
example:	Tanya	tells	funny stories.

	subject	passive voice of present tense	the old subject becomes object of the preposition by
	Funny stories	are told	by Tanya.

*   In the active voice, the **subject** performs the action.
*   In the passive voice, the subject **does not** perform the action.

✔ With a partner, try to convert the *underlined* present tense verbs to the present tense passive voice. If there are two objects, re-write the sentence twice using each of the objects as the subject.

1. Doctors <u>save</u> lives everyday.
2. My mother <u>cooks</u> a big meal on Sundays.
3. Chang and I <u>study</u> Italian at college.
4. Marta and Diego <u>give</u> me a ride.
5. You and Simon <u>take</u> classes at night.
6. We <u>telephone</u> our parents whom we love once a month.
7. The children <u>play</u> baseball in the park.
8. I <u>serve</u> dinner at five o'clock.
9. Alicia who is perfect never <u>makes</u> a mistake.
10. The professor <u>gives</u> us an exam which is very difficult every Friday.

Numbers 6, 9 and 10 all contained adjective clauses which were attached to either the subject or the object. When converting a sentence which contains an adjective clause to the passive voice, what must happen to the adjective clause?
The adjective clause must _____ the noun it is modifying.

adjective clause which
modifies the word Maria
example: Maria <u>who is from Argentina</u> loves Chinese food.
Chinese food is loved by Maria who is from Argentina.

✔ With a partner, try to convert the *underlined* present tense verbs to the present tense passive voice. Whenever it is necessary, omit the by phrase.

In adulthood, many people <u>acquire</u> a breathing disorder which is called asthma. Asthma <u>causes</u> an inflammation in the lungs. When an asthmatic's lungs <u>become</u> inflamed, they have trouble breathing. Asthma <u>causes</u> shortness of breath, fatigue and sometimes death.

An allergic reaction or severe bronchitis <u>triggers</u> asthma. People who suffer with asthma <u>use</u> an oral inhaler to relieve the symptoms. The oral inhaler <u>relieves</u> the symptoms by dilating or opening up the bronchial tubes in the lungs. Some patients also <u>use</u> a second inhaler to prevent attacks. This inhaler <u>contains</u> cortisone. When a person has an asthma attack, mucous <u>clogs</u> the lungs. If the lungs remain clogged, the person sometimes <u>dies</u>. The cortisone inhaler <u>prevents</u> this inflammation.

Asthma is a disease which is treatable, but many people are unaware of its symptoms. Therefore, they <u>suffer</u> unnecessarily. If a person suspects he/she has asthma, he/she should see a physician for an evaluation and treatment.

Why can't the verbs *become, die* and *suffer* be made passive?
Verbs such as <u>die</u>, <u>become</u> and <u>suffer</u> do not have an _____ . If there is no object, the sentence can not be made _____ .

Certain verbs are not followed by an object. What are these verbs called?
These verbs are called _____ verbs.

Verbs that are followed by an object are called_____verbs.

Rule 2

Transitive Verbs are verbs that are followed by an object. Only **transitive verbs** can be put in the passive voice. **Intransitive verbs** do not take an **object,** and they can not be made passive.

	subject	transitive verb	object
example:			
(active)	Martin	fixes	washing machines.
(passive)	Washing machines	are fixed	by Martin.

Because there is an object after this verb, the sentence can be stated in the passive voice. But, look at the next example.

subject   verb
My driver's license expired.

Because there is no object, this sentence can not be made passive.

 With a partner, convert each *underlined verb* to the active voice.

Each year one out of every five hundred infants dies from Sudden Infant Death Syndrome (SIDS). SIDS <u>is also referred</u> to as crib death by many people, and this is what typically happens. What seems to be a healthy baby <u>is delivered</u> by a woman. The parents take the child home and care for it without having any indication that the child is unhealthy. The baby <u>is examined</u> by his/her pediatrician, and everything seems fine. But, one day the baby <u>is put</u> down to sleep, and he/she never wakes up again.

When the baby doesn't wake up, someone checks on him/her to find the baby is not breathing and has an abnormal color. Usually, an ambulance <u>is called</u> by the parents or caregiver, and the baby <u>is rushed</u> to the hospital. Typically, these babies <u>are not revived</u>. Because the baby appeared healthy, an autopsy <u>is performed</u> by a pathologist. After performing the autopsy, usually nothing <u>is found</u> wrong with these infants. Therefore, these babies who die for no apparent reason <u>are labeled</u> SIDS babies which means there was no cause of death.

Many years of research have not provided any clear or definitive answer to this problem, but scientists continue to study this problem in hopes of finding an explanation and eventually a cure for this sudden and traumatic death.

Why wasn't it possible to convert *is put, is rushed, are not revived, is found,* **and** *are labeled* **to the passive voice?**
When there is no _____ , it is not possible to make a passive voice sentence active because it is not known who performed the action.

Why isn't it necessary to know who performed the action in these situations?
In some sentences, it is not _____ to know exactly who performed the action since the emphasis is not on the person or thing who performed the action.

R u l e

3

Frequently, there is no **by** phrase in the passive voice because it is not important to know exactly who performs the action.

example: The hat was made in France.

In this sentence, it is not important to know exactly who made the hat. What the writer is stressing is that the hat was manufactured in France. The person or people who made it are not important.

 With a partner, orally convert the following sentences to the passive voice.

1. Bronchitis causes asthma.
2. Asthma suffers use an inhaler to help them.
3. Some people call SIDS crib death.
4. The lungs contain a substance which is called mucous.
5. The pathologist performs an autopsy on the baby.

The Past Tense in the Passive Voice......................

✔ Read the following sentences and observe how the passive voice is formed.

1. a. Peter <u>bought</u> a motorcycle.
   b. A motorcycle <u>was bought</u> by Peter.
2. a. Jane and I <u>fixed</u> the flat tire.
   b. The flat tire <u>was fixed</u>.
3. a. We <u>cleaned</u> the house.
   b. The house <u>was cleaned</u> by us.
4. a. The girls <u>baked</u> a cake for the party.
   b. A cake <u>was baked</u> for the party.

What tenses are these sentences written in?
All of these sentences are written in the _____ tense.

What sentences are in the active voice?
In each sentence pair, letter _____ is written in the active voice.

What sentences are in the passive voice?
In each sentence pair, letter _____ is written in the passive voice.

How is an *active voice of a past tense* verb converted to the passive voice?
The _____ of the active voice sentence becomes the <u>subject</u> of the passive voice sentence. The <u>past tense</u> of the verb _____ is used, and the <u>main verb of the active voice</u> sentence is made a _____.

R u l e

4

How is an **active voice of a past tense** verb converted to the passive voice?

- The object becomes the **subject**.
- The verb **to be** is put in the **past** tense (was or were).
- The **main verb** becomes a **past participle**.
- If desired, the subject is followed by the preposition **by**.

example: The dog <u>ate</u> the food.

	simple past of the verb to be	past participle	
The food	was	eaten	by the dog.

✔ With a partner, convert the sentences to the passive voice. Be certain to use the correct tense.

1. My grandmother found a kitten in her yard.
2. The students completed the research study.
3. My doctor examines me twice a year.
4. A neighbor told my parents the news.
5. The mucous clogged his lungs, and it prevented him from breathing.
6. Maurice and I sent Katie a gift.
7. A heart attack causes chest pain and fatigue.

8. The doctor evaluated her patient carefully.

9. The physician gave her information about being pregnant.

10. The high pollen count triggered my asthma attack.

 With a partner, convert the following underlined transitive verbs to the passive voice. Whenever appropriate omit the "by" phrase and be sure to use the correct tense.

On September 28, 1998, the village police <u>caught</u> Samuel Smith exiting the window of a house. The police <u>questioned</u> Smith about his behavior, and he said, "This is my mother's house. I <u>lost</u> my key. So, I climbed up the trellis, and I <u>entered</u> my old bedroom window." Then the old woman who owns the house <u>walked</u> in the yard. When the police <u>asked</u> her if this man were her son, she said, "I've never seen this man before in my life." So, the police <u>arrested</u> Smith for breaking and entering. The following day a judge <u>arraigned</u> him at the county court, and he was held on $10,000 bail.

Since Smith couldn't pay for his bail, he <u>remained</u> in jail until the time of his trial two months later. At the trial, something interesting <u>happened</u>. Smith <u>produced</u> a birth certificate that proved he was indeed the woman's son. When the judge <u>asked</u> the woman why she lied, she said, "I was sick and tired of his losing his key all the time, and I thought I'd teach him a lesson."

The judge <u>dropped</u> the charges of breaking and entering and suggested to the woman that she find a better way to teach her son a lesson in the future.

The Passive Voice with Modals. . . . .

 Read the following sentences.

1. a. Ann <u>can help</u> Peter.
   b. Peter <u>can be helped</u> by Ann.

2. a. I <u>will cook</u> dinner.
   b. Dinner <u>will be cooked</u> by me.

3. a. Sara and I <u>might contact</u> the women.
   b. The women <u>might be contacted</u> by us.

4. a. Mary and Sue <u>should tell</u> her.
   b. She <u>should be told</u> by Mary and Sue.

5. a. You <u>could repair</u> it.
   b. It <u>could be repaired</u> by you.

What is a modal?

A _____ is a word which expresses meaning about ability, necessity, advice, possibility or other conditions.

What are some examples of modals?

Some examples of modals are _____.

When the active voice contains a modal, how can it be converted to the passive voice?

When the active voice contains a <u>modal</u>, it is converted to the <u>passive voice</u> by: making the _____ of the active voice the subject of the passive voice; second inserting the _____; third adding the simple form of the verb _____; fourth adding the _____ of the main verb of the sentence.

R u l e

5

An active voice sentence containing a **modal** is made passive by using the following rule.

- First, the **object of the active voice** sentence becomes the **subject** of the passive sentence.
- Second insert the **modal**.
- Third, add the simple form of the verb **to be** (be).
- Fourth, add the **past participle** of the main verb of the sentence.

example: I should clean the house.

subject	modal	+	verb be	+	past participle	
The house	should		be		cleaned	by me.

Convert the following sentences to the passive voice.

1. Irina and Boris can call me on Saturday.
2. We must buy our teacher a gift at the end of the term.
3. The teacher should test the students' ability to comprehend English.
4. You will prepare a wonderful meal.
5. Edward might buy a car next year.
6. We could not touch the exhibits in the museum.
7. Susan would not write such a letter.
8. Bong Chul must write a better paper.
9. Tomas might take a job.
10. They would never make such a remark.

With a partner, convert the underlined transitive verbs to the passive voice.

After a family has lost a baby to Sudden Infant Death Syndrome (SIDS), friends and relatives <u>can help</u> the parents, but they <u>can not take away</u> their pain. Family and friends <u>should acknowledge</u> the grief the parents are experiencing.

They <u>should allow</u> the parents to vent their feelings. The parents <u>will experience</u> depression, regret and anger. Some people <u>might tell</u> them this is inappropriate, but it is not. Friends and family must remember that most of us have never experienced such a sudden and tragic event. Therefore, the parents <u>may respond</u> in an unexpected way, but we <u>should not criticize</u> them for what we don't understand.

 With a partner, orally convert the following sentences to the passive voice.

1. A person will call the police when a burglar breaks into his/her home.
2. Samuel Smith would not carry his key.
3. The police should arrest the woman for lying.
4. The woman can not teach Spanish.
5. A judge should punish criminals with harsh prison sentences.

The Passive Voice in Other Tenses····················

 Read the following sentences carefully.

Column A

1. a. Ann <u>is helping</u> Paul.
   b. Paul <u>is being helped</u> by Ann.

2. a. I <u>am writing</u> a letter.
   b. A letter <u>is being written</u>.

Column B

3. a. Mary <u>was watching</u> the baby.
   b. The baby <u>was being watched</u> by Mary.

4. a. They <u>were reading</u> a mystery.
   b. A mystery <u>was being read</u> by them.

What tense is being used in Column A? _____

What tense is being used in Column B? _____

What voice is used in letter <u>a</u> of each example? _____

What voice is used in letter <u>b</u> of each example? _____

In example 1.b and 3.b, how is the passive voice formed in the present progressive tense?
The passive voice is formed by making the _____ of the active voice sentence the <u>subject</u> of the passive voice sentence. Second, use the _____ of the verb <u>to be</u>. Third, insert the_____ of the verb <u>to be</u>. Fourth, insert the _____ of the <u>main verb</u>.

In example 2.b and 4.b, how is the passive voice formed in the past progressive tense?
The passive voice is formed by making the <u>object</u> of the active voice sentence the_____of the passive voice sentence. Second, use the _____ of the verb <u>to be</u>. Third, insert the _____ of the verb <u>to be</u>. Fourth, insert the _____ of the <u>main verb</u>.

R u l e

6

The active voice of the **present progressive tense** is converted into the passive voice by:

* making the **object** of the active voice the **subject** in the passive sentence,
* using the **present tense** of the verb **to be** (am, is, are),
* inserting the **present participle** of to be (being),
* using the **past participle** of the main verb.

example: (active)   Jane <u>is serving</u> dinner.
(passive) Dinner <u>is being served</u> by Jane.

R u l e

7

The active voice of the **past progressive tense** is converted into the passive voice by:

* making the **object** of the active voice the **subject** in the passive sentence,
* using the **past tense** of the verb **to be** (was or were),
* inserting the **present participle** of to be (being),
* using the **past participle** of the **main verb.**

example: (active)   Jane <u>was serving</u> dinner.
(passive) Dinner <u>was being served</u> by Jane.

✔ Read the following sentences carefully.

Column A	Column B

5. a.   Ana <u>has helped</u> Tom.
    b.   Tom <u>has been helped</u> by Ana.

6. a.   We <u>have called</u> the school
    b.   The school <u>has been called</u>.

7. a.   Ana <u>had helped</u> Tom.
    b.   Tom <u>had been helped</u> by Ana.

8. a.   You <u>had watched</u> the program before.
    b.   The program <u>had been watched</u> before.

What tense is being used in Column A?_____
What tense is being used in Column B?_____
What voice is used in letter <u>a</u> of each example?_____
What voice is used in letter <u>b</u> of each example?_____

In example 5.b and 7.b, how is the passive voice formed in the *present perfect tense*?
The passive voice is formed by making the <u>object</u> of the active voice sentence the _____ of the passive voice sentence. Second, use the _____ tense of the verb <u>have</u>. Third, insert the _____ of the verb <u>to be</u>. Fourth, insert the _____ of the <u>main verb</u>.

In example 6.b and 8.b, how is the passive voice formed in the past perfect tense?
The passive voice is formed by making the _____ of the active voice sentence the
<u>subject</u> of the passive voice sentence. Second, use the _____ tense of the verb <u>have</u>.
Third, insert the_____ of the verb <u>to be</u>. Fourth, insert the _____ of
the main verb.

Rule

8

The active voice of the **present perfect tense** is converted into the passive voice
by:

- making the **object** of the active voice the **subject** in the passive sentence,
- using the **present tense** of the verb **have** (has or have),
- inserting the **past participle** of **to be** (been),
- using the **past participle** of the main verb.

example: (active)   Jane <u>has served</u> dinner.
             (passive)   Dinner <u>has been served</u> by Jane.

Rule

9

The active voice of the **past perfect tense** is converted into the passive voice by:

- making the **object** of the active voice the **subject** in the passive sentence,
- using the **past tense** of the verb **have** (had),
- inserting the **past participle** of to be (been),
- using the **past participle** of the main verb.

example: (active)   Jane <u>had served</u> dinner.
             (passive)   Dinner <u>had been served</u> by Jane.

 Convert the following sentences into the passive voice. Be sure to use the correct tense.

1. Marta has loved Manuel.
2. Marco and Louis had purchased him a gift.
3. We were watching movies all night.
4. You are eating too much junk food.
5. I am calling Ramon again.
6. Raj had failed that course before.
7. Rina and Pietro have given me their term papers.
8. Henrick is cleaning the car.
9. I was writing a letter.
10. You had memorized the new vocabulary by that time.
11. Silvana and Sven had eaten everything in the house.
12. The congressman has notified the press.

13. The police have arrested Sam several times.
14. The doctor is examining the child.
15. The parents were discussing the problem.
16. The teacher has discussed this topic many times.
17. You were learning French at that time.
18. I had seen the movie before.
19. Paul and I were enjoying the meal.
20. Our society has created and solved many modern problems.

 With a partner, whenever possible, *orally* convert the following sentences into the passive voice being certain to use the *correct tense*.

1. Svetlana is attending a small college.
2. The woman was not stealing the merchandise.
3. This attitude has caused a lot of pain over the years.
4. Theresa and I had assisted several new people in our community.
5. Rosemary and Cathy have run a soup kitchen for several years.
6. The police locked up the young man.
7. The man enters the house through a window.
8. The judge has not granted the man bail.
9. Pietro invites people to the meetings each month.
10. The people in the group bring snacks to the meeting.
11. Ann who is an attorney might defend Samuel in court.
12. Evelyn can contact the parents.
13. Peter will clean the room after the meeting.
14. Frank must mail the invitations by Friday.
15. The police have questioned this man in the past.

Read the following essay. Where ever possible, convert any underlined active voice verbs to the passive voice, and convert any underlined passive voice verbs to the active voice where possible.

As American people <u>enter</u> the "golden years" in the United States, they <u>make</u> lavish plans for their retirement. They <u>anticipate</u> their retirement finances for years so that they <u>can enjoy</u> their independence since many people want to maintain their current standard of living. As these golden years begin to slip away, these same people hope they will die peacefully in their homes, otherwise many of them eventually end up living in a nursing home when they are no longer self-sufficient. This seems to be the way life progresses in this country regardless of where a person comes from.

Many immigrants, however, have always believed the way to guarantee a happy old age was to have children since their children would take care of them in their senior years. Today many new immigrants <u>are actively giving</u> home care to their aging parents, but these care takers do not <u>know</u> what their Americanized children will do when they too become old. The new generation of immigrants <u>must make</u> the same decision many Americans have had to make regarding the care of parents, grandparents and other aging relatives. But, these decisions <u>are intensified</u> by cultural beliefs. Moreover, these people <u>are frequently prevented</u> from seeking the outside help they need by these traditions.

All cultures have ideas about family roles. The Chinese <u>follow</u> a concept called filial piety. That means their children <u>must honor</u> their parents and care for them. Most Hispanic families also live together, and this <u>is never questioned</u> by anyone. However, more and more immigrants <u>are finding</u> it is very difficult to keep up their family traditions in this country for several different reasons.

In most traditional foreign countries, it <u>is believed</u> women with children <u>should not hold down</u> jobs. Therefore, most women are available to tend to older relatives. However, a new struggle exists today because many immigrant women <u>find</u> it necessary to work out of necessity. As a result, when an older relative <u>needs</u> care and the family <u>must place</u> the person in a nursing home, the children <u>feel</u> a sense of guilt and shame. Worst of all, the person placed in the home <u>feels</u> rejected and abandoned.

Another reason many immigrants <u>want</u> to care for their relatives at home is because it provides a way to maintain their cultural roots. Home care <u>allows</u> them a deep sense of satisfaction in the ever changing world this new country brings. One woman said, "Taking care of my dying father was not easy since I work a lot, but I <u>did</u> it. Since my father's death, I feel that despite the difficulties involved I was able to complete my role as a loving and good daughter. This <u>has sustained</u> me throughout this period of grief."

It <u>has been said</u> by many that this new land can be a heaven or a hell. For many, the United States <u>has provided</u> them with a chance at a better life or freedom which <u>was denied</u> to them by their governments. But, for others it <u>has forced</u> them to compromise their strong cultural values in order to survive in this new world.

✔ *Writing:*

1. Write an essay explaining how the move to this country has forced you or your family to change your cultural values and beliefs. Be certain to explain how you feel about the change. Be sure to use the <u>passive voice at least eight times</u> and underline it.

2. Find a short newspaper article which describes a crime that was committed. The article need only have three or four paragraphs. Read the article carefully. Circle all the active verbs and underline all the passive verbs. Then try to rewrite the article converting the active verbs to the passive wherever possible. Then re read the article. Decide which version of the article sounds better and be prepared to explain why.

Articles

The objective of this chapter is to teach students:

- *the difference between count and non-count nouns and,*

- *the way in which articles are used with each type of noun to distinguish between the general and the specific.*

Review of Nouns

What is a noun?

A noun is the name of a _____ , _____ or _____ .

a. List five examples of a noun which functions as a person.

    1. _Mr. Chiu_   4. _____

    2. _____   5. _____

    3. _____   6. _____

b. List five examples of a noun which functions as a place.

    1. _the World Trade Center_   4. _____

    2. _____   5. _____

    3. _____   6. _____

c. List five examples of a noun which functions as a thing.

    1. _the pencil_   4. _____

    2. _sugar_   5. _____

    3. _love_   6. _____

What is a *count noun*?

A _____ noun is a noun that can be <u>counted</u> such as cars, fingers, people etc.

What is a *non-count noun*?

A _____ noun refers to a whole group of things that are made up of individual parts such as sugar, money, coffee, furniture. _____ nouns also refer to _____ such as milk, <u>solids</u> such as butter or cheese or <u>abstractions</u> knowledge, hatred etc.

Rule

1

A **noun** is the name of a **person**, **place** or **thing**.
Nouns can be divided into **two categories**: **count** nouns and **non-count** nouns.

Count nouns are nouns that can be counted. This category of nouns include items such as lamps, dogs, chairs, desks, pencils etc.

Non-count nouns are nouns that refer to a whole group of things such as sugar, sand, money and fruit. This category also includes liquids (milk), solids (cheese) or abstractions (excitement).

Divide the following list of nouns into count and non count nouns:

information	pen	shoes	fun	beauty
furniture	chairs	love	pride	peaches
teeth	excitement	noise	shirt	horses
hair	music	fame	knowledge	hatred
bravery	blanket	lamp	ignorance	computer
sex	pollution	honesty		

Count Nouns   **Non Count Nouns**

_____   _____

_____   _____

_____   _____

_____   _____

_____   _____

_____   _____

_____   _____

_____   _____

_____   _____

Read each of the sentences. Remember that * means that there is an error in the sentence.

*1. I have the <u>information</u>.
*2. Parents should share their <u>knowledge</u> with their children.
*3. <u>A hatred</u> is a terrible thing.
*4. I need <u>a sugar</u> to bake the cake.
*5. Many people experience <u>an anxiety</u>.

What type of noun is _underlined_ in each sentence?

A _____ noun is underlined in each sentence.

Explain why numbers 1 and 2 are incorrect.

A <u>non-count noun</u> can not be _____ .

Explain why numbers 3, 4 and 5 are incorrect.

A <u>non-count noun</u> can never use the articles _____ or _____ .

R u l e **2**	1. Non-count nouns can not be **pluralized.** They are always singular. 2. Non-count nouns do **not** use the articles **a** or **an**.

Articles with Count Nouns . . . .

✔ Read the following sentences and observe how the use of different articles changes the meaning.

1. a. I saw <u>a dog</u> in the yard last week.
   b. I saw <u>the dog</u> who belongs to my neighbor in the yard.

2. a. Ariel bought <u>a dress</u> in that shop last year.
   b. Ariel bought <u>the dress</u> she is wearing in that shop last year.

3. a. They sang <u>a song</u> to the baby.
   b. They sang <u>the song</u> I heard in the musical.

Are the words dog, dress and song count or non count nouns? _____

How does the use of the articles _a_ and _the_ change the meaning of the noun?

The article _____ or _____ is used in <u>general or non specific situations</u> in order to make a generalization. The article _____ is used when referring to <u>specific</u> things.

✔ Read the following sentences and determine how the use of the article changes the meaning of the noun.

1. a. I saw <u>dogs</u> running around in my yard.
   b. I saw <u>the dogs</u> that belong to my neighbor running around in my yard.

2. a. Ariel bought <u>dresses</u> in that store a few years ago.
   b. Ariel bought <u>the dresses</u> she wore to those parties at that store.

3. a. They sang <u>songs</u> to the baby.
   b. They sang <u>the songs</u> I heard on the radio to the baby.

How does the use of the article *the* or the *absence of the article the* change the meaning of the word *songs*?

When a <u>count noun is plural</u> and the article <u>the</u> is used, it refers to a _____ thing.
However, when a <u>count noun is plural</u> and <u>no article</u> is used, it refers to a _____ thing.

R u l e

3

**RULES FOR THE USE OF
ARTICLES WITH COUNT NOUNS**

	Specific	Non Specific or General
Singular Nouns	the	a/an
Plural Nouns	the	_____

✔ Read the following sentences.

1. I bought <u>a lamp</u>, but <u>the lamp</u> was broken.
2. She called <u>a doctor</u>. <u>The doctor</u> said to drink plenty of liquids.
3. I have <u>an orange</u>. <u>The orange</u> was grown in California.
4. Shani had <u>an interview</u> for a job. <u>The interview</u> went very well.

Why is the article a used in the first clause and the article the is used in the second clause for the same word?

The first time a <u>general or non specific</u> noun is mentioned, the articles _____ or _____ are used. The second time the same noun is mentioned the article _____ should be used since it has now become a <u>specific</u> item.

R u l e

4

The first time a **non specific or general noun** is mentioned, the articles **a/an** are used.

example: Marta saw <u>a</u> strange man in his yard.

The **second time** the **same noun** is used, it becomes something **specific** since it refers to an exact person, object or thing . Therefore, use the article **the** because it references a specific noun.

example: Marta saw <u>a</u> strange man in her yard. <u>The</u> man was picking apples.

✔ Complete the following exercises with *a, an, the* or leave the space blank.

1. When she glanced out _____window in her bedroom, she saw_____man she didn't know walking down the street._____man was wearing a black coat.

2. Tomas knows _____ woman she is talking about well.

3. Claude and Marie went to _____ store to buy some clothes, but _____ store was closed.

4. We need _____ curtains for our bedroom.

5. We saw _____ curtains that Mona has in her house in that shop.

Article Usage with Non-Count Nouns . . . .

✔ Read the following sentences.

1. a. I bought <u>furniture</u> for my bedroom.
   b. I bought <u>the furniture</u> in my bedroom at the department store last year.
   c. I bought <u>some furniture</u> for my bedroom.

2. a. Children gain <u>knowledge</u> from their parents.
   b. Children gain <u>the knowledge</u> they need to survive from their parents.
   c. Children gain <u>some knowledge</u> from their parents.

3. a. I dumped <u>sugar</u> on my kitchen floor.
   b. I dumped <u>the sugar</u> I needed to bake my cake on the kitchen floor.
   c. I dumped <u>some sugar</u> while I was baking a cake.

4. a. <u>Pollution</u> is bad for our environment and health.
   b. <u>The pollution</u> in the city air is bad for our health.

Are the words knowledge, furniture, sugar and pollution count or non count nouns?
They are _____ nouns.

When a *non-count* noun is *general or non-specific*, what article is used?
When a non-count noun is <u>general or not specific</u>, _____ is used.

When a *non-count noun* is *specific*, what article is used?
When a non-count noun is <u>specific</u>, the article _____ is used.

Can a non count noun be pluralized? _____

Why is the word *some* used with *non count nouns*?
The word _____ is sometimes used with non-count nouns when referring to something that is <u>general</u> or <u>non specific</u>.

R u l e
. . . .

5

USE OF ARTICLES WITH NON-COUNT NOUNS

	Specific	Non Specific or General
singular nouns	the	

Remember:
The article **A** or **AN** is **never** used with a non-count noun;
non-count nouns are **never pluralized**;
the word **some** is sometimes used with **non-count** nouns when referring to something that is **general** or **non specific**.
. . . .

✔ Complete the following sentences with the article *the* or no article at all.

1. I need to buy_____salt and pepper.
2. After I purchased _____ salt, I put it in the closet in my kitchen.
3. I love _____music. Yesterday, I listened to _____music which was coming from my neighbor's backyard.
4. The teacher gives the class _____homework every day, but yesterday_____homework she gave us was very easy.
5. Many people resent being given _____advice since _____advice they are given is sometimes inappropriate.
6. _____ money can't buy_____ happiness.
7. _____happiness I've found with my husband and child is priceless.
8. _____health is wealth.
9. _____health of an unborn child can be jeopardized if the mother smokes cigarettes.
10. _____ignorance is bliss.

Nouns Which Are Count or Non-Count · · · · · · · · · · · · · · · · · ·

✔ Read the following sentences and specify whether the underlined noun is a count or non-count noun.

1. a. I had <u>a glass</u> of wine with dinner.
   b. Mirrors are made out of <u>glass</u>.
2. a. I found <u>a hair</u> in my food.
   b. Tina has blond <u>hair</u>.
3. a. I bought <u>a chicken</u> for dinner.
   b. Would you like <u>chicken</u> for dinner tonight?
4. a. The teacher read the students' <u>papers</u>.
   b. <u>Paper</u> comes from the pulp of trees.

Each set of sentence pairs uses the same noun twice.
In letter <u>a</u> of each pair, the noun is a _____ noun. However, in letter <u>b</u>, the noun is a _____ noun.

How can the nouns in these pairs of sentences be both count and non-count nouns?
Some nouns can be either_____or _____ nouns depending on the context of the sentence.

6

Some nouns can be **both** count and non-count nouns depending on the context of the sentence.

example: I saw <u>a lamb</u> on the farm.
I saw <u>two lambs</u> on the farm.

In this example, the noun **lamb** is a **count noun** since it refers to a noun that can be counted. However, read the following example.

example: We had <u>lamb</u> for dinner.

In this example, the noun **lamb** is a **non-count noun** since it is not a countable concept.

✔ Complete each of the following sentences with the correct article or no article at all.

1. I bought _____ tea yesterday.
2. I drank _____ cup of tea with my breakfast.
3. Sara needs _____ flour for her cake.
4. The baker needs to buy _____ large sack of flour for his cakes.
5. We never eat _____ lamb in my house.
6. Mary had _____ little lamb.
7. I cooked _____ chicken for dinner last night.
8. I bought _____ chicken for supper.
9. Vegetables contain _____ iron and other minerals.
10. I have _____ iron in my basement which I use to press my clothes.

✔ Read the following sentences and observe what is added to make a non-count noun countable.

1. a. Francois drinks <u>coffee</u> in the morning.
    b. Francois drinks <u>a cup of coffee</u> in the morning.
2. a. We eat <u>fish</u> twice a week.
    b. We eat <u>two pieces of fish</u> once a week.
3. a. You drank <u>wine</u> with your meal.
    b. You drank <u>a glass of wine</u> with your meal.
4. a. They bought <u>bread</u> yesterday.
    b. They bought <u>a loaf of bread</u>.

In each sentence pair, the underlined noun in letter *a* is a *non-count* noun. However, the same noun is used in letter *b* as a *count noun*. What has been added to letter *b* that permits these non-count nouns to be used as count nouns?
When a <u>specific quantity</u> or <u>unit of measure</u> is added to a _____ noun, the noun becomes a _____ noun.

7

When a **specific quantity** or **a unit of measure** is used in conjunction with a **non-count noun**, the noun becomes **countable**.

example: We eat <u>fruit</u> and <u>cheese</u> for an evening snack.

In this example, the words fruit and cheese are non-count nouns. However, in the following example, a quantity and a unit of measure are added so that the nouns are now countable.

example: We eat <u>a piece of fruit</u> and <u>an ounce of cheese</u> for an evening snack.

✔ Complete each of the following exercises with the appropriate article or no article at all.

1. People need _____ knowledge to survive.
2. _____ little knowledge is a dangerous thing.
3. I bought _____ soda in the supermarket.
4. I drank _____ glass of soda with my meal.
5. Children need to drink _____ milk.
6. My son drinks _____ quart of milk everyday.
7. Toni puts _____ sugar in her coffee.
8. Toni puts _____ spoonful of sugar in her coffee.
9. Many restaurants serve _____ bread with dinner.
10. Many restaurants serve _____ loaf of bread with dinner.

✔ Read each sentence to a partner and have him/her orally complete each sentence with the article *a, an, the,* or *leave the space blank.*

1. Brian purchases _____ jewelry for his girlfriend every year.
2. Kevin bought _____ diamond ring for his girlfriend.
3. Kathryn has _____ homework to do tonight.
4. Frances has _____ assignment due on Friday.
5. Martin asked his teacher _____ question.

   _____ teacher answered _____ question carefully.
6. I put _____ book you want on _____ table in the kitchen.
7. Laura has _____ work to do in her apartment this weekend.
8. Karen has _____ information that I asked for this morning.
9. Maryjane learned all _____ new vocabulary words in her French book.
10. Regina has _____ good vocabulary because she reads a lot.
11. Let me give you _____ suggestion.
12. In my neighborhood, _____ mail is delivered by noon time everyday.
13. _____ junk mail is very confusing for a foreign person who's just arrived here.

14. Maria loves———— music, but———— music she listens to isn't my taste.

15. Tom bought ———— new equipment he needed for his car.

16. Teenagers shouldn't have———— sex because they are emotionally immature.

17. ———— poetry is beautiful.

18. ———— poetry we read in our class was unusual.

19. I heard———— news about the earthquake this morning.

20. Sharon doesn't have enough ———— food in her house.

21. ————traffic in the city is very heavy. I always hit———— lot of———— traffic when I drive into Manhattan.

22. There is———— sand on the beach, but this morning———— sand was wet from the storm last night.

23. The children like to play in ———— sand when they are at the beach.

24. The room was full of ———— dust.

25. ————dust on the table was so thick I could write my name in it.

26. Sarah knows a lot of ————songs.

27. ———— song that he sang at her wedding was lovely.

28. ————children all over the world love to jump in ———— puddles.

29. ———— children on my block never make a lot of———— noise.

30. ———— noise from her stereo is unbearable.

31. My father always respected ———— people who worked hard.
    ———— people who work hard feel good about themselves.

32. I bought———— gas for my car this morning.

33. ————sentences in this book are very short.

34. In high school, ————students read a lot of ———— classic literature.

35. There is ————box of white chalk on my desk.

36. I don't like the smell of ————chalk.

37. ————doctors help heal people. ———— doctor I went to see told me to rest.

38. ————criminals commit crimes.

39. That man is ————criminal because he murdered his wife.

40. ———— grass is green. But, ———— grass on my lawn is brown because of the terrible heat wave we had this summer.

✔ Read the following letter. In a small group or with a partner, insert one of the following articles *a, an, the* or *leave the space blank*.

Dear Rafaela,

My husband and I have ———— daughter, and we really don't want any more children because

of ———— financial and emotional commitments involved in rearing———— child. ————

problem is our parents keep informing us that our daughter is going to become ———— spoiled brat if she doesn't have _____ sibling. You had only one child, so I thought you could share your insight into this matter. Do you think most only children get spoiled? We're beginning to consider conceiving _____ baby just to give our daughter _____ companion.

Lana

Dear Lana,

There have been _____ lot of tall tales about how only children become spoiled or suffer from _____ loneliness. These stories are not true In fact, _____ only child reaps many benefits including more attention from both parents. One result of _____ extra care is that they are inclined to do very well in both _____ school and in _____ life.

_____ only child tends to be in _____ upper IQ groups, too. They also have _____ very good vocabulary and superior interactive skills. I also believe they are more autonomous and self-sufficient, and they interact better with _____ children.

Even children with _____ sibling can sometimes get spoiled or lonely, but as parents, we must try not to be overly indulging or permissive.

I think it would be _____ tragedy to have _____ baby just to create _____ sibling for another child. That would be unfair to _____ baby and _____ older child.

I hope you will consider _____ points I made before you consider having _____ baby. Only _____ two of you can decide what is right for your family!

✔ The following list of sentences contain typical errors in the use of articles. With a partner, read each sentence and correct the error.

1. It was nice summer evening.
2. She was raped by unknown man.
3. How can you find man in a city with population of two million?
4. He always tried to find the way to stay alone with me.
5. Next day he had accident.

6. I have heard a bad news on television.

7. We are civilized people, and physical abuse looks like a wild behavior.

8. If husband has the bad temper, he may think he can hit his wife.

9. It is only excuse for them.

10. I was teenager when this happened.

11. I prefer to take easy way in facing life.

12. Few months ago, I started smoking.

13. I went to hospital for lung problem.

14. If you are good student, you will do well.

15. People will not take a responsibility for their children.

16. It is a common knowledge.

17. It doesn't matter if you are just child.

18. She called my mother and told her to send me bunch of toys.

19. The parents' money is not children's concern.

20. They give each other hard time.

21. I read about this in newspaper.

 Writing: Write an essay explaining why it is better for a child to raised in a home where there is more than one child, or write an essay explaining why it is better to have only one child. Be sure to check all your articles to be certain that they are used correctly.

Phrasal Verbs

The objective of this chapter is to teach students:

- *a phrasal verb is the combination of a verb plus a particle and has a special idiomatic meaning and,*

- *to distinguish between prepositions and particles and,*

- *separable and non-separable phrasal verbs.*

Particles versus Prepositions . . . .

 Examine each pair of the sentences and observe the movement of the underlined word.

1. a. I picked <u>out</u> a gift for my friend.
   b. I picked a gift <u>out</u> for my friend.
2. a. The student handed <u>in</u> his paper.
   b. The student handed his paper <u>in</u>.
3. a. We called <u>back</u> my father.
   b. We called my father <u>back</u>.
4. a. You filled <u>out</u> the application form.
   b. You filled the application form <u>out</u>.
5. a. Peter and Laura put the gifts <u>away</u>.
   b. Peter and Laura put <u>away</u> the gifts.
6. a. Tomas picked <u>up</u> the crying child.
   b. Tomas picked the crying child <u>up</u>.

What is moved around in each sentence?
The _____ is moved around in each sentence.

Even though one word is moved around, does each pair of sentences have the same meaning? _____

In these groups of sentences, what part of speech are the words *up, in, back, away*?

_____

✔ If you thought *up*, *out*, *in*, *away* and *back* functioned as prepositions, examine these sentences and note * means that a sentence is not grammatical.

1. a. She looked <u>up</u> the word.
   b. She looked the word <u>up</u>.
2. a. She looked <u>up the driveway</u>.
   *b. She looked <u>the driveway up</u>.
3. a. He ran <u>over</u> the dog.
   b. He ran the dog <u>over</u>.
4. a. He ran <u>over the bridge</u>.
   *b. He ran <u>the bridge over</u>.

Why can the word *up* be moved in number 1 but not in number 2?
In number 1, the word <u>up</u> is not functioning as a _____. It is functioning as a _____.
When a <u>verb</u> and a <u>particle</u> are combined, they have a <u>special meaning</u>. However, in number 2 the word <u>up</u> is functioning as a _____ , and the <u>object of a prepositional phrase</u> can _____ be moved around.

Why can the word *over* be moved in number 3 but not in number 4?
In number 3, the word <u>over</u> is not functioning as a _____. It is functioning as a _____ . When a <u>verb</u> and a <u>particle</u> are combined, they have a <u>special meaning</u>. However, in number 4, the word <u>over</u> is functioning as a _____ , and the <u>object of a prepositional phrase</u> can _____ be moved around.

Explanation ·

Particles

Rule 1

Sometimes words like **up, over, out** work in conjunction with a verb in order to have a **special meaning**. In these situations, these words are called **particles,** and they **function differently from prepositions**.

example: I worked <u>out</u> the problem.
I worked the problem <u>out</u>.

Rule 2

The combination of the **verb** and the **particle** create something called a **phrasal verb,** and it has a special meaning.

example:

call up	= make a phone call
work out	= solve or exercise
look up	= search for
take out	= remove
run over	= crushed by a moving vehicle

Rule 3

Many phrasal verbs are **separable** which means the object can be placed either **after the particle** or **between the verb and the particle**.

example: I couldn't figure out <u>the answer</u>.
I couldn't figure <u>the answer</u> out.

Non-Separable Phrasal Verbs

 Read the following sentences which contain phrasal verbs.

1. a. I got on the plane at Kennedy Airport.
   *b. I got the plane on at Kennedy Airport.

2. a. I kept on studying.
   *b. I kept the studying on.

3. a. I got over the flu.
   *b. I got the flu over.

Why can't the particle be moved around in these sentences?
Some <u>phrasal verbs</u> are _____ which means the <u>particle</u> can not be _____.

Rule 4

Some phrasal verbs are **non-separable** which means the **particle can not be moved around**. The object can only be placed after the particle.

example: The professor always <u>calls on the students</u> who are unprepared.
Dolores <u>stayed up</u> all night.

 Read the next four sentences which contain separable phrasal verbs.

1. a. I wrote down the message.
   b. I wrote the message down.
   c. I wrote it down.
   *d. I wrote down it.

2. a. Sara brought up the topic.
   b. Sara brought the topic up.
   c. Sara brought it up.
   *d. Sara brought up it.

3. a. Juan cut out the article.
   b. Juan cut the article out.
   c. Juan cut it out.
   *d. Juan cut out it.

Why is letter d in each group of sentences incorrect?

When a phrasal verb is <u>separable</u> and the object is a pronoun, the pronoun must be placed

_____ .

R u l e

5

When a phrasal verb is separable and the object is a **pronoun**, the pronoun **must be placed** between the verb and the particle.

example: I looked **it** up in the dictionary.
I picked **her** up at her house.

✔ *Exercise:* With a partner, *underline* the phrasal verbs in the following essay, and specify whether they are separable or non separable. See Appendix A for a list of phrasal verbs.

During the holidays, I couldn't figure out how I was going to fix up my apartment. So, I called up a friend, and she suggested I throw my old artificial Christmas tree away. She said, "Throw that old tree out!" After I hung up the phone, I decided to get on the bus and go to the store to buy a real tree. Yet I hadn't considered how I would carry it away.

Just as I was putting my coat on, the bell rang. It was my sister. I was a little annoyed with her since I've told her to call me up before she drops in on me. But, she's the type of person who likes to take over, and she never listens. Well to make a long story short, she invited herself to come with me to pick out the tree and bring it back to my place.

We got into her car and drove around until we came across a discount Christmas tree store. When we got out of the car and walked into the store, we immediately noticed the store had the most wonderful selection of beautiful trees. I didn't even have to think it over. I immediately knew which tree I wanted, so I grabbed it before someone else could. It was the biggest tree in the store, yet I only paid twenty-five dollars for it.

We brought the tree back to my place and decorated it. Once my tree was set up, I really felt as if I had the holiday spirit this year.

Using Appendix A, which contains a list of phrasal verbs, with a partner replace all of the underlined words with an appropriate phrasal verb. Also, be sure to place any pronouns used between the verb and the particle.

In December I <u>meet</u> an ESL teacher I had for a course last summer. He asked me to <u>glance at</u> some literature he had about an intense ESL writing course that was being given at the college during January. He told me he thought this course would be ideal from someone like me. I said I would <u>consider</u> it. After he walked away, I was going to <u>put it in the garbage,</u> but I felt guilty. So, I took it home.

After I was home a few hours, I decided to <u>skim over</u> the brochure. It said that the students should <u>not delay</u> improving their writing skills and that the best way to improve these skills was to take an intense course with two of the most noted instructors in the college. It stated that the course would run for twelve days, and the class would start at nine in the morning and end at three in the afternoon. I began to think it might be worth it <u>to endure</u> this experience to <u>complete</u> the class which I was required to take any way. Moreover, I didn't think it could be that much work either, so the following day I enrolled in the class.

The first day of class was the day after New Years, and there had been a heavy snow storm the previous night. When I <u>got up,</u> the roads were still covered with snow and ice. So, the drive to the campus was terrible, and I also had to <u>give my friend a lift</u>, too. I arrived at the class half an hour late, and the first thing the professor said to me was, "You're late. Class begins at nine o'clock. Each lateness counts as half an absence. If you have one absence, you will fail my course." I was flabbergasted. I felt like <u>ripping up</u> the registration form and <u>not going to</u> the class. I knew immediately this teacher was going to be bad news.

The first day the professor had us write a paper which he <u>returned to us</u> after our only break which was a half hour long. He <u>drew lines through</u> every single error, and expected us <u>to find out</u> what the errors were and correct them. Very few people got any kind of decent grade. He indicated we would rewrite each composition at least three times since good writers wrote many drafts of all their papers. By the end of the day, I couldn't wait to <u>leave</u> this class. It was a nightmare.

The following day, every single student <u>returned</u> to class on time and <u>gave an assignment</u> which the professor eventually <u>destroyed</u>. He informed some people their papers were quite inadequate and told them <u>not to submit</u> an assignment they hadn't written carefully or proof read.

Each day he taught two new points of grammar which we were expected to use in our writing assignment that night. Through out the twelve day term, he <u>gave out</u> twenty-eight writing assignments and taught twenty-four different points of grammar. He never let us take a break, so we <u>continued</u> to work all day. The only time we could relax was during our half hour lunch break, and we didn't dare to take extra time, either.

But, something funny happened, after twelve days he had <u>made</u> many of our writing problems <u>disappear</u>, and we were beginning to get good grades. It was painful and tedious, but every one of us had drastically improved our writing. Moreover, most of us passed the departmental exit exam.

In the end, I can't say that I really liked this professor, but I respected him since he was the person who really taught me how to write well in English.

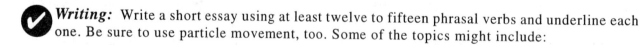 **Writing:** Write a short essay using at least twelve to fifteen phrasal verbs and underline each one. Be sure to use particle movement, too. Some of the topics might include:

- telling about a phone call you received and returned about picking up some friends for a party;
- describing a difficult class you took;
- describing a trip you took and all the arrangements you made;
- or, writing about any topic that allows you to use twelve to fifteen separable and non separable phrasal verbs.

Preposition Combinations

19

The objective of this chapter is to allow students to:

- *practice using prepositions by inserting them in short pieces of literature and,*

- *correct typical errors made by students.*

Reviewing Combinations

The following are a few typical compositions written by ESL students. In a small group or with a partner, read them and insert the best preposition for each selection. Refer to Appendices A and B for assistance.

1. _____ my opinion, teachers and college professors shouldn't be given tenure because they will become unmotivated or cruel _____ their students and forget the reason why they have been hired.

A few years ago, I heard _____ a professor who tried to get rid ____ all the students in his class ____ giving them a hard time _____ every test or assignment. Little ____ little, the students started _____ drop the class thinking they had a problem completing the class work. Finally, one girl, named Claudia, _____ the class noticed that even though she was doing very well ____ all her other classes, she just couldn't seem _____ satisfy this professor. Claudia spoke ____ one ____ her professors _____ the problem she was having _____ this course. Professor Wilson immediately knew what was going ____ since he'd been teaching at the college _____ over twenty years. He explained that this professor was trying ____ force many _____ the students to drop ____ the course so that he wouldn't have to teach such a large group ____ students ____ the end ____ a long day.

Professor Wilson also explained the concept _____tenure _____Claudia who wasn't familiar _____it . After this discussion, instead_____dropping the course which she had originally planned to do, Claudia and several other students spoke _____a senior college official in order _____try_____ resolve this problem, but they were told the college couldn't stop this teacher since he had tenure. In the end, Claudia who had a 3.6 index received a D_____ this course.

This is only one _____many stories I've heard_____the problem _____tenure. It is unfortunate that so many students have to suffer _____the hands of a professor because_____ such a policy. Therefore, I believe college professors and teachers should not be given tenure since some people don't know how_____use it without abusing it.

2.   My country tries to protect women's rights, but the respect _____these laws still isn't strong enough. Generally, many people still do not support women's rights.

Currently, a woman can accuse a man _____ raping her if she wants, but if a woman reports such a crime, she may bring disgrace_____her family and herself. She is also denounced _____ the public despite her being an innocent victim. _____olden times, people believed a woman could never get married unless she was pure. Therefore, being raped placed a stigma _____the girl and her family so that no decent man would want _____marry a woman _____a dishonored family. Although society has become more liberal, some_____these beliefs still exist _____ subtle ways.

I saw a movie based_____a true story_____my country_____ a woman who was raped _____ a neighbor. The young woman was engaged _____be married and confided _____ her fiancée who discouraged her_____reporting the crime. Finally, the young woman decided

_____ prosecute the man, but _____ the trial the defendant claimed the woman consented

_____ the relationship and was free with her sexual favors.

_____the end _____ many months in court, the man was found guilty, but the woman's

reputation and life were destroyed. Her fiancée left her, and her family felt disgraced and hu-

miliated _____this young woman whose virtue was called _____ question.

This was a tragic story which can only be altered _____ a change _____attitude towards

women _____ my homeland.

✔ Write a composition explaining why you agree or disagree with giving college professors and
teachers tenure.

or

✔ Write a composition explaining how your country deals with women's rights. Be sure to use
at least ten of the preposition combinations in Appendix B.

✔ In a small group or with a partner, complete each blank with the correct preposition. After
completing the sentences, verify your answers by checking the list of Preposition Combinations in Appendix B.

1. The little girl is afraid _____the dark.
2. Jane was so angry _____ her son that she couldn't concentrate _____ her work.
3. Mary is crazy_____ Andre.
4. Don't discriminate_____a person because of their race or religion.
5. Smoking is bad _____your health.
6. Anna believes _____ reincarnation.
7. When children grow up, they must learn not to depend_____ their parents.
8. I borrowed some money_____Susan.
9. We arrived _____Kennedy Airport at 6:30 PM.
10. The mother is aware_____the problems her child is having in school.
11. Many people disagree _____ racism.
12. My mother and father argue _____every little thing.
13. Theresa was absent _____school again.
14. Compared_____my teacher, your teacher is easy.
15. The sky cleared _____after the storm.

16. I discussed the problem _____ a psychologist.

17. I am extremely disappointed _____ your test results.

18. Mario is engaged _____ Tammy.

19. Alice is getting a divorce _____ Chang.

20. Paul always dreams _____ how life was in his country.

21. Maria Louisa always looks forward _____ her vacation.

22. We are interested _____ finding a vacation that is good for the whole family.

23. The Khalids were invited _____ their cousins wedding.

24. When he became involved _____ an extra-marital affair, his wife left him.

25. The child escaped _____ the fire.

26. I am exhausted _____ working so many hours.

27. People should always be kind _____ animals.

28. I didn't know anything_____ this problem she was having.

29. Henry never laughs_____ our jokes.

30. The teacher insisted _____ knowing the truth from the students.

31. I introduced Susan _____ Joseph at my wedding.

32. Because of the snow storm, the students were excused _____ their classes that day.

33. I have been looking_____ my good pen all day.

34. François always listens_____ the radio in bed.

35. She looked _____ the picture of the child.

Oral Exercise: Read the following sentences with a partner and determine if the *underlined preposition* is used correctly in each sentence and if necessary correct it.

1. My father insisted <u>in</u> paying for the bill in the restaurant.

2. That coat won't protect you <u>in</u> the bitter cold wind outside today.

3. Do you approve <u>of</u> his behavior?

4. The police arrested the thief. I wonder what will happen <u>with</u> him.

5. My friend apologized <u>for</u> me <u>for</u> forgetting to pick me up at the station.

6. It isn't fair to compare Professor Riccio <u>with</u> the other professors in the department.

7. Excuse me <u>from</u> interrupting you, but you have a telephone call on the other line.

8. My sister likes to feel sorry <u>with</u> herself.

9. I spoke to my attorney <u>about</u> your problem.

10. Did you hear <u>of</u> the plans to build an outdoor pool in the college parking lot?

11. Have you heard <u>from</u> your friend in Israel lately?

12. I'm not accustomed <u>with</u> such hot weather.

13. I disagree <u>about</u> your wanting to get another car.

14. I have to tell you <u>about</u> a crazy thing that happened to me last night.

15. The prisoner escaped <u>in</u> jail.

16. I'm ready <u>for</u> the test.

17. It is important to believe <u>in</u> yourself.

18. I applied <u>in</u> the job in the library.
19. Carol objected <u>with</u> the loud music being played at midnight.
20. It is not polite to laugh <u>over</u> other people's mistakes.
21. Canada belongs <u>with</u> the United Nations.
22. I am confused <u>with</u> this problem.
23. Is Sheila angry <u>about</u> you again?
24. I am always complaining <u>to</u> my husband because he is never home on time for dinner.
25. The English test consisted <u>of</u> a long list of grammar questions.

Error Analysis: The following is a list of real preposition errors made by ESL students. Read each sentence and make any necessary corrections in the use of prepositions.

1. They have many different opinions for that.
2. I agree people living together before marriage.
3. They didn't graduate in high school.
4. They lack confidence themselves.
5. She took advantage her sister.
6. Some people live at bad relationships where there is a lot of violence.
7. She takes care him.
8. She is engaged with him.
9. What are the benefits for living together?
10. I am concerned her.
11. She couldn't talk her problem anymore.
12. Some kids experiment drugs during their teenage years.
13. This is a custom to my country.
14. From my opinion, I don't think there is anything wrong with her.
15. When I asked the problem, they said it was corrected.
16. You have to listen older people.
17. The child played different kinds of toys.
18. I saw what my father did to her. He was so kind to her.
19. I saw what my father did for her. He was so cruel and unkind to her.
20. They work long hours on their work place.
21. Some young generation do not appreciate their older relatives.
22. Children have a lot to learn on life.
23. When I came USA, my grandfather met me at the airport.
24. A friend can introduce you with somebody.
25. She got married with him.
26. A child threw a glass of juice in the floor.
27. I looked for the window, and I saw your wife throwing cold water on the baby.
29. I was angry for her.
30. We search equality and freedom.

31. In the other hand, you never know with whom you are going out.

32. A good way to meet someone is for personal ads.

33. It depends from the culture that you are from.

34. We think that they are discriminating to us because of our religion.

35. The only thing I can suggest you is to work harder.

36. We can see the same similarity as the rich and poor.

37. They never talk their problems with their older relatives.

38. I would talk all the incidences that happened to me in my life.

39. Maria is different than Alice.

40. If public schools engage prayers, they will become religious schools.

41. I disagree praying in our public schools.

42. My cousin got married a man from another religion.

43. Understanding is important in dealing for different people.

44. There are a lot of reasons why couples should move together.

45. I will never forget him. He was the most important person for me.

46. If we hate someone, we can not do anything on it.

47. Before marriage, there should be a course given for being a good wife.

48. She ended on getting divorced to him.

49. Sometimes you don't think on having a baby until you find out you are pregnant.

50. My cousin got divorced with a man who beat her.

Write a composition about one of the following topics. Be sure to check your preposition usage carefully.

1. Describe how a husband or wife are selected in your culture and be certain to explain why you like or dislike this tradition.

2. In the United States, many people use personal ads to meet a partner. Explain why you think personal ads *are* or *are not* a suitable way to meet a mate.

Easily Confused Terms

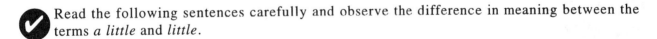

20

The objective of this chapter is to teach students:

- *to understand some easily confused terms which include:*
  - *a few versus few; and a little versus little,*
  - *other versus another,*
  - *and adjectives using the present and past participles.*

Few vs A Few and A Little vs Little

✔ Read the following sentences carefully and observe the difference in meaning between the terms *a few* and *few*.

  1. a. I have <u>a few good friends</u>.
       b. I have <u>few good friends</u>.

  2. a. He has <u>a few new shirts</u>.
       b. He has <u>few new shirts.</u>

  3. a. Sonia had <u>a few dollars</u> left.
       b. Sonia had <u>few dollars</u> left.

  4. a. You knew <u>a few people</u> in that school.
       b. You knew <u>few people</u> in that school.

✔ Read the following sentences carefully and observe the difference in meaning between the terms *a little* and *little*.

  5. a. Jean has <u>a little money.</u>
       b. Jean has <u>little money.</u>

  6. a. We have <u>a little time</u> to kill.
       b. We have <u>little time</u> to kill.

  7. a. They know <u>a little Spanish.</u>
       b. They know <u>little Spanish.</u>

  8. a. You have <u>a little patience</u> for children.
       b. You have <u>little patience</u> for children.

Which terms are used to modify *count nouns*?

_____and _____are used with count nouns.

Which terms are used to modify *non-count nouns*?

_____ and _____are used with non count nouns.

What does the statement *a few* suggest?

The statement <u>a few</u> suggest there is a _____ of something.

What does the statement *a little* suggest?

The statement <u>a little</u> suggests there is a _____ of something.

What does the statement *few* suggest?

The statement <u>few</u> suggests something is almost _____ or doesn't _____.

What does the statement *little* suggest?

The statement <u>little</u> suggests something is almost _____ or doesn't _____.

Rule 1

The terms **a few** and **few** are used with **count nouns**.

> *example:* a few good men
> few students

The terms **a little** and **little** are used with **non count nouns**.

> *example:* a little information
> little information

Rule 2

The terms **a few** or **a little** suggest there is a **small quantity of something**.

> *example:* There is <u>a little milk</u> in the refrigerator.
> There are <u>a few</u> students still taking the exam.

The terms **few** or **little** suggest something is **almost completely gone** or **almost doesn't exist**. These terms have a negative meaning.

> *example:* <u>Few people</u> meet their true potential in life. (not many people)
> The teacher gets very angry when a student answers incorrectly. She has <u>little patience</u> for their mistakes. (hardly any patience at all)

✔ *Oral Exercise:* With a partner, verbally complete each sentence with either: *few, a few, little,* or *a little.*

1. Do you have_____minutes? I'd like to ask you about your job experience since I have so _____information about you.

2. Ann received an award for her perfect work because she makes _____ mistakes.

3. After Joan tasted her steak, she added _____ salt and pepper to it.

4. I don't like a lot of garlic in my food. I add _____ garlic to my food when I am cooking.

5. The professor gave an excellent lecture. As a result, _____ students had questions.

6. Dane is having trouble getting used to his new school. Therefore, he has _____ friends there. But, his sister is very relaxed and has met _____ nice girls.

7. I have to go to the drug store because I need _____ things.

8. Dara checks her mailbox everyday even though she gets _____ mail.

9. We're looking forward to this weekend. We're planning on spending _____ days with my parents.

10. Driving to the concert was a pleasure. We arrived quickly because there was _____ traffic and _____ accidents on the road.

11. My sister arrived in New York _____ days ago.

12. We think they could use some help. Let's give them _____ advice.

13. Because their family is very poor, the children have _____ toys and _____ money.

14. Are you finished?
No, not yet. I need _____ more minutes.

15. _____ years ago, I met my husband at work. But, _____ people knew we were dating since we didn't want everyone to gossip about us.

16. In each person's life, _____ rain must fall sometimes.

17. I was hungry, so I ate _____ nuts.

18. I eat _____ nuts because they are high in calories and cholesterol.

19. Margaret likes her coffee to be sweet; therefore, she adds _____ sugar to it. But, I like my coffee plain, so I add _____ sugar or milk.

20. The prices in that store were very high, so I bought _____ things there.

The following is an entry from an ESL student's personal journal. With a partner complete each blank with either: *a few*, *a little*, *few* or *little*.

The other evening when I entered my class early, I was surprised to see only one student sitting in the classroom. _____ students in my evening class arrive early because they have _____ time to spare since they come directly from their jobs to school. However, when I glance around the room _____ minutes before the class begins, I see _____ students eating their dinner and talking to each other. Because they only have _____ minutes before class, many of them are eating when the professor enters the class.

I've also noticed in the evening classes there are a lot of people who have worked all day, and they have _____ patience for teachers who are unprepared or classmates who act like children. Typically, evening students are quite motivated even though they only have_____

time to do assignments and study. The limited time they do have, they manage very carefully

so that they can meet all the demands of being an employee, student, parent or spouse.

But, unfortunately in one of my classes, there were _____ students who weren't so mo-

tivated. They only did _____bit of the work assigned each night. They left the classroom

_____times each night and complained about every assignment they received.

Initially, most of us were tolerant of their behavior, but after a while, the rest of students made

_____ remarks to these people whose only goal was to pass by doing the least amount

of work.

In general, I've found in evening classes, there is_____tolerance for fooling around,

and this makes the classes quite productive.

✔ *Writing:* Write four or five of sentences describing something which you have *few* or *little* of. Next, write four or five sentences describing something of which you have *a little* or *a few* of.

Other versus Another ·

✔ Read the following sentences and observe the use of the underlined words.

1. a. Can I have <u>another</u> apple since I'm still hungry?
   b. Can I have <u>the other</u> apple since that one is bruised?
2. a. You can take <u>another</u> piece of cake if you want more.
   b. You can take <u>the other</u> piece of cake if you don't want that one.
3. a. Susan and Edgar bought <u>another</u> cook book since they only had one.
   b. Susan and Edgar bought <u>the other</u> cook book since it was less expensive.

What part of speech are the words *another* and *other* in these sentences?
The words <u>another</u> and <u>other</u> are _____ in these sentences.

What is the difference in meaning between *another* and *other*?
The adjective_____ means one more in addition to something that has already been
mentioned. The adjective _____means the last one in a group or the only one that remains in a group.

 Read the following sentences.

1. a. That piece of cake looks stale. Can I have <u>the other</u>?
    b. Mary just ate one piece of cake. She says, "Can I have <u>another</u>?"
2. a. There are two women in this picture. One is young, <u>the other</u> is old.
    b. That cookie was delicious. Can I have <u>another</u>?
3. a. That newspaper is torn. Please give me <u>the other</u>.
    b. I have to buy two newspapers today. Please give me <u>another.</u>

In the above sentences, what part of speech are the words another and other?
In the above sentences, the words <u>the other</u> and <u>another</u> are _____ .

What is the difference in meaning between the pronouns *the other* and *another*?
The pronoun _____means one out of a similar group; however the pronoun _____
means the last one in a group.

R u l e

3

The words **another** and **the other** can function as either a **pronoun** or an **adjective**.

example: Mary wants <u>another</u> drink. (adjective)
Mary had one drink. Now she wants <u>another</u>. (pronoun)
Please give me <u>the other</u> pear. (adjective)
I ate one pear. Paulette ate <u>the other</u>. (pronoun)

Another means **one** more in addition to something already mentioned.

example: That apple was delicious. I'd like <u>another</u>.

Other means **the last one in a group** or the only one that remains from a group.

example: Don't give me that piece of cake. It's too small. I want <u>the other.</u>

 Read the following sentences and observe what is being done incorrectly in numbers 1 and 2.

*1. I want <u>another</u>.
*2. I want the <u>other</u> candies.
3. I want the <u>others</u>.

When another and other are adjectives, can they be pluralized? _____

When another is used as a pronoun, can it be pluralized?
_____ , it (can or can not) be pluralized because the pronoun <u>another</u> means one more in a
group.

When *other* is used as a pronoun, can it be pluralized?
_____ , it (can or can not) be pluralized since it can mean several more out of a group of
items.

When *other* is used as an adjective, can it be pluralized?

_____ , it (can or can not) be pluralized because adjectives are never_____ .

R u l e

4

When **another** and **other** are used as **adjectives**, they can not be made plural since **adjectives are never pluralized**.

example: I want another apple.
I want the other apple.

When **other** is used as a **pronoun**, it may be **pluralized** since it means **several more** out of a group of items.

example: Elsie went home with the others.

When **another** is used as a **pronoun**, it is never **pluralized** because another means **one more** in a group.

example: I would like another. (This is asking for one more. It is always singular and can not be pluralized.)

✔ *Oral Exercise:* With a partner, verbally complete the sentences with the correct forms of: *another, other, others, the other, the others.*

1. Jaime has only two shirts, a blue one and a gray one. His wife wants him to buy_____ one.

2. Jaime has two ties. One is blue, and_____is gray.

3. Some ties are blue. _____are gray.

4. Some shirts have short sleeves. _____shirts have long sleeves.

5. The gym class was divided into two groups. Half of the children stayed inside and played tennis. _____ children went outside and played softball.

6. If you really dislike your job, why don't you look for _____ one? You don't have to be a secretary forever. There are lots of _____ careers.

7. A house has many different rooms. The living room is one room, and the bathroom is _____ . _____ rooms in a house are the dining room, kitchen and bedroom.

8. Some children have birds as pets. _____ have fish. Still _____children have hamsters as pets. But, there are _____kinds of animals that are house pets too.

9. When I was a kid, I had two friends. One was a tall. _____ was short.

10. The first time I went to my class when I walked into a classroom, it was the wrong room. So, I went to _____room and found my class.

11. The children at the camp have two choices for activities in the morning. One is to play soccer. _____ is to go swimming.

12. I have two pieces of candy. One is for Theresa. _____ is for Jamie.

13. My mother gave me a dress. I tried to put it on, but it was too tight. So, I had to return it and buy _____ dress. _____ dress fits perfectly.

14. We have two cars. One is old. _____ is new.

15. Pears and strawberries are good sources of fiber. _____ sources include lettuce, broccoli and tomatoes.

16. Mario received three gifts. One was from me. _____ one was from his mother-in-law. _____ gift was from his girlfriend.

17. Frank asked six people to our house for dinner. Out of those six, only Jorge and Stephanie could come. _____ couldn't come because they had to work.

18. I would like some more videos. Are there any _____available? _____I saw last week were really funny.

19. There are two women on the corner. One is Hedda. _____ is Paula.

20. _____ day I saw two movies. One was excellent. _____ was all right.

✔ With a partner or in a small group, complete the blank with the correct forms of: *another, other, others, the other, the others*.

Waitress: Would you like _____ cup of coffee, Sir?

Customer: No thanks. But, I was looking at what _____ people in my group are eating. It looks delicious. What is it?

Waitress: Well, _____ are having a very spicy bowl of chili. Would you like some, too?

Customer: No, I better not. _____ day I had some chili, and I had heartburn for the whole night. _____than chili what _____Mexican food do you serve?

Waitress: That's about it, Sir. We're just a plain diner. You'd have to try_____ type of restaurant to get Mexican speciality dishes. I'm sorry. How about _____ piece of pie?

Customer: Maybe I will have _____ . Ah... Wait a second. I'll take a piece from _____ one that hasn't been cut yet. It looks fresher.

Waitress: I'm sorry, Sir. I can't cut into _____ one until the first one is finished. I have a great idea, Sir. Why don't you do what_____in your group are doing.

Customer: And, what is that?

Waitress: They're paying their bills and leaving a healthy tip.

✔ *Writing:* Write a dialog between two or three people who are either eating in a restaurant or purchasing something in a store. Be sure to use *other* and *another* as adjectives and *other, others* and *another* as pronouns.

Adjectives Ending in ED and ING ·······················

✔ Read the following sentences.

1. Michael's books are very <u>surprising</u>.
2. Harry is very <u>interested</u> in biology.
3. Cathy was <u>fascinated</u> by the book she read.
4. We were <u>excited</u> about the birth of our first child.
5. You look <u>bored</u> with that book.
6. It was a very <u>embarrassing</u> situation.

In the above sentences, what part of speech are the words *interesting, fascinating, shocked,*
excited, bored **and** *embarrassing?*
These words are _____that end in <u>ed</u> and <u>ing.</u>

R u l e

5

The **present participle** and the **past participle** can be used as **adjectives**.

| past participle which functions as an adjective | present participle which functions as an adjective |

example: Mary was <u>surprised</u> at her remark.   The remark was <u>surprising</u>.

✔ Read the following sentences and observe the difference in meaning.

1. a. This is a <u>boring class.</u>
   b. This is a <u>bored class.</u>
2. a. This is a <u>frightening child.</u>
   b. This is a <u>frightened child.</u>
3. a. The old woman was a <u>loving</u> person.
   b. The old woman was a <u>loved</u> person.
4. a. The woman was <u>confused</u> because of her illness.
   b. The woman was <u>confusing</u> because she didn't communicate well.

Do the terms *boring class* **and** *bored class* **have the same meaning?**
_____, they (does or does not) have the same meaning.

What is the difference in meaning between the *boring class* **and the** *bored class?*
The _____ class gives <u>a reason</u> for the boredom which was because the class was
not interesting. However, the _____ class describes <u>how the students felt</u> when they
were not interested in the class.

Write a general rule explaining when to use and adjective ending in *ed* **or** *ing.*
The <u>present participle</u> ing is used as an _____to describe a _____for a feeling.

The <u>past participle</u> <u>ed</u> is used as an _____ to describe how the noun it modified felt.

R u l e

6

When a **present participle** is used as an adjective, it expresses the **reason** for a feeling. The feeling is created **internally** by the noun it modifies. This has a very **active** meaning.

example: That woman is <u>fascinating</u> because she speaks ten languages.

The word **fascinating** is an **adjective** that modifies the word woman, and the use of the present participle indicates the **reason** for her being fascinating.

When the **past participle** is used as an adjective, it express **how the noun it modified felt**. It has a **passive** meaning. The feeling is created by something **external** to the noun it modifies.

example: The woman was <u>excited</u> when she heard the news.

The word **excited** is an adjective that modifies the word woman, but **the excitement** was created by an external source which was **the news**. Moreover, it describes **how the woman felt**. Therefore, the past participle is used as the adjective.

 Oral Exercise: Read a sentence to a partner or a small group and have them select the correct adjective.

1. Cheryl didn't enjoy that movie. She said it was (boring, bored).

2. Cheryl was (boring, bored) because the movie didn't have a good plot.

3. My husband is (interesting, interested) in old cars. But, I don't find old cars very (interesting, interested).

4. Mr. Rush is an (exciting, excited) man. He has traveled all over the world.

5. The man was yelling and screaming. He was very (exciting, excited).

6. When the child heard the thunder, she became (frightening, frightened).

7. A person who waves a knife is very (frightening, frightened) to the people around him.

8. This class is not (boring, bored) because the professor is an (interesting, interested) person.

9. Rosemary isn't (interesting, interested) in dating because she is too busy with her work.

10. Tim is a (confusing, confused) story teller. I am always (confusing, confused) when Tim tells a story.

11. Gerard was (embarrassing, embarrassed) when his mother told him that she loved him. Sometimes it is (embarrassing, embarrassed) to hear such a remark in public.

12. Cynthia is (fascinating, fascinated) by marine life. I think it is a (fascinating, fascinated) subject.

13. Kathryn and Laura are (shocking, shocked) women because they sun bathe in the nude. Their relatives were (shocking, shocked) by their actions.

14. Eddie and Tina were (exciting, excited) about their wedding plans. Weddings are always very (exciting, excited) events.

15. She thought she was such an (exciting, excited) person, but all she ever did was sit in front of the television and drink beer.

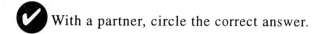 With a partner, circle the correct answer.

As a foreign student in an American college, I've had a great deal of difficulty getting accustomed to the American educational system.

The first time I came to the college was to register for my classes. I was very (excited, exciting) since I had just arrived in this new and (excited, exciting) country, but my excitement soon turned to (agonized, agonizing) frustration when I had to stand on line for over four hours because the (antiquated, antiquating) college computer system had malfunctioned.

When I finally got to the front of the line, I was already (exhausted, exhausting) from the long and (tired, tiring) wait. When I handed the woman my (completed, completing) program card, she told me I couldn't register since I hadn't seen a (qualified, qualifying) adviser. She indicated that I should go across the hall to the advisement office.

In the advisement office, I was informed that I'd have to take a placement exam before being able to register for any courses. Feeling completely (demoralized, demoralizing), I went to the Office of Student Testing to take the exam. As soon as I entered the classroom, I could tell this would be a really (stimulated, stimulating) experience since all the students looked completely (disinterested, disinteresting) in what they were doing.

After I showed my student identification card, a placement exam was handed to me, and I was told I could take as much time as I wished to complete it. I began to carefully read each passage in the reading test, but the material was so (bored, boring) that I had a hard time concentrating. After completing the (exhausted, exhausting) reading section, I had to write a (detailed, detailing) composition explaining why I agree or disagree with capital punishment. By the time I finally came to the Math section of the test, I was so (fatigued, fatiguing) my body began to ache. After three and a half hours of this (annoying, annoyed) experience, I was finally done but wasn't sure if I had really done my best. The director of this office told me to return to the college the following day so that I could register for classes.

When I went home, I felt less than (invigorated, invigorating) and (disappointed, disappointing) with my first experience at an American college. In my country, if a student is admitted to a college, he/she is automatically placed in a program which is predetermined by the college and attends classes with the same group of students throughout all four years. There are no (exacerbated, exacerbating) placement exams or elective courses. Each student is told exactly what must be studied and does it.

After I got used to the American college system, I began to appreciate the flexibility it gave me and felt a lot less (frustrated, frustrating) about some of the inconveniences which ultimately permitted me more input into my curriculum and education.

Writing: Write a composition explaining why you feel that working in groups and figuring out rules is useful or unproductive in learning. Be sure to use at least ten of the (ed, ing) adjectives listed below or some others that are suitable.

Column A	Column B
interesting	interested
troubling	troubled
exhausting	exhausted
tiring	tired
spoiling	spoiled
disappointing	disappointed
loving	loved
confusing	confused
alarming	alarmed
insulting	insulted
impressing	impressed
annoying	annoyed

····· *Infinitives and Gerunds* ·····

21

The objective of this chapter is to teach students:

- *the difference in meaning and form between infinitives and gerunds,*

- *the use of verb and adjective preposition combinations,*

- *infinitives of purpose,*

- *infinitives with <u>too</u> and <u>enough,</u>*

- *gerunds as subjects and,*

- *typical infinitive or gerund errors.*

Form ·

 Circle the *gerund* in the following sentences.

1. The child hated telling lies.
2. The teacher considered failing the student.
3. I finished reading the book.
4. We practiced writing a composition.

What is a gerund?
A gerund is a verb that has_____ placed on the end of it.
example: _____

 Circle the *infinitive* in the following sentences.

1. My husband promised to clean the house.
2. The teacher tries to instruct them well.
3. She manages to visit her mother every week.
4. I hope to go to Europe this summer.

What is an infinitive?
An infinitive is a verb with the word _____ placed in front of it.
*example:*_____

✔ Put the following verbs in the gerund and infinitive form.

Verb	Infinitive	Gerund
1. eat	_____	_____
2. drink	_____	_____
3. swim	_____	_____
4. yell	_____	_____
5. help	_____	_____
6. love	_____	_____
7. swim	_____	_____
8. teach	_____	_____

✔ Read each of the following sentences and determine what is being done incorrectly and correct it.

*1. Mary enjoys to drink wine. _____

*2. She needed call her mother. _____

*3. She expect winning it. _____

*4. They denied to steal the bike. _____

*5. She plans marrying him next year. _____

In these sentences what is used incorrectly?
The _____ and _____ are not used correctly.

R u l e

1

A gerund is a verb that has the letters **ing** placed on the end of it.
 example: talking,   walking,   singing,   yelling

An infinitive is a verb that has the word **to** placed before the simple form of the verb.
 example: to talk,   to walk,   to sing,   to yell

Certain verbs must be followed by a gerund.
 example: She <u>enjoys *playing*</u> softball.
 The child <u>goes *swimming*</u> everyday.

Certain verbs must be followed by an infinitive.
 example: Monica <u>plans *to become*</u> a nun.
 Roberto <u>hopes *to marry*</u> Sonja.

Infinitive versus Gerund Form ·

✔ Read the following sentences.

1. I always enjoy <u>eating</u> at Marie's, but many people avoid <u>eating</u> there.
2. I plan <u>to eat</u> at Marie's tonight. I want <u>to get</u> there before six.
3. She hoped <u>to win</u> the lottery.
4. Helen avoided <u>eating</u> clams after she got food poisoning.
5. They intend <u>to buy</u> a car next year.
6. The boys admitted <u>calling</u> the girl.

When is an infinitive or a gerund used?
A _____usually refers to a real activity that will or will not definitely occur.
An _____ usually refers to an activity that is planned, possible or probable rather than a real or definite event.

✔ Read the following sentences carefully.

1. Mary admitted <u>not knowing</u> the answer.
2. Paulette and I regret <u>not telling</u> our parents the truth.

How is a gerund made negative?
A gerund is made negative by placing the word _____before the gerund.

✔ Read the following sentences and determine which event occurred first.

1. I needed to take a nap.
2. He wanted to apologize to her.

3. She hopes to marry Guillermo.
4. The old woman appeared to be lonely.

When the action in the main verb occurred first, do we use an infinitive or gerund?

_____

2

A **gerund** usually refers to a real or definite activity that will or will not *definitely* occur. A gerund **does not** usually refer to something that might happen.

> *example:* We discussed getting married.
> We avoided talking to her for months.

Both these events definitely happened; therefore, a gerund is used.

A gerund is made negative by placing the word **not** before it.

> *example:* We discussed not moving to another country.

An **infinitive** refers to an action that is **planned**, **possible** or **probable** rather than real or definite.

> *example:* I intend to fix the broken pipe myself.

This is something planned but may not occur; therefore, an infinitive is used.

An **infinitive** is also used to refer to an action that occurs later than the main verb in the sentence.

> *example:* I needed to know the truth about him.

 Complete the following exercise with either *to drink* or *drinking*. Be sure to remember the rules discussed in Rule Two.

1. She admitted _____.
2. She wanted _____.
3. She detested _____.
4. She appreciated _____.
5. She decided _____.
6. She regretted _____.
7. She despised _____.
8. She seemed _____.
9. She prepared _____.
10. She denied _____.
11. She risked _____.
12. She postponed _____.
13. She would like _____.
14. She didn't mind _____.
15. She disliked _____.

16. She would prefer _____.
17. She pretended _____.
18. She agrees _____.
19. She promises _____.
20. They mean _____.
21. She expected _____.
22. She avoided _____.
23. She hoped _____.
24. She recalled _____.
25. She asked _____.
26. She needed _____.
27. She appeared _____.
28. She missed _____.
29. She resisted _____.
30. She agreed _____.

Communicative Practice

Using six verbs from exercise D, ask a partner to describe activities he/she did.

    example: *Mary, what did you postpone doing?*
                 I postponed having a baby for three years.
                 Carlo, what did Diego appear to do?
                 Diego appeared to be sleeping.

✔ Complete the following exercise with either the infinitive or the gerund of the word in parentheses.

Many students decide (go) _____to college without considering the commitment and

dedication which is needed (succeed) _____from the very first day.

As a teacher, I've always wanted (mention)_____some of the things students un-

wittingly do which directly impact their success or failure. First, if students would like (attend)

_____ college, they must plan on being available to register for classes, but many stu-

dents risk (be) _____excluded from classes by registering late or after classes have

begun. If a student hopes (be)_____admitted to a class, it is imperative he/she reg-

ister as early as possible and expect (attend) _____the first class meeting so that he/

she avoids (miss)_____important information the professor may give out dur-

ing the first class meeting.

Next if a student postpones (register)_____before classes begin, he/she is probably

going to miss at least one or more class. He/she will regret (do)_____this since the

teacher will count those missed classes as formal cuts which could ultimately impact the final

grade. Most instructors don't mind a student's (cut) _____a few times. But, if the

student becomes sick during the semester, the cuts begin (mount) _____up, and

the student risks (fail) _____the course. Students can avoid (be)_____penal-

ized by registering on time and planning (attend) _____each and every class.

Finally, many students have admitted (drop) _____ out of college because they did not keep up with the assignments as they were given by the professor. Students should not postpone (read)_____ a required assignment, (write) _____ a paper, or (study) _____ for a test until the last minute. There is no way a student can adequately prepare at the eleventh hour. Before deciding (attend)_____ college, a student must plan (do) _____ assignments and (study) _____ a certain amount of time each week. If a student can not make this type of commitment, perhaps he/she should postpone (enroll) _____ until a later date.

These are simple tenants which many students appear (misunderstand)_____ even though they are essential to succeeding in college. So, if a student agrees (sign)_____ up for classes, he/she can avoid (drop) _____ out by following these basic concepts.

Remember and Forget

The gerund and infinitive rules just learned should help to explain the difference in meaning in the following sentences.

✔ Write a number 1 over the action that occurred first and a 2 over the action that occurred second.

1. a. I remember locking the door.
    b. I remember to lock the door.
2. a. I forgot to take my medicine.
    b. I forgot taking my medicine.

The gerund is used to describe an action that _____.

The infinitive is used to describe an action that _____.

Rule

3

When using the verbs **remember** or **forget**, a gerund is used to describe an activity that happened before the main verb. However, when an infinitive is used, the action described in the main verb occurred first and the infinitive second.

example: 2   1
           I remember brushing my teeth that night.
           First I brushed my teeth, then I recalled doing them.

          1   2
           I remember to brush my teeth every night before bed.
           First I remember I must brush my teeth. Then I brush them.

✔ Complete the following exercise with the infinitive or the gerund.

1. I remember (go) _____ to France when I was ten years old.
2. Remember (set) _____ your alarm tonight.
3. I hope (graduate) _____ in four years.
4. Pierre forgot (call) _____ his mother yesterday.
5. Mary forgot (pay) _____ the paper boy that day.
6. Stan promised (stop) _____ practicing the tuba at midnight.
7. Stan stopped (practice) _____ the tuba at night.
8. I regret (not tell) _____ Betty my plans last week.
9. I regret (tell) _____ you that your husband has had an accident.
10. I never regret (tell) _____ the truth.
11. Juan dislikes (drive) _____ a truck.
12. The man appeared (be) _____ drunk.
13. Osman pretended (know) _____ Claudia well.
14. The teacher always remembers (give) _____ an assignment.
15. The teacher remembered (give) _____ her a passing grade.
16. We stopped (use) _____ the bathroom on the highway.
17. We stopped (use) _____ that bathroom because it was always dirty.
18. He quit (smoke) _____ ten years ago.
19. The woman quit (work) _____ so she could spend more time with her baby.
20. They can't afford (purchase) _____ a house yet.

✔ With a partner, write a list of five things you remember to do everyday.

example: I remember to take a shower every morning.

✔ With a partner, write a list of five things you forgot that you had done.

example: Ahmed forgot taking his medicine and took a second pill.

✔ With a partner, write a list of five actions you would like to stop doing.

example: Paolo would like to stop smoking.

✔ With a partner, write a list of five actions you stopped doing.

example: Rosa stopped working to stay home with her new baby.

The Object of the Preposition . . . .

✔ Read the following sentences and correct errors in the use of gerunds and infinitives.

*1. She insisted on li~~X~~en to your complaints.
*2. The professor insists on to~~X~~ome to class very late.
*3. She is excited about st~~X~~t college.
*4. I am accustomed to ha~~X~~e a lot of money.
*5. They can count on w~~X~~te a lot of essays.

What mistake was made in these sentences?
After a preposition, a _____ is always used.

✔ Read the following sentences and explain why the underlined word is wrong and correct it.

*1. My mother insists on <u>me</u> coming home early.
*2. The teacher objects to <u>them</u> coming to class late.
*3. You are afraid of <u>him</u> getting lost.

A gerund can not be modified by an _____ pronoun. It must be modified by a _____ adjective.

R u l e
. . . .

4

After a preposition, a **gerund** is always used not an infinitive.
  example: She insisted <u>on listening</u> to your complaints.

A gerund can not be modified by an object pronoun. It must be modified by a possessive adjective.
  example: My husband is opposed to <u>my</u> working after we have children.

. . . .

✔ What part of speech are the underlined words.

1. The child is <u>afraid</u> of crying.
2. I am <u>interested</u> in learning.
3. They are <u>opposed</u> to killing.
4. Mary is <u>crazy</u> about having fun.
5. We are <u>nervous</u> about getting married.
6. You are <u>used</u> to asking a lot of questions.

What part of speech is the underlined word in each sentence?
The underlined words are _____ .

What part of speech is each word that follows the underlined words?
These words are _____ .

What part of speech must a preposition be followed by?
A preposition must be followed by a _____ .

When using an adjective preposition combination, is a preposition followed by an infinitive or a gerund?
It is followed by a _____ .

✔ What part of speech are the underlined words?

1. She <u>believes</u> in telling the truth.

2. I <u>object</u> to her making remarks.

3. We <u>admitted</u> to playing a trick on her.

4. He <u>insisted</u> on paying for the dinner.

What part of speech is the underlined word in each sentence?
The underlined words are _____ .

What part of speech are each of the words that follow the underlined words?
These words are _____ .

What part of speech must a preposition be followed by?
A preposition must be followed by a _____ .

When using a verb preposition combination, is a preposition followed by an infinitive or a gerund?
It is followed by a _____ .

R u l e

5

In English, many common expressions are made up of:
    an adjective plus a preposition,
    or a verb followed by a preposition.

A preposition must be followed by a noun or a gerund.
   example: You can count <u>on earning</u> a lot of money in the stock market.
       The students are bored <u>with learning</u> about infinitives and gerunds.

Choose the appropriate preposition from the box. You will use some of the prepositions more than once. Then add the correct form of the verb in parentheses.

| at | on | of | against | instead | off | in | to | about | for |

1. Pete is very interested (listen) _____ to rock music.
2. New Orleans is famous (have) _____ great Cajun food.
3. You are not concerned (get) _____ bored.
4. We are not good (learn) _____ science.
5. I'm worried (not get) _____ a good job after I graduate.
6. Raul is excited (go) _____ back to Colombia, but he is nervous (fly) _____.
6. My parents insist (visit) _____ my grandparents every Sunday.
7. I'm really looking forward (stay) _____ home this weekend.
8. My girlfriend is very fond (study) _____ .
9. I'm crazy (play) _____ with computers.
10. I am fond (go) _____ to California.

Write the appropriate prepositions and the correct verb forms in these sentences.

I am interested _____ (eat) _____ at the East Coast Inn. In fact, I was excited

_____ (eat) _____there. Last night, in addition _____ (have) _____ a

good meal, I had a good laugh there too. A customer stated the chef was not capable _____

(make) _____ Italian food well. He said the loud music was responsible _____ (upset)

_____ his stomach. At first, the owner felt guilty _____ (spoil) _____ his din-

ner until he blamed him _____ (destroy) _____ his life too. Most restaurant

owners are accustomed _____ (hear) _____ complaints. Sometimes, it is im-

possible to keep people _____ (complain) _____ . Years ago we used _____

(get) _____ more complaints when we had a different cook. But, now the owner and the

customers are tired _____ (hear) _____ his constant objections. Even though some

people are rude, the owner always thanks them (come) _____ to the restaurant.

The following list contains frequently used adjective-preposition combinations and verb-preposition combinations. Write ten sentences about this class, the students or the teacher using this list and an appropriate gerund.

example: Juan Carlos *is afraid of receiving a bad grade in this course.*

Adjective-Prepositions

to be accustomed to
to be addicted to
to be aware of
to be capable of
to be content with
to be confused about
to be convinced of
to be crazy about
to be devoted to
to be envious of
to experiment with
to be exhausted from
to be fond of
to be grateful for
to be guilty of
to be happy for
to be innocent of
to be involved in
to be jealous of
to be known for
to be polite to
to prepared for
to be proud of
to be qualified for
to be ready for
to be relevant to
to be responsible for
to be satisfied with
to be sure of
to be terrified of
to be worried about

Verb-Prepositions

to apologize for
to approve of
to argue about
to believe in
to complain about
to deal with
to decide on
to depend on
to discriminate against
to dream about
to escape from
to feel like
to fight for
to forget about
to forgive for
to hear about
to insist on
to listen to
to look forward to
to object to
to participate in
to pray for
to prevent from
to provide for
to recover from
to rely on
to rescue from
to substitute for
to thank for
to think about
to vote for

 Correct each of the following sentences.

1. She insisted on him wearing a rain coat.
2. She is interested in learn a second language.
3. Our parents are opposed to us living together before we get married.
4. That restaurant is famous for make excellent food.
5. I am looking forward to them visiting us next fall.
6. We can count on you doing your work correctly.
7. You are afraid of get a bad grade in the course.
8. Her parents are nervous about us driving in the ice and snow.

9. Ali and Osman are opposed to live with a woman before get married.
10. The student objected to you call him a liar.

 Read the following composition and insert the gerund or infinitive for each word in parentheses.

Once a law has been passed, nobody should deliberately break it. However, not everybody can avoid (make) _____ mistakes, and they sometimes don't realize exactly what has happened. I got into trouble for (be) _____ involved in (jump) _____ a subway turnstile even though I didn't know it was happening.

A year ago, my friend Jadwiga and I were arrested for (not pay) _____ our car fare at a subway station. I, however, was not really guilty because I did not have any idea of what my friend was doing behind my back. By the time I realized my girlfriend had pushed through the turnstile on my card, it was too late. Within seconds of (witness) _____ this act, the policemen had handcuffed us and had us (face) _____ a wall.

When the police officer asked us some questions, my friend tried (tell) _____ them I was innocent, but they informed us that since we did it together I was also at fault. They took us down to the police station (take) _____ fingerprints and mug shots. Jadwiga smiled in her photograph; I cried. We stayed behind bars for five hours when finally an officer presented us with an appointment for a court hearing.

Several weeks had passed when we finally went before a judge. Prior to (go) _____ to trial, our lawyers explained to us what the potential penalties could be. We were found guilty of (commit) _____ the crime, and for our punishment we had (clean) _____ a subway station for two days.

I was surprised (see) _____ the trial only took two hours without (us, our) even (utter) _____ a word. Fortunately, our punishment was not too bad since all we had (do)_____was clean a subway station for a day with a group of other people who had been convicted of the same crime.

Is it possible to prevent yourself from (get)_____into trouble with the law? I don't always think it is since I am not a very lucky person. My little mistakes are usually recognized by the right people. This should warn me (make)_____ sure I am more careful. Will I be accused of (commit)_____ another crime? Did I learn a lesson from (be) _____ arrested? Those are question which I will have (answer)_____ in time.

Infinitives of Purpose . . . .

✔ Read the following sentences and observe the use of the infinitives.

1. I went to Macy's yesterday **to buy** a dress.

2. Why did you go to Models?
   I went **to return** a pair of sneakers.

3. I use a calculator in order **to prevent** mistakes.

4. Why did you buy a dictionary?
   I bought a dictionary in order **to spell** correctly.

Why is an infinitive used in each of these examples?
An infinitive is used it to explain a _____ .
Sometimes the **long form** *in order to* is used.

R u l e	
6	An **infinitive** is sometimes used to express a reason or a purpose for doing something.

> *example:* I went to Bloomindales **to purchase** a new dress.
> I went to Bloomindales **in order to purchase** a new dress.

✔ Answer the following questions using an infinitive of purpose.

1. Why did he enroll in Chinese 101?
   He enrolled in Chinese 101 *in order to meet* the requirement for a foreign language._____

2. Why did she take a bus to work?

_____

3. Why did she go to her lawyers office?

_____

4. Why did your professor call you this morning?

_____

5. Why did he turn on the radio?

_____

6. Why did she start jogging?

_____

7. Why did you turn off the air conditioner?

_____

8. Why did you disconnect the telephone last night?

_____

9. Why did John hide when he saw his wife walking down the street?

_____

10. Why did George color his hair red?

_____

✔ With a partner, write five sentences explaining why you came to this school using an infinitive of reason or purpose.

example: Marla and Ali came to this college in order to study art.

Infinitives with Too and Enough . . . .

✔ Read the following sentences and determine why these sentences are written incorrectly. Then correct them.

*1. The woman said she was too young die.
*2. She was too tired think straight.
*3. She was to slow to answer the question.
*4. He isn't old enough smoke.
*5. Teenagers aren't old enough having sex.
*6. A child is not old enough to buying cigarettes.

What format is used when using the word *too* with an infinitive?
When using **too** and an infinitive, the rule is to use the word
        too + _____ + _____ .

What format is used when using the word *enough* and the infinitive?
When using **enough** and infinitive, the rule is:
        _____ + **enough** + _____ .

7

The rule used with **too** and an **infinitive** is:

too   +   adjective   +   infinitive.

example: Maria is too young to get engaged.

The rule used with **enough** and an **infinitive** is:

adjective/adverb   +   enough   + infinitive.

example: Marta is old enough to drive a car.

✔ Write sentences by putting the following in correct order.

1. time/to go to the party next week/ We don't have/ enough
   We don't have enough time to go to the party next week.

2. to touch the sky/ too / He's / short

3. to pay his credit card bills/ money/ Tim doesn't have/ enough

4. this coffee is / cold/ to drink / too

5. to eat lunch / time/ Claude didn't have/ enough

6. enough/ to take a vacation alone/ old/ Sara and Emily aren't

7. too/ to get married/ young/ Shifra and Yoni are

8. early/ to go to a restaurant for dinner/ too/ it's

✔ Complete the following sentences.

1. The weather is too warm ⎯⎯⎯⎯⎯⎯⎯⎯⎯⎯⎯.
2. Teresa is five years old. She's too young ⎯⎯⎯⎯⎯⎯⎯.
3. Ali isn't old enough ⎯⎯⎯⎯⎯⎯⎯⎯⎯⎯⎯⎯.
4. That book is too old ⎯⎯⎯⎯⎯⎯⎯⎯⎯⎯⎯⎯.
5. Alicia isn't pretty enough ⎯⎯⎯⎯⎯⎯⎯⎯⎯⎯.
6. Last night I was too tired ⎯⎯⎯⎯⎯⎯⎯⎯⎯⎯.
7. Yesterday, I was too busy ⎯⎯⎯⎯⎯⎯⎯⎯⎯⎯.
8. A BMW is too expensive ⎯⎯⎯⎯⎯⎯⎯⎯⎯⎯.
9. I don't have enough time ⎯⎯⎯⎯⎯⎯⎯⎯⎯⎯.

10. Yesterday Franco didn't have enough time _____ .

11. A teenager is old enough _____ .

12. A toddler isn't old enough _____ .

13. This hot chocolate is too _____ .

✔ With a partner, describe two activities that your partner is too young/old to do.

example: Marc is too young to drive a car.

✔ With a partner, describe two activities your partner is young/old enough to do.

example: Sari is old enough to get married.

Using Gerunds as Subjects and It + Infinitive . . . .

✔ Read the following sentences.

1. a Riding a camel is fun.
   b It is fun to ride a camel.

2. a. Doing homework is important.
   b. It is important to do homework.

3. a. Resting is important.
   b. It is important to rest.

4. a. Learning to read is important.
   b. It is important to learn to read.

Is there any difference in meaning between the two sets of sentences? _____

In letter <u>a</u> of each pair, a _____ is used as the subject of the sentence.

The verb is singular because a _____ is always singular.

In letter b of each pair, the word *it* is used as the subject of the sentence. But, the word <u>it</u> refers to the _____ in the sentence.

Rule	
8	A gerund can be used as the subject of a sentence, and the verb is always in the third person singular.
	example: Jogging is good for your health.
	The dummy it can be used as the subject of a sentence in order to refer to the infinitive.
	example: It is essential for a foreigner to learn English.

✔ Make the sentences with the same meaning by using *it + infinitive*.

1. Having good friends is important.
   It is important to have good friends.

2. Playing baseball is exciting.
   _____

3. Being courteous to people is important.
   _____

4. Learning about other cultures is exciting.
   _____

5. Walking is good for your health.
   _____

6. Is learning a second language easy?
   _____

7. Having a baby is painful.
   _____

8. Studying chemistry is difficult.
   _____

9. Raising children is not an easy job.
   _____

10. Being a teacher is challenging.
   _____

✔ Revise these sentences to use a gerund instead of an infinitive.

1. It is important to eat properly.
   Eating properly is important.

2. It is fun to watch movies.
   _____

3. It is easy to boil water.
   _____

4. It is boring to look at a wall.
   _____

5. It is relaxing to read.
   _____

6. Is it easy to learn to sew?
   _____

7. Is it hard to get a college degree?
   _____

8. It is wrong to cheat on a test.
   _____

9. Is it dangerous to smoke cigars?
   _____

10. Is it expensive to live in Manhattan?
   _____

Using the following list, create six sentences using a gerund as the subject.

watch television   clean the house   do homework
exercise   cook dinner   smoke cigarettes
raising children   get an education   practice English

example: Walking is good for your health.

 Using the following list, create 6 sentences using an infinitive and the dummy *it*.

take a walk   paint a house   listen to music
write a composition   walk a dog   buy a new car
have a baby   practice English   take a bath

example: It is important to drive carefully.

Complete the following sentences with either the infinitive or the gerund.

1. I need (study) _____ tonight.

2. We enjoy (cook) _____ gourmet meals.

3. Ellen started (talk) _____ about her problem.

4. Bud and Sue have decided (get) _____ married.

5. We finished (eat) _____ around 8 o'clock.

6. Are you planning (take) _____ a vacation this year?

7. I like (meet) _____ new people.

8. The Wilsons went (camp) _____ in Yellowstone National Park.

9. My roommate offered (help) _____ me with my English.

10. I'd just begun (watch) _____ a movie when the phone rang.

11. Please stop (crack) _____ your knuckles.

12. Did you remember (feed) _____ the cat this morning?

13. I won't be late. I promise (be) _____ on time.

14. Soshi is considering (move) _____ to a new apartment.

15. What time do you expect (arrive) _____ in Denver?

16. Some children hate (go) _____ to the dentist.

17. They forgot (lock) _____ the door when they left my house.

18. I don't mind (live) _____ with ten people!

19. Don't put off (write) _____ your composition until the last minute.

20. Ken had to quit (jog) _____ because he hurt his knee.

21. The company will continue (hire) _____ new employees.

22. That's not what I meant! I meant (say) _____ just the opposite.

23. You want (go) _____ (shop) _____ this afternoon.

24. Alex seems (want) _____ (go) _____ (sail) _____ this weekend.

25. Cindy intends (go) _____ to work next year.

26. Pierre can't afford (buy) _____ a new car.

27. Janice is thinking about (look) _____ for a new job.

28. My boss refused (give) _____ me a raise.

29. Mr. Carter continued (read)_____ his book even though the children were making a lot of noise.

30. My roommate is trying (take) _____ a nap.

31. I keep (hope)_____ that I'll get a letter real soon.

32. Would you like (go) _____(dance) _____tonight?

33. Children like (play)_____ make believe games. Yesterday Raul pretended (be) _____ a doctor, and David pretended (be)_____ a patient.

 Find the errors in the following sentences.

1. Do you enjoy to go to parties?

2. I went to the store for getting some toothpaste.

3. Did you go to shopping yesterday?

4. We usually go to the cafeteria for get coffee in the morning.

5. Osman needed to went downtown yesterday.

6. Sojin cut the rope without look.

7. I thanked him for drive me to the airport.

8. Is difficult to learn a second language.

9. It is important getting an education.

10. Tulip isn't enough old to get married.

11. Do you want go to swimming tomorrow?

12. Justina went to the bank for cashing a check.

13. Edson was sleepy to finish his homework last night.

14. Is easy this exercise to do.

15. Does me smoking annoy you?

16. Learn to speak a second language takes many year.

17. The professor insisted on him rewriting the paper a fourth time.

Correct any errors in the use of infinitives or gerunds.

It was 1998, and life was good. It was a time enjoy the fruits of me having been successful. My family and I were living in a modern luxury apartment, and I had a great job which paid me well. My family and I could afford to getting whatever we wanted. We had a nice car, beautiful clothes and fine food. We were also able spending a great deal of money on entertainment. Was good to have an easy life .

Then it happened. My boss took me aside and reprimanded me for do something wrong, but I thought his concerns were unjustified and unreasonable. We argued, and I lost control of my temper. I was so enraged I wound up to quit this great job.

When I went home, I was still fuming. I was especially angry at me being so foolish and no just agreeing with the boss. However, as I walked in our apartment, it suddenly hit me that I had no way to providing for my family without work at this great job. My wife was angry for me doing such a stupid thing. I had no idea of what I was going doing.

I had get another job immediately. I had not planned on this happen and hadn't saved much money for a rainy day. I went from place to place beg for a job, but there was nothing being found. What was I going do about my family? The bills were piling up to the ceiling. My wife had selling many of our lovely belongings just to feeding us. It was a nightmare. I finally packed up my family and sent them to live with some relatives who were willing help us out for a while.

It took a long time get another good job and save up enough money so that I could bring my family back home. I felt disgraced and humiliated, but I learned something very important. Don't let pride getting in your way. It is important using good judgement and common sense when dealing with a superior. I now try keeping these thoughts in mind when my supervisor has criticism of me.

 Write a composition telling about a time you or someone you know lost your temper and responded negatively. Be sure to use: gerunds; infinitives; a dummy it with an infinitive; a gerund as the subject; too + adjective + to; adjective + enough + to; and an infinitive of purpose.

·······Editing Your Papers·······

22

The objective of this chapter is to teach students:

- *how to edit their own grammatical errors and,*
- *different compositions that contain typical ESL student errors.*

✔ These papers require many grammatical corrections. In a small group, read each composition carefully and make any necessary corrections to the grammar.

✔ *Topic One:* Is it better to have a small family or a big family?

I am agree with that it is better to have a small family with only two childrens. This way people have a family, but the children have always a brother or sister for company. In a small family, parents gives more attention to their children and financially it's better too.

My first belief is it is better if a parents have the small family with only the two children because it is easier to give attention to fewer childrens. If parents have two children they can pay more attentions to them. The childrens always plays together, they doesn't fight often. If parents have two children. They can teach them to share their toys and other things. So when the children are going to school. They don't have no problems. They always shares their things and never fights with their friends.

Financially, it's easier for parents to take care of the small family. Parents with big family can't educated their children, and everyone stay poor. In the small family both parents can work to helped pay for the childrens education. The parents can save enough money to live in nice place too. In the big family, the parents never get ahead of themself. My cousin had a big family, and they always had the financial problems. None of his children were able to go to college, but my brother had a small family. My brothers family lives nicely and everyone can go to school and be happy, too.

In conclusion I think that small families with only the two childrens are better off because parents can given they children more attention, have better financial resources and the childrens aren't lonesome. In my opinion, life is better for everyone in a smaller family.

 Topic Two: Should Cigarette Companies be permitted to advertise their products?

In todays world many cigarette companies are advertise their products, but some people ask if the cigarette companies should be permit to advertised. My answer to this questions is no the cigarette companies should not be allowed to advertise. To support my answer, I have few reasons why advertising cigarettes is wrong.

Cigarette advertisements are most of the time very interesting, that's why we should stop it. Teenagers who look at the advertisement, and they see a beautiful girl or handsome guy who is smoking a cigarette. The teenagers wanted to be like that person in the picture, so they started to smoke When they realize what they do. They end up having bad habit which is smoking.

Teenagers also when they seeing these advertisement think that smoking will make them more mature or they will had more dates. But, they wrong it's only making they health worse. Smoking will not make them more of anything, it will only made them more foolish to jeopardize their lifes with the risk of getting lung cancer.

Cigarette advertisements also encouraged adults to take up the habit. When an adult sees an advertisement of a person relaxing with a cigarette. They want to relax with a cigarette too. The only problem is the real person has problems that won't go away with the cigarette. Every time my uncle has the problem he lights up a cigarette. This cigarette just create a second problem for him. It doesn't solve nothing.

Although advertisers make cigarette smoking glamorous in the advertisements, I would not like to be a chimney and end up dying. Therefore I against advertising cigarettes.

Topic Three: Should public high schools be permitted to distribute condoms to their students?

In my opinion, given out Condom in the public school is a terrific idea. It is going to help students make a wise decision before having sex. Since sex among teenage is very common and dangerous.

Teenage have sex without using a condom because they don't want to deal with the embarrassment of going to a drug store to purchased the pack of condoms. They afraid everyone is watching them, and might get the wrong impressions of them, or if they seen a friend of the family, they think the friend would go to tell they parents. My friends aunt catched him buying condoms in a store, and she told his parents. Now my friend is scare to be catched and don't buy none. Instead he have unsave sex. This is very dangerous. If he could get free condom at school, he would probably have save sex.

When a teenager is thinking about having sex. They should take the responsible of using protection. The best protection is abstinence or no sex at all, but this advice is frequently ignore by teens in public schools. Some teenager who have sex without using protection says, that it's okay they wrong because having unsave sex can caused unwanted pregnancy, sexual transmitted diseases and many other illnesses contagious. For example, before my graduation. Eighteen students got pregnant after returning from the prom and five got infect with the AIDS virus. I think if they had gave out condoms at school that many student would not have got pregnant or caught AIDS. Parents should get together with school administrators to maked them realize that given out condom in school is going to helped students make the right decision before having sex, but not provoking them to have a sex.

In my case, if I have the relations with a person I will used the protection I get at school to prevent any kind of illness or diseases.

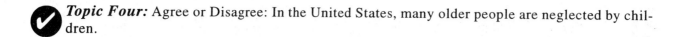

Topic Four: Agree or Disagree: In the United States, many older people are neglected by children.

Today many older people in this country are not appreciate by their families. Many of they are send to old peoples home by their children or living alone. The others that living with their children often lack of love and attention.

I think it ashame old people in this country have this type of life. The old people had spend almost half of their life working for their children, take good care of them and teach them a lot of things. But when their children grows up. they think that the old parent are the burden to them. The children should realized that someday they will become older. And how they would feel if their children ignored them. The adult childrens should take good care of the older parents, and do it as a good example for their childrens to follow.

My grandmother is eighty-five years old lady. She is a healthy and smart. We lived with her together after I am born. My father takes good care her and pay much attention to her. When I was growing up, I saw what my father did to her, it stays so deep in my mind. So I follow what my father did. I love my grandmother, and my grandmother love me. She always share her experience with me, too. But, now that my parents have immigrate here, she left alone. We miss her. We keep in touch by phones or letters. I think our love will never change. If she will come here, we will welcome her and take good care her.

In my opinion, I think parents need to take care their children when they were young. Also, children need to take care their parents when they old. This is a circular process, everyone must follow in every part of the world, but in this country they don't do this, and it is shame.

Topic Five: A wedding makes a statement about each family. It is an extension of their culture, lifestyle and values. What are weddings like in your homeland? How does a wedding in your homeland differ from American weddings? How does it reflect the difference in cultures?

In my country, the way how a wedding is ran is very important because that shows you lifestyle, values and social positions. Traditionally in our culture, the grooms family pay for the wedding. So, they ran the wedding. They will feel ashame if they can't afforded the wedding. This is very serious thing in my country.

I remember when I came to the United States and heard that in American the bride family pay for the wedding. I was very surprised. This is just the opposite from my country But, sometimes the bride family isn't agree with them about the reception so the bride family can talk them and ask them for some changes. Here is one example. Last week I went to the Canada for a wedding. The bride family is vegetarian, but the groom family is not. The bride family want to serve only vegetables at reception. They don't want meat and seafood. The bride parent talk to groom parent and groom family agree to made some change. The two family made compromise to keep everybody happy.

Next, at our weddings, there is no party favor for the guests. On the contrary, the guests has to give the couple a gift or money. Usually, they give them a red envelop with money inside. This mean good luck. This is a very traditional custom in our wedding.

There are a lot of rules which are follow at our weddings. Some of them are very old tradition and superstitious. For example, the mirror in the groom house should be cover with paper, this way the mirror won't reflect another woman who could tempt the groom. This means another person won't come between the couple. Furthermore, they also ask a four or five years old boy to jump in the the bride and groom's bed. This means the couple will have son soon. But, never a girl should do this. That is bad luck. My people are very superstitious about these rules and follow them carefully.

There are one more wedding difference in my culture. That is a bride wear at least two dresses at the reception. One at the beginning of the reception and another one at the end. However, Americans don't do this. I saw a video tape of a wedding and the bride wear the same wedding dress from the beginning of the wedding until the end of the wedding. The American bride don't change her dress.

In short, I think the way how the wedding is ran is very important. Weddings are very memorable and reflect the culture beliefs of a couple.

✔ *Topic Six:* Agree or Disagree. If a person wants to be successful in an American college, he/she must be prepared to do a lot of hard work.

In order to accomplish your education in the school. Students need to get acceptable grades in their courses. These grades will be determine whether or not the students are capable of graduate from the school. Therefore, every student must put a lot effort to get good grades.

When I took a English composition course for a second time. The teacher explain the students so many grammar rules that must be used in writing. We practice many essays in class with different topic, but at that time, I was taking other course like mathematics, Computer engineering, Communication and electrical circuits. I never had no time to study for all this courses, so I neglect my English course.

A week before the big exit examination, I started worry about my grammar and how to explained my thought in an essay because I had only concentrate on my other courses. I said to myself this test must be a piece of cake, so that why I don't put to much effort into it.

When the day came to took the test. I was so nervous. They given me fifty minutes to write a essay. The topic was so confused. By the time I began to write the essay I only had 30 minutes left. I could not organize my idea properly because English it not my native language. I don't have no time to checked my grammar and spelling error on the paper. When the time expired, I gave my test to the teacher.

The next meeting class I receive the result of the test. I felt so terrible when I heard I had failed. I could not control myself, and I started almost crying. Many questions came to my head and I could not answered. But, now I realize that every course need a lot of practice especial in English courses.

The school is not a easy process. It require so much effort and many painful situation. For me is like a battle that you must be prepare for at anytime. Some of the professor made your life easy other given you hard time on test. Taking a test proves mental knowledge to others. Every test give either a green light or a red light. That mean you failed or passed the test. When you passed the test you fell so happy about it. When you failed the test you fell so sad that you wanted ran out of the door. To receive a college diploma, the students must go through this long process and prove that you deserve to receive a diploma.

✔ *Topic Seven:* Explain how you survived the blizzard that dropped over two feet of snow in the city.

The big Blizzard was an unforgettable event which caught me by surprise.

Actually I was working in a restaurant on weekends. I went to work on Saturday, I finish work at 4 am, I get home around 4:30 am and I went to sleep at 5 am. When I got up Sunday afternoon and I was too tired to go back to work that afternoon. I began to walk around the house trying to decided if I would called in sick. Suddenly, I looked through the window, it surprise me. What I saw was a beautiful scene, everything was white as my teeth. The streets and the cars were cover with a thick layer of snow which was already more than one foot deep.

I turn on the TV and I hear the bad News that no personal cars were allowed to be in the streets. Because the city was declare in a state of emergency. I took my car out anyway even though we not allowed to do so. I couldn't went more than a block, my car get stucked on the snow. So, I come back home and went to bed.

To be honest, I needed this short vacation, I have been very busy since school started in September. This was the only time that I could relaxed and rest. But, after time passed by. I felt scare because the city was in a state of emergency and my daughter wasn't with me. She had to stay for the weekend with cousin because I had to worked.

On monday, I got up and I went to the supermarket to get some food, but there wasn't much left. They didn't have no milk, no bread or no meat. I was bored on Monday, I decided to go to picked up my daughter and have some fun with her. I had to travel by subway. Because the buses and cars couldn't operate in the very deep snow. I had a good time with my girlfriend, my daughter and my cousins. We played snow, we make a snow man we put my daughters scarf him. We also took a lot of pictures.

In conclusion, I needed a good rest and had lot of fun with my daughter during the big blizzard.

 Topic Eight: Why are there so many homeless people in the city and what life circumstances cause these people to become homeless?

In todays world there are many people who lives in poverty, because of the bad economy and the govt. failure to help sick people. In Los Angeles, also there are many people who are homeless because of these problem.

The economy problem is the main reason for homeless. Even though in LA, the economy is better than the other cities. But, still there are many people who are homeless, and they do not have any shelter or place to live. For instance, when one of the building in LA catch fire and it got destroy the government don't take any quick action about it. Because they didn't have money to give these persons a place to live. Therefore, the people who lives in that building lost everything and they don't even get a safe place where they can find the shelter. This is one reason why people become homeless, and they government don't do nothing for them.

The another reason people get homeless because some people have the mental illness and was in special hospital. But now the govt. don't give the special hospital the money they need to take care of these sick people, so these people were thrown out on the street. These person can't work or take care themselves, so they live on the street like animals This is sad the govt. should open up the special hospital for these homeless people.

According to me, the government should do something about homeless, because if the government don't do nothing about it, then all of LA will be destroyed by homelessness.

 Topic Nine: Write a composition about a time you failed a test.

The time that I finally pass my drivers' license written test for the third time was the most unexpected moment that I can remember.

When I live in New Jersey for a year. I had to take the written test to get a New Jersey Driver's License. I thought would be easier than the New York test. I took the test in English. Although I didn't yet have ability to read and write well in English, so I failed the test. On one hand, I couldn't believed that I failed, but on the other hand, I honestly didn't studied for the test either. I embarrassed myself. Since most of the people pass the test. When they take it. When I went back to work. My boss and my friends at work started to make fun of me. Because I fail.

When I took the test a second time. I didn't study again. Since I had this idea it would make me feel good to pass the test without studied. I still don't know what I was thinking at that time, but I took it anyway. Obviously, I fail the test again. Then I started to make excuses for myself. I kept telling myself that I failed because the new computer system made me fail, but, I knew it only an excuse.

After I failed the second time. A funny thing happened. I took the test for third time without study and I passed the test. Since I took it in my native language.

After I finally passed the written test. I realize that if there is any available opportunity to get something easily. I should definitely take the chance. I know that it wasn't right for me to expect good results from the test without put any effort into it. However, I was happy that I got what I wanted. Because I just kept taking the test.

 Topic Ten: Write a composition explaining what you would do if you won the lottery.

If I won the lottery. I will have three very important goals which I would be determined to accomplish them.

My first goal to which I would give top priority to is to buy two houses which is located in Great Neck. The two houses would be right next to each other, the first house would be for my wife, children and me. The second one would be for my parents with who I am very close with them. They could live with me, if they had wanted but I think they will want their own home. How much will these two houses cost will not be a problem. Because I would have loads of money to blow on anything I want. My house which would have five bedrooms and three bathrooms. My parents who are only two people would have a smaller place although my father wants a big garden. Even though he has never grown a thing.

My second goal which is to buy a fancy car. It would be a Jaguar I would also want a sun roof. So that I could pop my head out the window and wave to all the pretty ladies. I would also buy my father a Ford Explorer which it has four wheel drive. Even though he doesn't have a license. The reason why does he want a four wheel drive is because he has to take a bus and train to work even if there is a lot of snow and ice. This would save him lots of inconvenience he would never have to wait on a cold wet street again.

My third and final goal would be to invest the remainder of the money in stocks and bonds, I've always wanted to play the stock market. Additionally I will trade my own stocks like a real stock broker using the fancy computer that I will buy it. Although my friends who they work on Wall Street have told me that I can lose all my money. I don't believe what did they say to me, because I am a very smart guy which know all about what is he doing. If I win this money, I would turn my investments into billions of dollars, and donate a building to Queensborough Community College which it will be named after me.

In the end, if I won the lottery. I would be the happiest guy who everyone would love. Because I am rich.

Part Two

Composition

Selecting a Topic

The objective of this chapter is to help students:

- *narrow down a writing topic so that it is not too broad and confusing,*

- *brainstorm to create a list of sub-topics, and*

- *develop a more specific topic or thesis statement before beginning to write.*

Narrowing Down the Topic

Most students have a general idea about what they want to write, but sometimes their topic is too **broad** and includes too many sub-categories so that the writer becomes confused and unable to organize a clear concise academic composition. Therefore, before writing, students should examine their topics to determine exactly what they want to write about.

For instance, a student may want to write about education, but this topic can include volumes and volumes of information related to the field of education. Therefore, before writing about this topic, a student will want to determine exactly what aspect of education will be discussed in this composition. If unsure, a student can begin by simply listing all the words that come to mind when thinking about education. This process is called **brainstorming**.

✔ Brainstorm and make a list of all the words or terms that come to mind when hearing the word **education**.

elementary	early childhood	learning problems	computer
young children	trends in education	foreign students	
_____	_____	_____	_____
_____	_____	_____	_____
_____	_____	_____	_____
_____	_____	_____	_____

This list specified different topics about education. Now the writer should select one item and try to develop details about it. For instance, to develop details about foreign students, make a list of any words that relate to education and foreign students. Each of these words that are put on the list may also produce other words about the subject and will help the writer create a very specific or "narrowed down" topic for a composition.

Make a list of sub-topics for foreign students.

Education and Foreign Students

friendships
learning new language
cultural clashes

learning a new culture
writing difficulties

preparing ESL teachers
speaking difficulties

_____   _____   _____

_____   _____   _____

_____   _____   _____

_____   _____   _____

_____   _____   _____

 Now select one of sub-topics that is interesting and write about it.

example: When I arrived in this country, I didn't speak a word of English, and I was immediately placed in an American high school where hardly anyone spoke my language. In fact, most of the students had been born here and only spoke one language: English. Because there were only four foreign students in the school, there wasn't any special English as a Second Language program; therefore, my English teacher used to work with the four of us after school. Although she was a very dedicated and concerned lady, I now realize she didn't have a clue as to how to teach a foreign student how to read and write in English. Consequently, this made our learning process even more difficult.

 Re-read the free writing sample that was written about foreign students and determine what topic this student should write about.

Public schools should have teachers who are specifically trained to teach English as a Second

Language (ESL) to foreign students because regular teachers are not familiar with the pedagogi-

cal techniques used to promote successful learning. As a result, this lack of teacher training

creates many difficulties for ESL learners.

This is one technique used to help writing students create a topic which can be easily written about in a composition. The rest of this chapter will give writing students the opportunity to practice this technique.

Student Practice in Narrowing Down a Topic

✔ Select a sub-topic from the list on Education and make a list of words that relate to that sub-topic.

_____

_____   _____   _____

_____   _____   _____

_____   _____   _____

_____   _____   _____

_____   _____   _____

✔ Now select one of the sub-topics from the above list and write about it.

_____

_____

_____

_____

_____

_____

_____

_____

_____

_____

_____

✔ Re-read the free writing sample that was written and determine what topic this student should write about.

_____

_____

_____

_____

✔ Brainstorm and make a list of all the words or terms that come to mind when hearing the term Acquired Immunity Deficiency Syndrome (AIDS).

origin of AIDS	cure for AIDS	vaccine for AIDS	transmission
_____	_____	_____	_____
_____	_____	_____	_____
_____	_____	_____	_____
_____	_____	_____	_____
_____	_____	_____	_____

✔ To develop a more specific topic or thesis statement about the transmission of AIDS, make a list of sub-topics that relate to this subject. Each of these words on the list may also produce other words about the subject and will help determine a specific or "narrowed down" topic for a composition.

✔ Complete the list on the Transmission of AIDS.

Transmission of AIDS

transfusions	_____	_____
_____	_____	_____
_____	_____	_____
_____	_____	_____
_____	_____	_____
_____	_____	_____

✔ Now select one of the sub-topics and write about it.

_____

_____

_____

_____

_____

_____

_____

_____

_____

✔ Re-read the free writing sample and determine the topic this student should write about.

_____

_____

_____

_____

✔ Brainstorm and make a list of all the words or terms that come to mind when hearing the term **marriage**.

Marriage

young marriages   arranged marriages   second marriages   _____

_____   _____   _____   _____

_____   _____   _____   _____

_____   _____   _____   _____

_____   _____   _____   _____

_____   _____   _____   _____

✔ Pick one of the terms listed under the general category of **marriage**. For instance, a writer might choose to write about **arranged marriages**. In order to develop a more specific thesis or topic for a composition about **arranged marriages**, the writer should make a list of any sub-topics that relate to this subject. Each of these sub-topics on the list may also produce other words about the subject and will help produce a specific or "narrowed down" topic for a composition.

✔ Pick one sub-topics listed under **marriage** and make a list for that sub-topic.

_____

_____   _____   _____

_____   _____   _____

_____   _____   _____

_____   _____   _____

_____   _____   _____

✔ Now select one of the terms from the list that was just made and write about it.

_____

_____

_____

_____

_____

_____

_____

_____

_____

✔ Re-read the free writing sample and determine what thesis or topic this student should write about.

_____

_____

_____

_____

✔ Brainstorm and make a list of all the words or terms that come to mind when hearing the term **eating**.

Eating

healthy eating	eating disorders	unhealthy eating	_____
_____	_____	_____	_____
_____	_____	_____	_____
_____	_____	_____	_____
_____	_____	_____	_____
_____	_____	_____	_____

✔ Pick one of the terms listed under the general category of **eating**. For instance, a student might choose to write about **eating disorders**. In order to develop a more specific thesis about **eating disorders**, the writer should make a list of any sub-topics that relate to this subject. Each of these sub-topics on the list may also produce other words about the subject and will help to determine a specific or "narrowed down" topic for a composition.

✔ Make a list of related terms for the specific sub-topic **eating** which has been selected.

_____

_____ _____ _____

_____ _____ _____

_____ _____ _____

_____ _____ _____

_____ _____ _____

✔ Now select one of the words or terms from the list that was just made and write about it.

_____

✔ Re-read the free writing sample and determine what topic this student should write about.

Organizing a Composition and Introductory Paragraph

24

The objective of this chapter is to help students:

- *understand how an academic composition is organized,*

- *write an introduction which:*
    1. *states the topic clearly,*
    2. *captures the reader's interest, and*
    3. *clearly states the author's opinion, if necessary, and*

- *identify common mistakes made when writing.*

Organizing a Composition

A composition usually contains three main parts:

- an <u>introduction paragraph</u> which clearly tells the reader what the topic is,
- two or three <u>body paragraphs</u> which each discuss and develop a different point or reason for an opinion and only discuss the idea in the composition, and
- a <u>conclusion paragraph</u> which signals that the composition is ending.

The Introduction Paragraph

The introduction paragraph is used to begin a composition, and it usually contains a <u>thesis</u> statement which describes the topic the writer wants to discuss in the composition. If the introduction doesn't clearly state the topic, it is inadequate and unacceptable. Moreover, the introduction <u>should try to entice or excite the reader</u> so that he/she will want to read the composition.

As a writer becomes more advanced, it becomes possible to suggest or imply what the thesis or topic of the composition is. Since most students who use this book are beginning composition students, it is advisable for students first to learn to state the topic in a direct, clear manner before attempting to imply or suggest what the thesis is.

Techniques for Writing an Introduction

 Read the following introduction paragraph carefully and underline the thesis statement.

1. When I first came to this country, I entered a high school without knowing a word of English and needed special assistance in learning my new language. Since my high school didn't have many foreign students, there was no English as a Second Language (ESL) program; therefore, I only received tutoring from my English teacher who had never really worked with ESL students. Although she tried desperately to assist me, she didn't have a clue as to how to teach me to read and write. I believe if my school had had a teacher who was trained to instruct ESL students that I would have acquired the language with more ease and would have had fewer problems developing my language skills. I think it is essential for schools to provide ESL students with teachers who have been specifically trained to address the needs of second language learners in order to facilitate and streamline their learning.

What was the thesis statement or topic in this introductory paragraph?

_____

_____

How did the writer introduce the topic?

_____

_____

 Read the following introduction and circle the thesis statement.

2. Many people think they can contract the Acquired Immunity Deficiency Syndrome (AIDS) by donating blood or by touching a person with this disease although this is completely inaccurate. In light of this gross misinformation, I would like to explain the three different ways AIDS can be contracted. They are through unprotected sex, blood transfusions and the sharing of IV drug needles.

What was the thesis statement or topic in this introductory paragraph?

_____

_____

What technique did the writer use to introduce the topic?

_____

_____

 Read the following introduction and circle the thesis statement.

3. I recently read an article about a young man who received a rather unusual gift for his thirteenth birthday. Since this boy had never had sex, his friends hired a teenage prostitute for him as a birthday present. The teenager was delighted with his gift and couldn't believe how lucky he was. On his birthday, he went to the hotel where he was treated to his first sexual experience by a sixteen year old beauty. After the young woman left the hotel, he immediately noticed a message she'd written on the mirror in lipstick. It read, "Welcome, to the wonderful world of AIDS!" Six months later, this child found out that he had contracted this deadly disease. Ten days before his sixteenth birthday, he died. I wonder if this youngster had ever received any information about how this deadly disease is contracted. What would you tell a child if you had to explain how the AIDS virus is transmitted?

What was the thesis statement or topic in this introductory paragraph?

_____

_____

What technique(s) did the writer use to introduce the topic?

_____

_____

 Read the following introduction and circle the thesis statement.

4. "Pretty is as pretty does." That is an old saying my grandmother used to tell me when I was a little boy although I never quite knew what it meant until I met Daniella. She was the most beautiful woman I'd ever encountered, the first love of my life but the most selfish and insensitive person on earth.

What was the thesis statement or topic in this introductory paragraph?

_____

_____

What technique did the writer use to introduce the topic?

_____

_____

 Read the following introduction and circle the thesis statement.

5. It seems we're always hearing stories about people who die of cancer or emphysema because they smoked from the time they were youngsters. These same people might have lived and enjoyed good health for another twenty years if they hadn't been enticed into smoking as teenagers by seductive advertisements. I personally think it is tragic that our society allows the cigarette industry to manipulate young people into smoking by using glamorous ads which are directed at teenagers at a time in their lives when they naively think they are invincible.

What was the thesis statement or topic in this introductory paragraph?

_____

_____

What technique did the writer use to introduce the topic?

_____

_____

 What were the five techniques used to write an introductory paragraph?

1. A short story or stimulating incident can be used as long as it <u>directly relates</u> to the thesis or topic that is going to be discussed. (See examples 1 and 3.)
2. The topic can be stated along with the major points that will be discussed in the composition. (See example 2.)
3. A thought provoking question can be asked which leads into the thesis of the composition. (See example 3)
4. An appropriate quotation can be used to introduce the thesis statement. (See example 4.)
5. The writer can try to stress the importance of a current situation or problem demonstrating how this problem can impact our lives. (See example 5.)

Practice in Writing Introduction

Below is a list of five different topics. With a partner, write a stimulating introduction for each topic. Be sure to state the thesis statement or topic clearly and specify the technique used to write the introduction.

If a person is convicted of driving while under the influence of alcohol, his her license should be suspended for a year and his/her car should be impounded to guarantee that this person does not drive during the period of suspension. Explain why you agree or disagree with this statement.

_____

_____

_____

_____

_____

_____

_____

_____

_____

_____

Children should be taught that it is always wrong to lie and that there is no such thing as a white lie. Explain why you agree or disagree with this statement.

_____

_____

_____

_____

_____

_____

_____

_____

_____

_____

_____

_____

Explain how hard work builds character in a person.

_____
_____
_____
_____
_____
_____
_____
_____
_____

Explain why many urban college students must take more than four years to graduate from college.

_____
_____
_____
_____
_____
_____
_____
_____
_____
_____

Explain why a college student who receives tuition assistance from the government should or should not be required to maintain a grade point average of at least 3.0

_____
_____
_____
_____
_____
_____
_____
_____
_____
_____

Practice in Correcting Introductions

 Read the following introduction and explain what the writer has done incorrectly.

I agree with this topic because cigarettes cause serious diseases such as lung cancer and they can stunt the growth of a child.

What is the topic the writer wants to discuss? _____

Why is the reader unable to determine the exact topic of the composition?

_____

_____

The topic of this composition is whether or not cigarette companies should be allowed to advertise their products. Re-write this introduction so that it clearly states the topic in an interesting manner.

_____

_____

_____

_____

_____

_____

_____

_____

_____

_____

_____

 The topic for the following introductory paragraph is:

Explain why it is or is not worthwhile to work too hard or too much to succeed in school or work.

People always think if they want to succeed in school or work, they should get a good education and job related experiences. Even though these people become very successful in school or at work, they don't have good relationships with their family or friends. However, good relationships are a very important part of success because these interpersonal relationships help people acquire experiences and accumulate a wealth of knowledge.

What is wrong with this introduction?

_____

Re-write this introduction to make it acceptable.

_____
_____
_____
_____
_____
_____
_____
_____
_____
_____

✔ The topic for the following introductory paragraph is:

Explain why it is or is not worthwhile to work too hard or too much to succeed in school or work.

Some folks work too hard and too much in order to succeed so that they often don't have time to build relationships with their friends and families. In a survey in the New York Times, it showed that many working parents don't have time for their children and the children end up committing criminal acts. I read a story about a teenage boy who kept asking his father for help with a problem he was having with a friend, but the father was always too tired to listen to his son. Eventually, the son made his own decision and decided to rob a store so that he could get the money he needed. If this father hadn't worked too hard and too much, his son would have received the guidance he needed.

What is wrong with this introduction?

_____
_____
_____
_____

Re-write this introduction to make it acceptable.

_____
_____
_____
_____
_____
_____
_____
_____
_____
_____

✔ The topic for the following composition is:

Explain why in the United States old people are or are not appreciated by their families.

I agree that old people in the United States are not appreciated by their families for two reasons. The first reason is their children do not want to take care of them but put them in a nursing home where they are mistreated and neglected. My second reason is the younger generation doesn't respect them because they don't earn money. Instead, they view them as a nuisance and a burden. I will explain my reasons in the next two paragraphs.

Does this introduction state the topic clearly? _____

What is the topic? _____

Why is this introduction boring? _____

Rewrite the introduction to make it more interesting.

_____
_____
_____
_____
_____
_____
_____
_____
_____

Body Paragraphs

25

The objective of this chapter is to help students organize body paragraphs by learning to:

- *write a clear topic sentence for each body paragraph,*

- *discuss only one reason or point in each body paragraph,*

- *use appropriate details to develop each body paragraph to include:*

  1. *examples,*
  2. *facts,*
  3. *statistics,*
  4. *anecdotes,*
  5. *comparisons or contrasts,*
  6. *definitions, and*

- *verify that each detail relates directly to the point being made in the body paragraph.*

The Topic Sentence

The Purpose and Location of the Topic Sentence

After having written a clear interesting introductory paragraph, the writer is now ready to go into specific detail in the composition. These details must be presented in a highly organized fashion so that the reader knows exactly what point the writer wants to make about the thesis (topic) being discussed. These details are presented in the body paragraphs of the composition although <u>each body paragraph</u> only discusses <u>one explicit distinct point or reason</u> the writer wants to make.

In order to guarantee a beginning writer only discusses one specific point or reason, it is advisable to begin each body paragraph with a <u>topic sentence</u>. Although some highly experienced writers do not directly state the topic sentence or will state it at the end of the body paragraph, it is advantageous for beginning composition students use a topic sentence in the first sentence of each body paragraph to assure that the writer has a clear precise point to make in each body paragraph and to avoid just writing anything that comes to mind that may not be directly related to the topic.

For instance, if a student is writing a composition explaining the ways in which the AIDS virus is transmitted and the first paragraph plans to explain that AIDS can be transmitted by sharing intravenous (IV) drug needles, the topic sentence for this body paragraph could read as follows.

One way in which AIDS is frequently transmitted is by sharing intravenous (IV) drug needles.

After a writer has drafted a topic sentence, he/she should re-read carefully to verify:

- if the topic sentence describes what the paragraph will discuss and
- if the topic sentence contains one clear main idea.

It is important to remember the topic sentence is the introduction to the body paragraph and prepares the reader for what will be discussed, and it usually contains one main idea.

Practice Writing Topic Sentences

If a student has already written one body paragraph which explains AIDS can be transmitted by sharing intravenous (IV) drug needles, what are the other two ways in which this disease is spread?

1. _____
2. _____

Each of these two additional ways AIDS is transmitted can be used for a topic sentence for two separate body paragraphs. Write a different topic sentence that could be used to begin a body paragraph for each of these ways that AIDS can be transmitted.

✔ Write a topic sentence for transmitting AIDS through unsafe sex.

_____

_____

_____

✔ Write a topic sentence for transmitting AIDS through blood transfusions.

_____

_____

_____

Developing a Body Paragraph··························

Frequently, a writer has an introduction and a topic sentence for a body paragraph but develops writer's block and can't think of details to help fill out the body paragraph. There are several different methods which can be used to help develop a body paragraph.

example: Sometimes a writer will give an example which <u>directly relates to</u> the main point of the body paragraph. For instance, in a composition which discusses the ways in which AIDS is transmitted, the writer might start with the following topic sentence and then give an example.

One way in which AIDS is frequently transmitted is by sharing intravenous (IV) drug needles.

For example, if, Khalid, an AIDS infected man is using a needle to inject drugs into his veins and lends his dirty needle to Vladimir, who is another drug user, Vladimir can catch AIDS by using this contaminated needle.

 Using the topic sentence that indicates that AIDS can be spread through unsafe sex, write an example which explains this concept.

The next way in which AIDS can be spread is through unsafe sex. For instance, _____

_____

_____

_____

_____

 Using the topic sentence that indicates that AIDS can be spread through blood transfusions, write an example which explains this concept.

The next way in which AIDS can be spread is through blood transfusions. For instance, _____

_____

_____

_____

_____

Stories, Incidents or Anecdotes

Many writers like to call on their own experiences in order to develop their paragraphs, so they use brief stories to augment their main idea. But, be careful because these stories must directly relate to the main point the writer is trying to make in this particular body paragraph. If the story does not directly tie into the main idea or has strayed off the topic, it is inappropriate. Also, these little stories should not be prolonged or lengthy giving excessive details, but they should be concise and get directly to the point.

 Read the following topic sentence and example.

One way in which AIDS is frequently transmitted is by sharing intravenous (IV) drug needles.

My dear friend, Katerina, was at a wild party where the guests were shooting up heroine and passing the same needle from person to person. She used this dirty needle because she didn't realize the consequences of her actions. A year later, Katerina and five other people who had been at the party found out they had contracted AIDS from one of the guests who was infected with the virus.

It is important to note the writer <u>only included the most important facts surrounding this story</u> and didn't included insignificant details.

 Read the following body paragraph and explain why the story is unacceptable.

One way in which AIDS is frequently transmitted is by sharing intravenous (IV) drug needles. I had a friend that I met in high school in the United States. Her name was Katerina. She was in my home room class. She was a quiet and shy girl who didn't go out often, but one night she was coaxed into going to a party at her cousin's house. Her cousin lived in Boston. It was a wild party. Everyone drank a lot and used drugs such as cocaine and heroine. Some of the guests were shooting up heroine and passing the same needle from person to person. Katerina didn't realize she could catch AIDS by sharing an IV drug needle. Moreover, she wanted to fit in with the crowd, so she injected herself with the needle when it was passed to her. A year later, Katerina and five other people who had been at the party found out they had contracted AIDS from one of the guests who was infected with the virus.

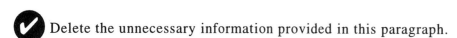 Delete the unnecessary information provided in this paragraph.

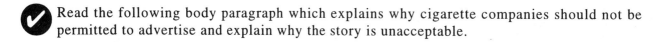 Read the following body paragraph which explains why cigarette companies should not be permitted to advertise and explain why the story is unacceptable.

The first reason why I don't believe cigarette companies should be permitted to advertise is because these ads are very seductive and entice vulnerable teenagers into smoking. My girlfriend, Gita, started to smoke when she was fourteen years old because she wanted to look like her other friends. At first, she didn't even enjoy smoking but continued since it made her feel like one of the crowd. Now Gita is an adult woman who is addicted to smoking and can't stop even though it is bad for her health.

Explain what is wrong with this story that was used in this body paragraph.

_____

_____

_____

Re-write this body paragraph so that the story relates directly to the topic of the composition.

_____

_____

_____

_____

_____

_____

_____

_____

✔ Using the topic sentence that indicated that AIDS can be spread through unsafe sex, write a brief story which supports the topic sentence which has already been written.

The next way in which AIDS can be spread is through unsafe sex. _____

_____

_____

_____

_____

✔ Using the topic sentence that indicated that AIDS can be spread through blood transfusions, write a brief story which supports the topic sentence.

The next way in which AIDS can be spread is through blood transfusions. For instance, _____

_____

_____

_____

_____

Facts

Many writers develop their body paragraph by including <u>facts</u>. Facts include any information which can be proven and frequently contain numbers or statistics about the subject being discussed. Facts can be taken from newspapers, magazines, or research studies although they must <u>directly relate</u> to the topic sentence which is the point the writer is trying to make. For instance, if a writer is discussing the fact that many people acquire AIDS by sharing IV drug needles, the following fact might be provided.

One way in which AIDS is frequently transmitted is by sharing intravenous (IV) drug needles.

A recent study which was done by the Center for Disease Control indicates that forty percent

of new AIDS cases resulted from sharing intravenous (IV) drug needles.

✔ Using the topic sentence that indicates that AIDS can be spread through unsafe sex, write a fact to support this point.

The next way in which AIDS can be spread is through unsafe sex. _____

_____

_____

_____

_____

_____

✔ Using the topic sentence that indicates that AIDS can be spread through blood transfusions, write a fact to support this point.

The next way in which AIDS can be spread is through blood transfusions. _____

_____

_____

_____

_____

_____

Read the following topic sentence and the fact which is provided and explain why this fact is unacceptable.

The first reason why I don't believe cigarette companies should be permitted to advertise is because these ads are very seductive and entice vulnerable teenagers into smoking. It has been proven through research that sixty-five percent of the teenage population will have tried smoking by the age of fourteen.

Explain what is wrong with the fact that was used.

_____

_____

_____

Re-write this paragraph so that the fact that is used relates directly to the topic of the composition.

_____

_____

_____

_____

_____

_____

_____

_____

_____

Definitions

Another technique which is used to develop a body paragraph is a <u>definition</u>. For instance, if a student is writing a body paragraph which explains that AIDS can be contracted through unsafe sex, the student might want to define what unsafe sex is.

The next way in which AIDS can be spread is through unsafe sex. Unsafe sex means engaging in any type of sexual activity without using a latex condom.

 Using the topic sentence that indicates that AIDS can be spread through blood transfusions, write a definition to explain what a blood transfusion is.

The next way in which AIDS can be spread is through blood transfusions.

_____

_____

A writer might also include a definition which is taken from a textbook or dictionary. For instance, if a student is writing a composition about whether or not it is worthwhile to work too hard to succeed in school or work, he/she might write the following.

> I don't think it is worthwhile to work excessively to succeed because success is a state of mind. According to psychologist, success is a feeling of accomplishment which differs from one person to the next. It is a highly individualized feeling which varies according to a person's self-image, personality and experiences.

✔ Using the topic sentence that indicates that old people are neglected in the United States write a definition for <u>neglect</u>.

I believe old people are neglected in the United States. _____

_____

_____

_____

_____

_____

Comparison and Contrasts

Many writers develop their body paragraphs by showing how two situations are similar or dissimilar. That is writers can compare, show how situations are alike, or contrast, show how situations are different. Once again, it is important to be sure that these <u>comparisons and contrasts are brief and relate directly to the topic</u>, otherwise they are inappropriate.

If a writer is discussing why old people aren't appreciated and wants to demonstrate a <u>contrast</u> between his/her homeland and the United States, it could be written as follows.

> The elderly are not respected in the United States because the younger generation does not value their opinions or advice. In my country, when a young person has a problem, he/she will automatically discuss it with the older members of the family because these people are revered and believed to have the most knowledge and experience in life. However, in the United States,

when a teenager has a problem, he/she will never consult an older relative because the elderly's advice is considered outdated and old fashioned.

✔ Read the following topic sentence and provide a comparison/contrast which appropriately supports the point of this body paragraph.

I don't believe cigarette companies should be permitted to advertise because these ads are very seductive and entice vulnerable teenagers into smoking.

_____

_____

_____

_____

_____

_____

✔ Using the topic sentence which indicates that it isn't worthwhile to work to hard and too much, write a comparison/contrast to support the point of this body paragraph.

It isn't beneficial to work too hard or too much because overworking can negatively impact a person's health. _____

_____

_____

_____

_____

_____

Conclusions

26

The objective of this chapter is to help students learn to write effective conclusions, which:

- *close a composition by drawing conclusions which will leave the reader thinking about the topic which has been discussed, and*

- *do not conclude points or ideas that were not developed in the composition.*

Why Is a Conclusion Needed?

Purpose of a Conclusion

1. Have you ever been enjoying a piece of music when it suddenly comes to a halt without any reason for stopping? How does such an abrupt ending make the listener feel? Most people feel confused and frustrated when a musical piece ends in such a fashion. The same feelings of confusion and frustration occur when a composition ends without a <u>conclusion</u> because a conclusion signals the end and allows the reader to feel complete and satisfied.

2. Have you ever finished reading a book or watching a movie and wished it would never end? Have you ever finished reading a story or watching a movie that leaves you with unanswered questions which you must imagine or resolve on your own? That is what a good writer can also try to do when creating a conclusion because the writer tries to leave the reader thinking, questioning and interested in what has been written.

How to Write an Effective Conclusion

The writer can <u>draw conclusions</u> about what has been said. For instance, if the writer has written a composition explaining why old people are not appreciated in the United States, he/she might make the following conclusion.

It is obvious the older generation is not respected but neglected in this country, but I firmly

believe this attitude will come back to haunt the younger generation when they become elderly

and victims of their own children's negligence because what goes around comes around.

The writer can <u>summarize the main points</u> that were made in the composition. For instance, if the writer has discussed the three ways in which AIDS can be contracted, the conclusion could be written as follows.

AIDS is a very serious disease which has destroyed many innocent lives because of lack of adequate information about how it is transmitted. Therefore, to prevent the spread of AIDS people should have safe sex, not share IV drug needles and be sure all blood is carefully tested before it is given to a patient.

The writer can try to <u>leave the reader thinking</u>. For instance, if the writer has discussed the three ways in which AIDS can be contracted, the conclusion could present a provocative statement or question which will leave the reader in deep thought.

I can't imagine any parent wanting a child to die from AIDS, so why don't parents sit down and explain to their children how this deadly disease is transmitted? If they don't, it may be a matter of life or death.

Practice Writing Effective Conclusions . . . .

✔ Write a conclusion which draws a conclusion about why it is <u>not</u> worthwhile to work too hard or too much.

_____

_____

_____

_____

_____

_____

✔ Write a conclusion which summarizes why you think the elderly are not appreciated in the United States.

_____

_____

_____

_____

_____

_____

✓ Write a conclusion which leaves a reader thinking about the ways in which AIDS is transmitted.

_____

_____

_____

_____

_____

Error Analysis

✓ Read each topic and the conclusion written about the specified topic and determine why each conclusion is inappropriate. Then rewrite it.

✓ *Topic:* It is not a good idea for a woman to work outside the home after she has children.

Generally, I believe children, especially teenagers, need a lot of supervision to guarantee they don't get involved with the wrong people or illegal activities because they are easily influenced and can get into serious trouble.

_____

_____

_____

_____

_____

_____

✔ *Topic:* Couples who are from different cultures or religions should be permitted to get married even though there may be many differences between them.

In conclusion, I believe if couples from a different religion or cultures aren't ready to get married, they shouldn't because it will not only affect them later on but also their children.

_____

_____

_____

_____

_____

_____

_____

✔ *Topic:* Cigarette companies should not be permitted to advertise their products because cigarettes are dangerous and unhealthy.

I believe cigarettes are extremely dangerous and unhealthy and can cause severe health problems; therefore, cigarettes should be banned just like drugs such as cocaine.

_____

_____

_____

_____

_____

_____

_____

Appendix

Phrasal Verbs

ask for	request
ask out	ask someone to go on a date
blow down	knock down
blow out	extinguish
* break into	enter some place by force
break up	to end a romantic relationship
bring back	return
bring out	produce or present
bring up	raise a child
bring up	present an issue for attention or discussion
burn out	stop functioning, become useless
buy out	purchase a business
call off	cancel
* call on	ask to answer a question
call up	make a phone call
carry out	accomplish or execute something
cheer up	make someone happier
clear up	clarify something
cross out	draw a line through something
cut off	shorten something
cut off	end or terminate something
cut out	remove something by cutting
cut out	stop doing something, discontinue an action
drop in	visit without calling first
drop out of	stop going
figure out	find an answer or solution
fill in	complete an answer by writing in the blank
fill in	write information on a form
find out	discover something
* fool around	joke and waste time
* get along with	have a good relationship with someone
* get away with	do something forbidden or illegal
* get back	return from some place
* get back from	return from some place
* get in	enter
* get off	leave a bus, airplane, subway etc.
* get on	enter a bus, airplane, subway etc.

Note: * means that it is a non separable phrasal verb.

*	get out	leave a car, bus, taxi etc.
*	get over	recover from an illness
*	get over with	complete an activity
*	get through with	finish or complete something
	give back	return
	give up	quit or stop doing something
*	grow up	become an adult
	hand in	give an assignment to someone
	hand out	give something to someone, distribute something
	hang up	end a telephone conversation
	hang up	put clothes on a hanger
	hold up	rob at gunpoint
	hold up	delay someone or something
*	keep on	continue to do something
	kick around	discuss a subject or ideas
	leave out	omit something
*	look at	watch
*	look forward to	anticipate an event pleasantly
*	look out	be careful
	look up	search for information in a reference book
	make up	tell a lie or invent something
	make up with	become friends again after a disagreement
	mix up	become confused
	pay back	return money to someone
	pick up	lift
	pick out	select
	point out	see and notice something
	put away	place something where it belongs
	put back	place something in its original space
	put down	stop carrying someone or something
	put down	criticize someone or something
	put off	delay or postpone
	put up	erect or build
*	put up with	tolerate or endure
	read over	glance at something
	run across	find someone or something accidently
	run into	meet someone by accident
	run over	strike or pass over someone or something with a moving vehicle
*	run out of	finish a supply of something
	sell out	sell or vend everything
	shut off	turn off
	start over	begin again
*	stay up	remain awake
	take off	remove clothes from the body
	take over	assume direction
	talk over	discuss something
	tear down	destroy a building
	tear off	remove a piece of paper from a book
	tear up	rip into small pieces
	think over	contemplate or consider something

throw out	put in the garbage
try on	put on clothes to see if they fit
turn down	lower the volume
turn off	stop a machine or shut off
turn on	start a machine or light
turn up	increase the volume
wake up	stop sleeping
* watch out for	be careful or cautious
wear down	reduce gradually by making someone or something weak
wear off	disappear gradually
wear out	become shabby or useless
work out	find a solution to a problem
write down	write a note on paper

Preposition Combinations

to be absent from
to be accused of
to be accustomed to
to be acquainted with
to be addicted to
to be afraid of
to agree with
to be angry at
to be angry with
to be annoyed with
to apologize for
to apply to
to apply for
to approve of
to argue with
to argue about
to be associated with
to be aware of

to believe in
to belong to
to blame for
to be bored with
to borrow_____ from

to be capable of
to care about
to care for
to clear up
to compare to
to complain about
to be composed of
to be concerned about
to be connected to
to be confused about
to consist of
to be content with
to contribute to
to be convinced of
to count on

to cover with
to be crazy about
to be crazy for
to be crowded with

to deal with
to decide on
to decide upon
to depend on
to depend upon
to be dependent upon
to be devoted to
to be different from
to be disappointed with
to discriminate against
to distinguish from
to be divorced from
to be done with
to dream about
to dream of
to be dressed in
to be dressed up in

to be engaged to
to be envious of
to be equipped with
to escape from
to be excited about
to be excused from
to be exhausted from
to experiment with
to be exposed to

to be faithful to
to be familiar with
to feel like
to feel sorry for
to fight for
to be filled with

to be finished with
to be fond of
to forget about
to forgive for
to be friendly to
to be friendly with
to be furnished with
to get divorced from
to get married to
to get rid of
to be good for
to graduate from
to be grateful for
to be grateful to
to be guilty of

to be happy about
to be happy for
to happen to
to hear from (someone)
to hear about (something)
to hide from
to hope for

to be innocent of
to insist on
to insist upon
to be interested in
to introduce (someone) to
to be invited to
to be involved in
to be involved with

to be jealous of

to be known for

to laugh at
to lack confidence in
to be limited to
to listen to
to look forward to

to be mad at
to be made of
to be married to

to be nice to

to object to
to be opposed to

to participate in
to be patient with
to pay for
to be polite to
to pray for
to be prepared for
to prevent from
to prohibit from
to protect from
to be provided with
to be proud of
to provide with

to be qualified for

to be ready for
to recover from
to be related to
to be relevant to
to rely on
to rely upon
to be remembered for
to rescue from
to respond to
to be responsible for

to be satisfied with
to be scared of
to search for
to be similar to
to speak about
to stare at
to stop from
to subscribe to
to substitute for
to succeed in
to suggest to (someone)
to be sure about
to be sure of

to take advantage of
to take care of
to talk to
to be terrified of
to tell about
to thank for
to be thankful for
to think about
to be tired of
to be tired from

to be upset about
to be upset with
to be used to

to vote for

to wait for
to wait on
to be worried about

Irregular Verbs

SIMPLE VERB	PRESENT	SIMPLE PAST TENSE	PAST PARTICIPLE
be	am/is/are	was, were	been
become		became	become
begin		began	begun
bend		bent	bent
bite		bit	bitten
blow		blew	blown
break		broke	broken
bring		brought	brought
build		built	built
buy		bought	bought
catch		caught	caught
choose		chose	chosen
cling		clung	clung
come		came	come
cost		cost	cost
cut		cut	cut
dig		dug	dug
do	do/does	did	done
draw		drew	drawn
drink		drank	drunk
drive		drove	driven
eat		ate	eaten
fall		fell	fallen
feed		fed	fed
feel		felt	felt
fight		fought	fought
find		found	found
flee		fled	fled
fling		flung	flung
fly		flew	flown
forbid		forbade	forbidden
forget		forgot	forgotten
forgive		forgave	forgiven
freeze		froze	frozen
get		got	gotten
give		gave	given
go	go/goes	went	gone
grind		ground	ground

SIMPLE VERB	PRESENT	SIMPLE PAST TENSE	PAST PARTICIPLE
grow		grew	grown
hang		hung	hung
have	has/have	had	had
hear		heard	heard
hide		hid	hidden
hit		hit	hit
hold		held	held
hurt		hurt	hurt
keep		kept	kept
kneel		knelt	knelt
know		knew	known
lay		laid	laid
lead		led	led
leap		leapt	leapt
leave		left	left
lend		lent	lent
let		let	let
lie		lay	lain
light		lit	lit
lose		lost	lost
make		made	made
mean		meant	meant
meet		met	met
pay		paid	paid
prove		proved	proved/proven
put		put	put
quit		quit	quit
read		read	read
ride		rode	ridden
ring		rang	rung
rise		rose	risen
run		ran	run
say		said	said
see		saw	seen
seek		sought	sought
sell		sold	sold
send		sent	sent
set		set	set
sew		sewed	sewn/sewed
shake		shook	shaken
shoot		shot	shot
shut		shut	shut
sing		sang	sung
sit		sat	sat
sleep		slept	slept
slide		slid	slid
speak		spoke	spoken
speed		sped	sped

SIMPLE VERB	PRESENT	SIMPLE PAST TENSE	PAST PARTICIPLE
spend		spent	spent
spill		spilt	spilt
stand		stood	stood
steal		stole	stolen
stick		stuck	stuck
strike		struck	stricken
swear		swore	sworn
sweep		swept	swept
swim		swam	swum
take		took	taken
teach		taught	taught
tear		tore	torn
tell		told	told
think		thought	thought
throw		threw	thrown
understand		understood	understood
wake		woke	woken
wear		wore	worn
weave		wove	woven
win		won	won
wind		wound	wound
withdraw		withdrew	withdrawn
write		write	written